ASTRO POETS

✳

ASTRO POETS

Your Guides
to the Zodiac

Alex Dimitrov
and
Dorothea Lasky

FLATIRON
BOOKS
NEW YORK

www.flatironbooks.com

Library of Congress Cataloging-in-Publication Data

Names: Dimitrov, Alex, author. | Lasky, Dorothea, 1978– author.
Title: Astro poets : your guides to the zodiac / Alex Dimitrov and Dorothea Lasky.
Description: First edition. | New York : Flatiron Books, 2019.
Identifiers: LCCN 2019032702 | ISBN 9781250313300 (hardcover) |
 ISBN 9781250313317 (ebook)
Subjects: LCSH: Zodiac. | Astrology.
Classification: LCC BF1726.D56 2019 | DDC 133.5/2—dc23
LC record available at https://lccn.loc.gov/2019032702

Our books may be purchased in bulk for promotional, educational, or business use.
Please contact your local bookseller or the Macmillan Corporate and Premium Sales
Department at 1-800-221-7945, extension 5442, or by email at
MacmillanSpecialMarkets@macmillan.com.

First Edition: October 2019

10 9 8 7 6 5 4 3

This book is dedicated to poets
and freaks everywhere.

CONTENTS

✳

ASTRO POETS

✳

WELCOME TO OUR BOOK

*

We're glad you're here. We wrote this book for you and all the people you'll ever date, and all the people you've ever dated, and for your mom and sister and the dog you will adopt soon, and the stranger on the street you want to say hello to but have not (not yet, at least). We wrote it for your current boss and your asshole ex-boss and your annoying, overbearing co-worker. We wrote it for your friends, the ones who've both saved and disappointed you, and those who never left no matter what. We hope you'll find some part of them right here in these pages. You'll also find the moon, the sun, obsession, oceans full of time, and even a small mirror where you'll sometimes see yourself.

Astrology reveals how we're connected. It's like a map half dipped in water, burned at the edges, and just decipherable enough to take with you wherever you're going. It won't ever indicate exactly where that is. But it will tell you some things about love and eternity, the past and the future, and what you should do right after you put down this book (which is to get closer to your true passion).

We both carried that map with us when we met at a party after a poetry reading in April of 2011. There was an instant fire sign connection and of course so many ideas, one of which was Astro Poets, but it wasn't called that then. At first we started an astrology Twitter called Fire Signs 4 Life (because being a fire sign is such a glorious struggle). After a few weeks of tweeting, we were bored. That's really how fire signs work: getting high on possibility, a lot of energy and a short attention span. But in November of 2016, we returned to the idea and decided to start Astro Poets. This time poetry would be at the heart of it, and it became what made the entire thing work. Just like astrology, poetry—all language, really—has to do with the past and the future. Language is the way into who we are and have been, and who we still might become. It's the way into a holy present, where the sounds of our ancestors meet the sounds of our future selves. In other words, poetry returns us to ourselves.

Before you begin reading the rest of this book, you might want to know some basic things about astrology. Here are some answers to some of your most burning questions.

What is a sun sign?

A sun sign is usually the first thing people learn about when they encounter astrology. It's what people are asking for when they meet you and say, "What sign are you?" When someone says, "Hey, I'm a Virgo," what they really mean is Virgo is their sun sign. (And if you aren't compatible with Virgos, that's your cue to run. And fast. Because any Virgo will know how to find you.)

Your sun sign is determined by the day, time, and place you were born; it refers to the placement of the sun the moment you were born. There are twelve signs in the zodiac: Aries, Taurus, Gemini, Cancer, Leo, Virgo, Libra, Scorpio, Sagittarius, Capricorn, Aquarius, and Pisces. Each sign has both an element (fire, earth, air, water) and an essence (cardinal, fixed, and mutable). You can see the breakdown here:

	Cardinal	Fixed	Mutable
Fire	Aries	Leo	Sagittarius
Earth	Capricorn	Taurus	Virgo
Air	Libra	Aquarius	Gemini
Water	Cancer	Scorpio	Pisces

Your sun sign is the single most important piece of information if you want to know how astrology affects your general personality. It can be thought of as your ego, or as your soul's potential. It's in many ways the most hopeful possibility of who you can be this time around on earth. Think of it as your karmic guidebook.

People often want to know: Which signs are good, and which signs are bad? Usually it's because someone met a Scorpio and they want to know if all Scorpios are in fact 100 percent evil. The answer, even when it comes to Scorpios, is that no sign is more "bad" than another. Every sun sign has good and bad traits, and what matters is how people use their potential to be who they want to be.

All this is to say, that your star chart isn't fate but an outline, with plenty of places to fill in the blanks however you wish. We are influenced by a multitude of forces, and a sun sign is only one part of them. All people, no matter what their sign, are influenced by their own free will. Your sign doesn't decide your fate—there are many things along the way that will complicate things.

Prince (a Gemini) famously said, "Ain't no particular sign I'm more compatible with," and in many ways he was right. First, all Geminis are pretty compatible with most signs, due to their easygoing attitude, brutal charm, and willingness to please. But speaking more universally, all signs can be compatible—what's important is the amount of work people are willing to do to get along.

When people think about astrology, they often think about love. There are some basic laws that influence love compatibility, but again, they're not the full picture. A sun sign will generally get along with signs of the same element. For example, Aries and Leo are both fire signs, and for the most part, they're going to get along well. Signs of compatible elements (fire and air; water and earth) will be drawn to each other as well. So, if you're a Taurus and eyeing a Pisces, by all means go for it. But if you're a Scorpio and feeling some vibes for a Leo, all things being equal: good luck. You're gonna need it.

What is an element?

There are four elements in the zodiac: fire, earth, air, and water. They fall in that order along the karmic wheel, repeating three times to make the twelve signs. Every sign has an elementary influence, which drives people's motivations and actions and can give you some idea of someone's nature. If you are confused about what traits you should associate with each element, consider your associations with that specific element. If you meet an intriguing Pisces, don't fret and run to your astrology app to direct you. Think of all your memories of water and you'll get a lot of information you need. Your instincts will guide you. For example, fire signs (Aries, Leo, Sagittarius) are often thought of as feisty, independent, and impulsive, while earth signs (Taurus, Virgo, Capricorn) can be thought of as sensual, loving, and practical. Water signs (Cancer, Scorpio, and Pisces) are spiritual, moody, and empathetic; air signs (Libra, Aquarius, and Gemini) are—mostly—brainy, communicative, and restless. Remember that within you, as a human being, you hold an implicit understanding of the signs.

What is an essence?

Every sign has an essence, and there are three types of essences: cardinal, fixed, and mutable. The four cardinal signs of the zodiac are Aries, Cancer, Libra, and Capricorn. The four fixed signs are Taurus, Leo, Scorpio, and Aquarius. And the four mutable signs are Gemini, Virgo, Sagittarius, and Pisces. Understanding essences can be just as simple as understanding elements. If you ever get confused and find yourself in a place with no Wi-Fi, think of your understanding of the words themselves: "cardinal," "fixed," "mutable." Cardinal signs want to be first, in charge and running the show. Every show, especially if it isn't theirs. They want to conquer. They crave followers and can get very frustrated if others don't fall in line easily. For this reason, although signs like Aries and Cancer will feel deep love for each other's can-do attitudes, they are destined for historic (and histrionic) power struggles. Any workplace with any sort of power differential between two cardinal signs, whether it be in title or salary or both, is asking for conflict. It's best to make sure all things are equal when it comes to these four signs. Though they will find a way to fight with each other regardless.

Likewise, fixed signs are exactly what they sound like—they stay put. They can be extraordinarily stubborn and do not like change in any form. For this reason, fixed signs can be thought of as loyal and ready to do anything for loved ones and friends. Once a fixed sign has committed to something or someone, they are not likely to change their mind and reverse course. Their loyalty can almost be a fault, as their need to stay in one place may cause them to be delusional—divorced from certain aspects of reality and unaware of partners' and friends' possibility for betrayal. A classic fixed sign is Taurus. Tauruses have been known to not move from a comfy couch for hours on end unless you present them with some damn good reason to. In fact, if there's chocolate and red wine within arm's reach, they might just stay there forever. Scorpios have been known to stay with cheating partners—for millennia, if need be—because they hate the idea of the unknowable, the nature of being alone. Fixed signs get the job done and are definitely the people you can count on. That is, as long as you want to count on something that won't budge. Most people do. Others find it frustrating.

Mutable signs are the fun ones. They are truly down for just about everything and although they have varied natures, depending on their element, they will go with the flow. They love other mutable signs, but two mutable signs together can be an exasperating pair, as neither will take the lead. And even if one does, it won't be a real lead but a halfhearted attempt to control the situation. Mutable signs crave cardinal and fixed signs. Cardinal signs especially appreciate mutable signs, as the latter are open to their antics. In contrast to fixed signs, mutable signs enjoy change and chance, and are often the life of the party (even in the case of a Pisces who is still in the mode of "feeling things" at a party). And although cardinal signs will steal the show and fixed signs will definitely attend the show, mutable signs are the show. In the karmic wheel, all essences work together to make harmony.

What is a moon sign?

No person is just their sun sign. In fact, each person can be thought of as a kind of fingerprint of many different planetary influences. Just as the sun was in a particular constellation at the time of your birth, so too was the moon (and Mars, and Venus, and Neptune, and so forth). There are indeed ruling planets that influence us generationally and spiritually. One key to understanding a person's motivations is knowing their moon sign.

If your sun sign can be thought of as the sign of your ego, your moon sign is your id. It's what moves you to do things when you're acting on your first instincts, without complex thought. It's what your base emotional response to a situation is, or what you might do in a situation if you're more tired than usual or altered in some fundamental way. It's the essence of your interiority. Distilled into one. Like a shot of unadulterated personality.

It's for this reason that people find it helpful to know a person's moon sign if they're in an intimate relationship with them. Oftentimes when two people are together, it's their moon signs that are in conversation. When all daily performance is stripped away, and it's you and your partner in bed watching a movie—no guard up, no ulterior motives or acting—that's your moon signs showing. Your moon signs filling the room.

You can find out your moon sign the same way you find your sun sign (date, time, and place of birth). Laws of compatibility generally function the same as they do with sun signs. So if your crush has a Gemini moon and you have a Libra moon, chances are, in an intimate setting your moons will be vibing. People who have compatible sun signs but incompatible moon signs may have some trouble getting along despite their apparent compatibility. If you're a Taurus with an Aries moon and your lover is a Capricorn with a Virgo moon, no matter how much your earth sun signs crush hard on each other, your partner will find you wildly impulsive and impractical. And you will find your partner . . . well, downright boring.

Think of a moon sign as the concentrated version of that sign, all of the energy contained in a shot glass. For example, Scorpios are pretty intense in every way. But if you compare them to someone who has a Scorpio moon, the moon version wins in intensity. The moon sign has hidden pressure and can be like a burst of air—unexpected, delightful, or, frankly, terrifying.

What is a rising sign?

Like sun and moon signs, a person's rising sign can tell you some fundamental things about them. It's their social mask. The person they are in formal and professional settings. It's the sign that people often see first and form quick opinions about. Many astrologers, us included, don't put a lot of stock in a person's rising sign. Sure, it's there, and it influences the way people see you, but in many ways it's a façade.

Your rising sign, or your ascendant, is the planet that was on the eastern horizon at the moment of your birth. Rising signs are a thin layer over a person. Someone with a Sagittarius rising may seem fun, flirty, and philosophical, but unless that person is a Sagittarian sun or moon, you can't count on that energy to be there as you get to know them better. In fact, a rising sign can be an impediment to getting to know some people well, depending on their astrological configurations. The person who is attracted to a Sagittarius rising may be disappointed to find that the real person inside, with a Scorpio sun and a Pisces moon, is a very different person indeed. In fact, rising signs can be a source of great unhappiness if we don't take the time to understand their implications and how they can distort core components of a person's true personality.

If you are interested in seeing the phenomenon at play in the real world, ask a close co-worker their sun and rising. You'll probably end up realizing how much you see their rising when they are talking to your boss and how their sun sign comes into play when the two of you are conspiring at lunch together. When people aren't sure of a situation, they put their rising sign mask on and hope for the best. A rising sign is great armor for the everyday, but it just doesn't paint a true picture. A lot of the time it's what you need to do to get by.

A question we're often asked when we tweet our weekly horoscopes is whether a person should read for their rising or sun sign. To set the record straight here, always read for your sun sign— although it's a common practice for horoscopes to address rising signs, because of the connection between your ascendant and your social mask. When horoscopes are written with worldly or practical pursuits in mind, it makes sense that you read for your rising sign. But our horoscopes are written with an eye toward your progression along the karmic wheel, and thus the sun sign is the best way to consider your predicted future path.

What is the karmic wheel?

The karmic wheel is a way of understanding the progression of a soul along its journey. It starts with Aries and ends with Pisces. It can sometimes correspond to the "ages" of the signs. For example, astrologers often think of Aries as the baby, yet to learn important lessons, and Pisces as the oldest sign, spiritually at the end of life, having collected all the karmic lessons of the zodiac. In between are the other ten signs, which move in graduations of age accordingly. So, for example, a Libra will often feel "older" than a Gemini, and a Taurus will feel "younger" than a Scorpio.

Signs next to each other have a karmic connection and, although quite incompatible, can be sexually attracted to each other. A Leo and a Virgo might seem at first to have nothing in common, but according to the laws of the karmic wheel, the Leo is looking to the Virgo for lessons they have yet to learn in this lifetime. For some, having a romance with the sign following them can be a way to grow karmically.

Every soul in the universe doesn't grow karmically in a systematic way, from one sign to the next, entering a "heaven" or whatever you want to call an afterlife. Existence is too complex for that. And astrology does not function as religions do. To the contrary, astrology provides many ways to think about living one's given life, and it's hard to know much about what happens after death (poetry might let you know that). It's our feeling that astrology is practical magic for your specific set of lifetimes. The karmic wheel is the spinning top along this twirling universe of possibilities.

What are opposite signs, and do opposites actually attract?

When people talk about opposite signs, they are referring to signs that are diametrically opposed on the karmic wheel. Every sign has an opposite, and it's always in the element that is most (not least) compatible with yours (so: fire/air, earth/water) and shares its essence (cardinal, fixed, or mutable). Aries/Libra, Capricorn/Cancer, Leo/Aquarius, Taurus/Scorpio, Sagittarius/Gemini, and Virgo/Pisces are the possible opposite combinations.

Opposite signs can go both ways in terms of getting along well or absolutely hating each other. Because each sign has something the other lacks, they can be ferociously attracted to and repulsed by each other. It can be a dance that turns them on yet also drags them to their deepest depths. An opposite pairing is not one to take lightly.

If you are interested in getting to know a sign that is your opposite, remember that power will always be an issue. Some signs (all cardinal signs, for example) are more power-hungry than others. And if you're sleeping with a sign that is your opposite, there's a good chance that things will work out, though communication may feel brutal. Don't forget how deeply different your other half is, despite similar motivations.

What does it mean for signs to be compatible?

Many people come to astrology to see how romantically compatible two signs are. A sign will usually get along with the other two signs in their element, signs that are two signs away on the karmic wheel (Aries/Gemini), and signs in their opposite element (earth/water and fire/air). But these rules don't tell the whole story, because every sign has varying temperaments. On the following pages is a table that rates compatibility on a scale of 1–10, with 10 being "let's get in bed now" and 1 being "please never talk to me again."

What are ruling planets?

Every sun sign is "ruled" by a planet. This means that every sign has a lens through which you can better understand it, and this lens is determined by characteristics that are associated with certain planetary influences. This goes back to ancient Greek and Roman mythology, as planets were named after gods, and these gods have been associated throughout time with certain personality traits. Ruling planets (and their corresponding gods) determine which forces are at play with each sign and can be a guide to help you understand the signs better. On page 16 is a table of the signs, their ruling planets, and the traits we associate with them.

	Aries	Taurus	Gemini	Cancer	Leo	Virgo
Aries	6	8	9	4	9	2
Taurus	8	7	6	9	4	10
Gemini	9	6	7	6	8	3
Cancer	4	9	6	9	8	8
Leo	9	4	8	8	8	6
Virgo	2	10	3	8	6	8
Libra	7	6	10	2	7	7
Scorpio	6	8	6	10	4	9
Sagittarius	10	5	8	6	9	5
Capricorn	3	10	2	8	7	9
Aquarius	9	2	9	3	7	4
Pisces	7	8	1	9	4	7

Libra	Scorpio	Sagittarius	Capricorn	Aquarius	Pisces
7	6	10	3	9	7
6	8	5	10	2	8
10	6	8	2	9	1
2	10	6	8	3	9
7	4	9	7	7	4
7	9	5	9	4	7
7	6	9	6	9	4
6	8	6	9	5	9
9	6	9	7	8	6
6	9	7	9	4	8
9	5	8	4	7	5
4	9	6	8	5	8

Sign	Ruling planet	What the planet brings to the sign
Aries	Mars	Loud, brash gestures
Taurus	Venus	An aesthetics of sensuality
Gemini	Mercury	A quick wit
Cancer	Moon	Nourishing spirituality
Leo	Sun	Brightly bold streamers
Virgo	Mercury	A sharp mind
Libra	Venus	Real true beauty
Scorpio	Pluto and a little Mars	A ferocious intensity
Sagittarius	Jupiter	A positive life force and luck
Capricorn	Saturn	Never giving up

Aquarius	Uranus and a little Saturn	Powerful genius
Pisces	Neptune and a little Jupiter	Creativity associated with the occult

Why do I care if Mercury is in retrograde?

If you've been following discussions about astrology in recent years, undoubtedly someone has said to you in passing, "Oh, Mercury's in retrograde. No wonder everything feels fucked up." "Mercury retrograde" has become a catchall phrase, used to explain just about any bumbling encounter, misworded email to your boss, or strangely emotional conversation with a potential crush. It's the horrible monster that can seemingly justify any complication about communicating with other humans. We are lucky that the phrase has entered the language, as it really does perform a service for us in our everyday existence. Let's take a moment right now to say, "Thank you, Mercury in retrograde, for always taking all the blame!"

Long ago, people believed that Mercury moved backward, and they termed the period during which it did so "retrograde." We now know that Mercury's orbit around the sun is simply shorter than Earth's. When Mercury seems to come forward again, after going "backward," everything relating to communication goes haywire.

The truth is that most people aren't exaggerating when they blame Mercury's retrograde. If you want to understand it, consider that Mercury is the planet of communication. Mercury is Gemini's ruler, and if there is something one might say about Geminis, it's that they love to talk (and talk and talk and talk). They get that from Mercury. In Roman mythology, Mercury is the tricky god of talking, persuading, traveling, and thievery. When Mercury is not in retrograde, the planet helps us all communicate (and sometimes manipulate each other, if necessary) through language. But in retrograde, its language-lubing qualities are at a standstill, or, worse yet, there is a major clog in the pipeline.

Any good astrologer will tell you not to make important deals when Mercury is in retrograde. We would tell you to basically sit quietly alone in a room (with no windows!) until the horrible period is over. Don't bother bringing a phone with you either, because you'll find yourself texting all your exes, awkwardly.

What is a Saturn return?

Since we're getting more outer-spacey in our discussions at this point, it might be a good time to tell you about Saturn return. Like Mercury in retrograde, Saturn return is something you have undoubtedly heard about from friends and lovers. You probably understand it as a thing to either revere or fear (and probably both).

When Saturn returns, it means that almost thirty years have passed since you were born and it's now high time to figure some shit out. Saturn is a planet that rules Capricorn, so it is an industrial one: its influence is to get us to work hard and start building foundations in order to create an empire. About the time people turn thirty, they start to realize that life doesn't last forever and they begin to think about the mark they want to make on the world. They might start thinking about a career versus a job, what they want from relationships in the long term, and what kind of person they want to be while they're alive. All the illusions of youth and childhood start to fade and they enter a middle-age phase (which lasts for another thirty years, when Saturn returns again). Influenced by the same forces that govern all Capricorns, people in Saturn return can get a little formal in their approach to things, which can be exciting (or not), depending on their individual vision of formality.

What you should remember is that Saturn return is a transformational phase giving you the ability to change and shape your life. The first one has to do with becoming an adult (around the ages of 27–30), the second (55–60) is you realizing all the things you won't be able to do no matter your planning, making your focus on what you do want even sharper, and the third (85–90) is reflective and has to do with gratitude—it's your soul preparing to take on another form while honoring the one you're in.

One reason people fear their Saturn return is that it can dredge up childhood memories and traumas they are forced to deal with head-on. Because of this, and as a result of a deeper understanding of mortality gained during this period, we may also experience profound sadness, which can be difficult to overcome.

If you are in this period it's important to a) remember that it will pass and b) consider taking some advice from Capricorns (don't worry, they love to give it): that with every age there is possibility. Growing into yourself doesn't mean that with the passing of youth you've lost something. Instead it means that you have become and are becoming the person you are meant to be, and that you are that much closer to your soul's potential. For most of us (we've both been through one cycle), it's pretty much one of the most exciting times of your life. So much necessary change, both exterior and interior, can occur.

A little something about date cutoffs

Reading this book, you will see that each sign fits into a specific time frame, as is customary. We did this because it would have been confusing to not give you some definite dates. But the truth is that there is variability in terms of when the signs cut off, even from year to year. Certain people born a Pisces in Cleveland in 1992 might not have been a Cleveland Pisces if born in 1963. These people are called cusps. If your birthday falls in the cuspy category—from around the twentieth to the twenty-third, depending on the month—you should investigate and find out what planet was shading your birth the moment you were born, and read accordingly.

Generally, the date cutoffs we use are pretty standard. You will find that, if you aren't a cusp, reading within your date range will give you a good understanding of your sun sign's influence on your personality.

But, yeah, what about cusps?

If someone says they are a cusp, it means that they are born within a few days of when the sun was transitioning from one constellation to another. These individuals often have traits of two signs, and it can be hard to really place them squarely as one sign or the other.

This can cause stress when thinking about love compatibility. It can be hard to know what sign is best for them. In these cases, it's good to look to the other planets (like a moon sign) for direction, as the dual sun sign influences won't always give a clear answer.

A lot of people ask us about cusps and if we believe in them. We have slightly different views between us, but generally speaking, we do believe in cusps. They are a real thing, albeit sometimes confusing. They can be hard to understand, but if you or a loved one is a cusp, it's best to come to terms with some ambiguity. If you are a cusp, try to quell your anxiety about "who you are" and realize that you are in many ways both signs that you inhabit, and that is truly great. Like poet Walt Whitman (Gemini) says, you contain multitudes.

The way things are divided in this book

We wrote this book together but we also divided the chapters up evenly, so that each of us is giving you a take on six signs. We picked the signs that we thought we knew the most about (for example, we each took our own sign) and went from there. We thought we'd be happiest writing about the signs we love to think about most. And our goal is always to feel happy and free. We're an Aries and a Sagittarius, after all—both fire signs.

Here is who wrote what:

Aries   Dorothea Lasky
Taurus   Dorothea Lasky
Gemini   Dorothea Lasky
Cancer   Dorothea Lasky

Leo	Alex Dimitrov
Virgo	Alex Dimitrov
Libra	Alex Dimitrov
Scorpio	Dorothea Lasky
Sagittarius	Alex Dimitrov
Capricorn	Dorothea Lasky
Aquarius	Alex Dimitrov
Pisces	Alex Dimitrov

As fellow fire sign and honorary Astro Poet Edmond Jabès says, "All the distance of stars is in writing by night. In the morning, the word becomes the link of a new chance." So, too, the karmic wheel keeps going, whether you choose to acknowledge it or not. Always remember that astrology is your companion, and the zodiac wears the glamorous perfume of magic wherever it goes.

ARIES

March 21–April 19

> I look
> at you and I would rather look at you than all the portraits in the world.
> *Frank O'Hara, born March 27, 1926*

The Aries

It was the year 2016. New Year's Eve. The United States was still reeling from a pretty intense election, and the mood was raw. Apocalyptic.

During the ritual New Year's celebration in Times Square, almost everyone was looking for even a momentary distraction. A night of song and dance, with the giant disco ball dropping from the sky at midnight, might prove that things were normal and as they should be.

Cue the quintessential Aries: Mariah Carey. Born March 27, the same day as the poet Frank O'Hara, the moviemaker Quentin

Tarantino, the actress Halle Bailey (and me, the poet Dorothea Lasky—hi!).

Mariah has been here before. New Year's Eve is practically her own show. So she proceeds to try and save the world in her own strange Aries way. As her first song begins, she stands framed in an endless arc of hot male dancers worshipfully holding these white feathers in the air at odd angles to frame her, her body wrapped in a slinky glittery gold dress. It's just all so . . . comforting.

But as the opening notes of the Aries-apropos song "Emotions" comes on, Mariah realizes quickly that she can't hear the song in her earpiece. In a flash, she becomes very angry. That is to say, Aries angry. Which itself is a mix of the immense red flame—ready to scorch anything in its path—and the intense cold blue flame at the center of all fires. Yeah, she's really mad, but she doesn't freeze up the way a Cancer might. Instead, she visibly blames an unseen other for the technical problems. She performs her displeasure. Into the mic: "We didn't have a sound check for this song, so we will just sing. It went to #1. And that's what it is."

Oh yes. No Aries would ever miss a chance to let you know something they did was #1. If it didn't go to #1, they might tell you it did anyway. Because Lord knows, it probably should have.

The show goes on, somewhat painfully, as Mariah smiles while seething in anger, but it does still go on. To an Aries, the saying "the show must go on" has vital meaning in everyday life. An Aries will let you know they're angry, but they will also always perform their way through adversity.

Because above all, Aries are great charmers. Even the deadly sparkle of Gemini or the deep seductive power of Scorpio is no match for an Aries in full power. Not even the slick cunning of a Capricorn can stop an Aries with a job to do. As the performance tanks, Mariah thinks of a way to make it better. "I am gonna let the audience sing, okay." And she holds her microphone out. "We didn't have a sound check but it's New Year's, baby, so that's okay, you guys," she tells the audience half-convincingly, with a fiery smile.

The terrible performance goes on so insanely long that you have to wonder if there wasn't a vengeful Pisces at the controls. "I want a holiday, too," she tells the audience at some point, half dancing. "Can I not have one?" The audience has no answer. But the universe itself has answered that question for every Aries who has asked it, every second of every day, or at least once in a while. *Uh, no,* says the universe. *You came here to entertain, not to sleep your days away. We have Libras for that.*

At the end of it all, Mariah, in partial despair, partial exhilaration, partial ruthlessness, says, "It just don't get any better." And then she leaves the stage without much fanfare.

She was just being honest, something all Aries are known for. A stage, a crowd, some tunes, and glitter. To an Aries, no, it just doesn't get any better than that. Mishaps and all. It's what they live for.

Things you might want to know about Aries

Aries is a cardinal fire sign, and the first sign of the zodiac, which means that it kicks off the karmic trip around the zodiac wheel. Because of this, Aries is often associated with new beginnings: the start of spring in the Northern Hemisphere and all of its symbolic associations—new flowers, baby birds in love with their mothers, fresh pea shoots out of a freshly mown grassy landscape, holding a person softly in the warm electrical floral air, lightly dusted dryer sheets, the possibility of summer somewhere on the horizon. A fresh start. Aries is the chance we have to get it all right again.

Aries is the sign of birth, and indeed it could be said that all babies begin life as Aries. It's just that everyone else changes into something else, while every Aries kind of just sticks with it.

Like a baby, an Aries carries tremendous energy and potential. An Aries can also be naively innocent and forgiving. They crave your attention and try to get it with all means at their disposal. Like a baby, an Aries will approach you with the expectation that you will love them. Truth be told, most of the time, it will be very hard not to. The world is always a bit new to them, even if they are not young in age, and they tend to assume that good will always overcome evil. To anyone searching for a shred of optimism left in this crazy world, that's intoxicating. Hence that famous Aries charm.

Most of all, like a baby, Aries needs love. Have you ever heard a baby cry in the middle of the night? It may need something in particular—it may be hungry or need to be diapered. But more often than not, that baby is crying because they want to know that the expression of their discomfort gives rise to some profound human emotion in you, and that you will come running to them. Aries cry out into the night because they want to see that someone will care. And, as with a baby, you can never come running fast enough, but if you do get there quickly, all will be right with the world again. If you don't, you will begin to see the Aries's dark side. If you have an Aries in your life, remember this.

Another way to think of an Aries is through the word classically associated with them: passion. When an Aries is into something, they are definitely really into it, and they will do absolutely anything for it. Their passion can sometimes border on obsession, and to an Aries, this is what makes it all the more exciting. This obsession can be a new project or an idea (an Aries usually believes they invented all new ideas). Or it might just manifest as the pallets of water bottles you notice in their apartment after they read a 100-word article online that said drinking alkaline water can help them live longer (which I do believe it can).

If an Aries is into you, then buckle your seat belt. If you have shown anything remotely resembling interest, they are three seconds away from being at your front door. Don't worry, they won't move in. Although for a little while, they may try to.

Some believe that the key to understanding an Aries is their contagious laugh. Whenever I listen to audio of myself laughing, I cringe with disbelief that I sound that ridiculous most of the time, but I have to believe all the people who've told me my laugh gets them laughing along with me. Certainly, as an Aries, it's nice to get lost in humor for a few moments, allowing my heavy ego to be dissolved into the ether. But I don't think laughter is the key to my personality. That's just performance; that's just Mariah on a good (or bad) day. The key to understanding an Aries isn't to be found in their display of charm. Instead it's revealed when they very much are not trying to charm you.

If you have ever known an Aries for longer than a moment, then you have undoubtedly begun to know another important characteristic of their personality: anger. Again, think of a baby clenching its fist in rage. Aries can get mad about a lot of things (and they reserve the right to get mad about anything AND everything, thanks so much), but the thing that drives their temper mostly is control.

That is to say, they need it. They strive to have control of their lives in almost every moment, and anything that stops them from having control over themselves and the situation at hand is going to make them more than a little cranky. They need to be free.

Generally, this means that the Aries in your life is going to need to plan their days as they wish and you'd best not do anything that cuts into their absolute freedom to do whatever the fuck they have planned. This means no obligations, especially ones that involve routines or rituals that they find meaningless or that have nothing to do with them, or in which they cannot engage as the ultimate winner.

Hence the conspicuous lack of Aries at any school reunion. I've never been to any of mine. Because isn't that shit beyond depressing. Am I right, my other Aries out there? It's asserting that period of time was a peak in life, and no Aries wants to believe that they've already peaked.

When an Aries plans their days, these plans will not have any foreseeable focus or goal, the way a Virgo's might. Their to-do list doesn't say "Write important contacts," like that Virgo's does, but they will have in their head some tasks to do that they feel will keep them at the top of their game. What this looks like varies from Aries to Aries, of course, but usually it means creating something that hasn't ever been there before. The most happy Aries will start something new every day where they can be the top boss and delegate tasks. They always want to top something or someone, if they can, because being in charge cures their underlying and ever-present sadness. Every Aries detests being bored. Calling the shots can be a natural antidepressant to an Aries.

This is not to say that they can't sometimes work well with others. If an Aries sees some interaction as important or they truly like someone or something, they can be dutiful and work the long hours no one else would ever dream of putting in. But Aries aren't ever that good at finishing things. If you tell them they have to do it because you said so, that's the quickest way to: a) make sure the Aries never does it; or b) drive them into a complete desperate melancholy. I have a magnet I keep on my fridge at all times that says: "I like group work, as long as I'm in charge." Nothing could be more Aries than that statement.

As mentioned, Aries do get very angry from time to time (read: every hour, on the hour). This is kind of a fucked-up thing to say, but if you know an Aries and they haven't gotten angry at you yet, chances are they don't care about you. If they used to get angry at you in the past and have stopped, they likely think you aren't worth the effort of their anger, for a variety of reasons. More likely than not, you are a battle that they don't care to win. If you care about them still, you should hope that somewhere in there, some tenderness is left in their feelings about you, and that they still remember the one time you came running when they cried in the middle of the night. But like when you need liquid from a sink with a broken hot water faucet, there is only the cold one left to give you water. If an Aries has stopped getting angry at you, likely their blood runs cold. If you love them, let's hope it's a coldness you can overcome and turn around. That's always possible. It's never that hard to get a baby to smile again, even seconds after it has been crying. They love life too much not to.

Aries as a lover

If you are interested in an Aries, DO NOT be shy. Although they are capable of making the first move, if need be, they love it when someone else makes the first move. Aries thrive on sexual attraction, particularly being the object of it. When someone is into them, it gives them reason to think life is worth it. A look that is quasi-intense with desire is enough to make any Aries high with happiness for at least twelve to two hundred and fifty years. Or at least fifteen seconds. But who's counting?

The best love signs for Aries are Sagittarius and Leo, and they also get along very well with Geminis and Aquarians. With Libras, there is an immediate attraction, but unless one agrees to be the submissive one, things could get ugly fast. Aries can get easily obsessed with Scorpios, but this love won't usually be reciprocated with the same intensity. If it is, their love will endure through just about everything and will be real, but it will take effort in communicating their feelings for the attraction to last, something neither sign is that good at. Aries will like other Aries because they basically like themselves, but usually no one has the attention span to make it work. Pisces will dote on Aries, and Aries will usually cave in and date them for a while, but it won't last too long. Aries and Taurus will have a fierce fall-in-love feeling in the beginning, but this will taper off once they get to really know each other. Aries-Capricorn is a doomed match, and Aries-Virgo is just as ridiculous. Aries and Cancer have a deep connection, but they will keep squandering opportunities, and eventually the Aries will walk away angrily and the Cancer will retreat for all eternity.

If you like an Aries, you should probably try to master your skills in eye contact, flirtation, and all forms of PDA. Aries have a reputation for being cold and aloof, but the people who say that probably didn't try hard enough to get an Aries to pay attention. Aries love displaying their relationships in the open, for all to see. One of the greatest memories of my life is when my high school Libra boyfriend and I first walked through the halls of our school, holding hands. The performance of love means more to an Aries than the love itself. I still remember all the gestures of affection that lovers have shown me, even simple ones like a Cancer hugging me sweetly in a coffee shop, or an Aquarius wiping the tears from my eyes when I had been crying. I still get chills remembering making out with a Gemini at a boring and buttoned-up dinner party when everyone else at the table was like *what the fuck*. Honestly, someone could be an ax murderer, but if they kiss me in public, I will turn all dewy-eyed for them, handing over my wallet and my underpants. On the flip side, as soon as these visible forms of affection are gone, so is my Aries heart.

For Aries, affection is cousin to passion, which is always the real key to the Aries heart. If you are sleeping with an Aries and you want to gauge their interest in you, you should become attuned to the fly-across-the-country method. How much an Aries is bonkers for you is directly proportional to how willing they are to get on a plane at a minute's notice, spend at least half a month's rent, and fly across the country to have sex with you. Because there is nothing that turns an Aries on more than someone who tells them they need to be with them immediately in a physical way, and if they feel that way (which they will, if you tell them how much you want them), they will show up at your door, butt-ass naked, even if you live in Australia and they live on Mars (which, duh, they do).

The only other thing that turns an Aries on as much as really disgusting PDA, and them getting on a plane to profess their love in the form of four days of constant, no-holds-barred sex in semi-private and definitely public places near where you live, is when you get on the plane first. I still remember my college boyfriend, an amazing Aquarius, running over to my apartment in the rain (of course, he only had to travel half a block to do so, but go with me here), just so that we could hold each other and stare into each other's eyes in a room filled with low lights. Opening that door and seeing him in that rain-soaked dirty green hoodie ignited every fire cell in my fire sign heart, and to this day I fantasize about sweet men in hoodies showing up in the rain, saying *I love you I love you* over and over again. If you want to keep your Aries, you should be willing to do this at least once in a while. Or maybe every Tuesday (and Thursday). And Wednesday, too. And oh yeah, don't forget about Friday (and also, Saturday and Sunday).

If you want to warm an Aries up, find some way to touch their face lightly. Even a head pat, which seems so patronizing, I know, will oftentimes really entice an Aries to give you a second look.

And if that worked, and you've got an Aries alone, the fastest way to get them really hot and bothered is to keep touching their head a lot. Their actual head—the thing near their face. Nothing gets them going more than a long, in-depth head massage, followed by a neck massage, to release their pent-up tension and anger from being alive as an Aries on earth for however long they've been around. Note: no matter how long that is, there will be a lot of pent-up anger. Probably more than you bargained for.

I'm biased, but I think having sex with an Aries is generally pretty fun. As long as the Aries is into the person, they are pretty much down to try anything once, and they love when people are secretly kinky (which is why they love Aquarians so much). They will engage in group sex, but usually only if it's with people they don't know well. If you want your Aries to be open to these sorts of experiences, the best thing you can do is to manage their jealousy. Being in a threesome where their long-term partner seems into the other person more than them is pretty much their biggest fear, aside from nuclear war and dying in obscurity. But you are going to want to understand their jealous side no matter what you do with an Aries. An Aries must be your #1 at all times. Even if you just met them five minutes ago. Especially then.

In the early stages of a relationship, an Aries can be compulsive and will relish the excitement of having sex multiple times a day over many days with their new person. These displays help their insecurity, because the passion can be quantified. On the flip side, if the passion is gone or if you have pissed them off, their body will be like an ice block. If this happens, warming the ice is not impossible. When I am in an ice age with someone, all they need to do to turn things around is to shower me with warmth. If the Aries matters to you, go to them. Drive across the country, if you have to. Almost nothing else quite gets those warm jets flowing again than knowing that you care enough to be impulsive.

Aries love to flirt, especially after things have been consummated and they know you belong to them. They love constant attention. Or, in truth, they love it for most of the day, with you sending them sexy photos at least every few hours, asking how they are, and generally expressing your earth-shattering desire for them. It's the "most" that's a little confusing. This instinct in them can be a little hard to understand, as you must be willing to do this but must also appear to be independent and have your own thing going on, so that when they are busy working or, more specifically, creating a tableau of three hundred glow-in-the-dark plastic cats in their bathtub, you can chill until they are ready for more attention.

To put it another way, Aries do not like clingy people but often find themselves around them. They want to be wanted, not obligated to respond to a million texts that are about someone else's feelings. This is not to say that if an Aries is into you, they aren't willing to go there emotionally. But because Aries is charismatic, they can attract their fair share of clingers. And then Aries can sometimes be fooled into thinking the clinginess of, say, a Capricorn is about some overwhelming desire, when really it's about how the Aries makes the Capricorn feel alive for once. This dynamic might work for a more nurturing sign like a Cancer, but to an Aries, it spells doom. They need someone who picks them up in the middle of the day with the effervescence of life. My advice to you: be that person.

Aries as a friend

Because Aries aren't calculating, the way all earth signs and all the water signs apart from Pisces are, they aren't necessarily good at making strategic friendships. They will have a sense that certain people are important in their profession, and they will try to win them over if it helps them, but they probably aren't going to be too great at maintaining these types of friendships unless there is a genuine connection. They are attracted to friends who are loyal, who can put up with their angry outbursts, and who respect their need to control their own lives. They love to be complimented, and they love friends who tell them how great they are and how much they mean to them. You can think of an ideal Aries friend as an ideal Aries lover, minus the sex. However, if you are a good enough friend, chances are the Aries has thought about having sex with you at least a few times. Yes, you can take that insight to the bank.

Aries are worth the anger and the effort to constantly stroke their egos, as they will do anything for their true friends. If you are truly in need, you can trust that an Aries will be there for you. If anyone crosses you and they love you, they will get super-fiery and potentially kill the person. At the same time, if you are friends with an Aries then you should be okay with last-minute cancellations and changes in plans, and someone being late to meet up or to get back to you. They will be there for you when they need to be, but not before. An Aries thinks friendship should be fun and easy, because there are plenty of other things in life to worry and stress about (which they do relentlessly), and they won't put up with people who don't agree. Whereas if an Aries is into a person romantically, it is hard for them to completely walk away cleanly; any friend who makes their Aries buddy feel bad will be cut off easily. Aries just have way too much to do to care if you are hurt that they were six minutes late to meet you. It would be better if you understood that you are lucky they showed up at all and brought their magic to your life. If you can't handle this kind of friend, find a sweet Virgo to go to drinks with: they'll be on time, at least. You probably didn't deserve an Aries anyway.

Aries style

Aries are not known for being shy, and this is very evident in their dress. Aries like lots of colors, especially bright colors, and if there is one word to sum up their style, it might be "colorful." If there is a neon shirt anywhere within a two-hundred-mile radius, they will find it swiftly, like a vulture circling around for some dead carcass. Aries are also drawn to fire tones—like all variations of orange. But the color that may best characterize Aries is red. Even if you meet the occasional Aries who is more subdued than the one I am describing, you will find that they have many pieces of red clothing populating their closet. More likely than not, that person you notice in a crowd with a blindingly red sweater on is an Aries. If you get a chance to meet them, be sure to tell them how much you like it.

Because Aries love to perform, they use the everyday as their stage. No matter what they say, and you will find some who deny it, they want to get noticed. Dress becomes a way to charm people; the excitement of the social world is always about overpowering everyone else around them. They want everyone they meet to not only like them but find them the most spectacular person in the universe. This extends to fashion. It's a sure bet that telling an Aries they are the best dresser in the room is a good way to get them to become your friend.

Aries tend to be quite compulsive when it comes to clothes buying, and no matter what their budget is, they will have lots and lots of clothes. Just as they hate committing completely to anything, they hate to commit to one particular style forever. They will purchase things that are cheap both in price and, frankly, in taste. Aries is more apt than most other signs to dress "sexy." In fact, the most direct way to win over an Aries is to tell them how hot they are. (Although I do appreciate when people I meet tell me I am a powerful genius at every turn, I really just want them to say how hot I am.) At root, of course, is that deep insecurity of Aries, who are never sure you will pick them up in the middle of the night from their crib when they are crying. So no matter what you say, compliment them on their sexy shirt, and you will start off on the right foot with them.

Texting with an Aries

Aries aren't known to be the best texters in the zodiac, particularly because text messages can feel like a trap to them. We all know that thing that happens while texting where you are having a conversation that goes back and forth and suddenly no one is sure when it will all end. It's like endless small talk but in emoji form, and to an Aries nothing is more boring and pointless. For that reason, I have my phone on "Do Not Disturb" (but allow calls from certain people); why should everybody's texts interject a million thoughts and emotions into my day without my say-so?

So I admit it is a paradox when I advise: you should text your Aries a lot and often. Although I am slightly annoyed when I see a bunch of texts on my phone, another part of me is happy. Text messages are just another way to get endless attention, and I am sad when it feels like people aren't texting me, because then I am just a baby alone in the world, emotionally starved and cut off from my well-deserved sea of admirers. The best kinds of texts to an Aries are ones that cheer them on, as Aries tend to pack a lot into their days and can suffer easily from exhaustion. Aries love to see that their friends are thinking of them. Aries love to hug, and if your text message is a virtual hug, they will be very excited.

Aries will respond to your text quickly if it involves work or important business, like making money (which they love to do in theory but aren't always good at in the long term). If your text at all feels like it's going to get them in a conversation they don't feel like having, they won't write you back for a long time, or at all. Sometimes an Aries will be silent over text because they are angry and they don't want to give you the power of getting into a fight with them, especially in writing. Texting makes Aries feel vulnerable—it's on the record, and they tend to blurt things out constantly that they haven't thought through or, usually, didn't mean. Nothing is worse to an Aries than you having evidence of their asshole tendencies in a screenshot. If your Aries isn't responding, don't keep writing. It will actually make them explode.

Aries prefer texting pictures, because these show you exactly what they are doing during the day. It's their way of saying "Wish you were here" or "I miss you" or "You matter a lot to me" without having to actually say so. It might even be a way for them to hint: get on that plane.

Aries 1: Happy Birthday!!!!
Aries 2: Happy Birthday!!!!
Aries 1: I love you!!!!!
Aries 2: Talk to you next year!!!!!

Aries: What are you doing now?
Taurus: Sleeping.
Aries: Want to come over?
Taurus: Is 10 hours from now ok?

Aries: I think you are so cute.
Gemini: I was just reading a book about birds who are capable of flying faster than the speed of light! Their wings are actually made entirely of light and they aren't even birds and also I think that the aquariums are just so exquisite. Do you like my new outfit? [sends pic]
Aries: Yes I love it!!!!! Do you like this field of purple flowers? [sends pic]
Gemini: YES! Maybe we can hang out in the next five months?

Aries: Will you marry me? [25 heart emojis]
Cancer: I miss you. [kissing face]
Aries: Can I come over now?
Cancer: Sure. I was just making CBD and kale soup for you.

Aries: You are the hottest person I have ever met.

Leo: I'll be over in 10 min.

Aries: Move faster.

Leo: 6 min.

Aries: Can you help me?

Virgo: Of course!!

Aries: [no response for one week]

Virgo: Everything ok?

Aries: You really upset me when you told me my shirt was ugly.

Libra: You really should learn to chill.

Aries: [10 min later] Want to go see that French film tonight?

Libra: Duh.

Aries: I need to see you.

Scorpio: [no response]

Aries: [The next day] I miss you so much!

Scorpio: [Four years later] Can I have your boss's personal email?

Aries: Oh my goodness, you are the best!!!

Sagittarius: You are!

Aries: Do you want to move in?

Sagittarius: [silence for the rest of eternity]

Aries: [20 emojis all in blue]

Capricorn: Can you talk?

Aries: Not until later.

Capricorn: I'm calling you now. You'd better pick up or else.

Aries: [sends poem they wrote about bees]

Aquarius: I love that. [sends drawing they made of Aries naked]

Aries: You are such a good artist!

Aquarius: What are you doing now?

Aries: I feel so sad.

Pisces: I'll be right over with blankets and bananas. I don't have anything to do tonight so don't worry, I can stay up all night talking.

Aries: I actually have a date.

Pisces: Ok, sure. I'll just stay in your apartment until you come back.

The Aries imagination

If Aries were a city, it would be Rome, with its frantic, almost militaristic energy, deep history of decadence, and lavish worship of power. If Aries were a kind of weather, it would be the sunniest day at the start of spring, with tulips and daffodils everywhere and the smell of hyacinths in the air, a kind of unfocused electricity everywhere, the temperature veering toward hot but not quite. If Aries were a punctuation mark, it would be an exclamation point, and at least three of them. If Aries were a type of clothing, it would be anything seductive that you can take off quickly, so definitely anything involving ties and Velcro. If Aries were a time of day, it would be morning, like the crack of dawn, because life is too short to not cram every day full of life. If Aries were a stuffed animal it would be a non–stuffed animal and instead a beautifully decorated sparkling and glittery figurine that you covet as your most special knickknack. If Aries were a nightmare, it would be full of gore and would creep you out for days but also have a happy resolution. If Aries were a dance, it would be improvisational, as plans ruin dancing, don't they? If Aries were a utensil, it would be a butter knife, because Aries want to cut things but they detest actually hurting anyone. If Aries were a flower, it would be all flowers.

Aries are the pioneers of the zodiac, and they love to think of themselves as discovering new things and saving the world. They are not liars by nature, and they can smell your insincerity a mile away. An Aries's imagination is a landscape of endless enthusiasm. If an Aries is into something, they are all in to the extreme. Aries usually have a set of obsessions, like a particular food, activity, or idiosyncratic type of object, that they will collect and hoard and think about constantly. If they like to eat bananas, then probably they will eat everything banana-flavored, compulsively getting anything that even looks like a banana for as long as they want to.

I once was into strawberries because, I mean, they are so cute, right? I didn't really like to eat them, but I wanted to wear them and I had entire strawberry outfits that I would wear constantly. I am sure people thought my strawberry period was weird, but I didn't even consider what other people thought, so pure was my love for the red and green image of the fruit. I remember one day I found myself dressed as a strawberry, eating strawberry ice cream, and talking on a strawberry phone, and I thought, okay, this is getting a little odd. You can't really reason with an Aries that their obsessions are excessive. They don't even fully understand what the word "excessive" means. But when they are done with something, they are done for good. One day I got so bored with strawberries, and I put all those clothes (and pencils and phones and lamps and pillows) away and never went back. My feeling for strawberries now is a cold indifference.

The idea of a special destiny gets an Aries to do almost absolutely anything. It's not that an Aries even necessarily believes in a universe that cares specifically about them, because despite being narcissistic at times, they are too rational to think this way. But they do want to think that all of the boredom and gross parts of life are somehow worth it. They want to think that somewhere, someone—somehow—is waiting to love them in exactly the way they feel they deserve to be loved. They never really give up hope for this perfect bliss, even when they are in more mundane and seemingly solid relationships or professional paths. Somewhere an Aries is reading this paragraph ready to go back to school, or leave whatever country they are living in, in search of The One. They want to feel that everything isn't completely futile. Ever since birth, they have had this sneaking suspicion that they were put on this earth for a reason.

And of course their suspicion was right. All of us were put here to do something. We all are in search of our destiny. And if we don't find it this time around, we hope that next time we will.

The Famous Aries

One Famous Aries, Lady Gaga, has a song, called "Applause," that pretty much sums up everything about what it's like to be an Aries:

> *I live for the applause-plause, live for the applause-plause*
> *Live for the way that you cheer and scream for me*

Trust me, she means what she sings. Every Aries is a Famous Aries who is trudging through their days, mindlessly doing laundry or cooking (just kidding, no Aries cooks, unless you mean the microwave, or unless they are a world-class chef, dominating all competitors) or staring off into space, waiting for when you feel so moved by their greatness that you put those two hands together and do what they've been waiting for. Clap clap clap. Every Famous Aries loves that sound.

Vincent van Gogh is a good example of a Famous Aries. With his optimistic paint swirls and hyper-bright colors, Van Gogh attempted to represent his intense feelings about life in his art. He wasn't that concerned with depicting reality but instead sought to represent how he, the king of his canvas, felt about reality. There is also the famous story of him being so obsessively in love with a woman that he gave her his ear. For some people, this seems like a sign of illness and very icky, but any Aries who has heard that story gives a little "Eh" in response to it. *I could do better*, they are probably thinking, imagining what body part they'd cut off for their lover. Anything but their genitalia is fair game.

Chaka Khan is another great example of a Famous Aries. Her song "Ain't Nobody" could be the love ballad for any Aries relationship. I like to listen to it whenever I am particularly obsessed with someone. I am sad that Van Gogh couldn't have listened to it when he delivered his ear. In this song, Chaka perfectly captures what every Aries is thinking for the first five minutes after they meet someone they find attractive, which is usually anyone at all. She is a true representative for the Aries cause, which is to live blissfully and peacefully fascinated with something for all time and into eternity.

Aries wants to use their power to achieve not only ecstasy but a higher state of understanding for everyone, especially themselves. The Aries poet Octavio Paz wrote about this possible otherworldly state in his famous poem "Sun Stone" and called it "an actual presence like a burst of singing."

Every Aries is "an actual presence like a burst of singing." Aware of their and others' presence on earth, they also search for something that will take them higher, whether that be art, politics, theater, or love. All of those things and more. Always more.

Other Famous Aries

1. Eddie Murphy
2. Bette Davis
3. Alec Baldwin
4. Tim Curry
5. Elton John
6. William Wordsworth
7. Tracy K. Smith
8. Robert Frost
9. Hugh Hefner
10. Chance the Rapper

Aries playlist

- Akon, "Locked Up"
- Aretha Franklin, "Respect"
- Tracy Chapman, "Fast Car"

- Loretta Lynn, "Somebody Somewhere (Don't Know What He's Missing Tonight)"
- Fergie, "Glamorous"
- Diana Ross, "Ain't No Mountain High Enough"
- Jill Scott, "The Fact Is (I Need You)"
- Billie Holiday, "You Go to My Head"
- Celine Dion, "My Heart Will Go On"
- Selena, "Dreaming of You"

The Aries (a poem)

You are a forest edged in fire. What else can we say about it. Except the red rushing of leaves is not what anyone else had expected. Do you get mad. Yes, you do. You do get angry. You are the ramming thing, coming in full with horns on a jet made of flames. You scorch anything and everything, as if it is nothing. A giant renegade of pure steel. With palm trees and periwinkle bells, you stop reading the sullen hellish book. But who stopped you? Answer me! Because when they said that The Creator does not like the weak, they did not mean you. You are not anything tired, but at times, you acquiesce. You simmer down. When appropriate, of course. And then you light back up again. It's a curse really. You edge your lips in blue and green, and find it very simple to go backwards. Meanwhile, you aren't going anywhere at all. Wild yellow lights where you see it all and can agree that you aren't looking for anything in particular. Sheer life, and an endless trumpeting in the woods. But love is real. Love is real, you said. But no one was asking.

TAURUS

April 20–May 21

To be old is
to be ode.

Tan Lin, born April 24, 1957

The Taurus

If you are ever feeling sad, like nothing in the world matters, all you need to do to feel better is watch a Taurus speak about their hopes and dreams. Listening to a Taurus's words reminds us that if we, too, view life as a slow and deliberate process, we can get back on track toward a goal. And this goal should be (most of the time) to live life as happily as possible, and full of peace. They say that the happiest people are the ones who live life in the present. A Taurus does the present very well—by being meticulous and on a path. They teach us that we should always be on our way toward something we want, if we want to feel whole forever.

If you don't have any Tauruses in your life, extend an SOS into the universe. If you plan to live a long time, you will need at least one. I almost married a Taurus, which would have been a mistake in a lot of ways, but I miss that stable Taurus energy in my day-to-day. That is, until I remember his Taurus anger. Which was nothing to mess around with. If you have never seen a Taurus mad, then seriously, count your blessings. Whereas an Aries can lose both their temper and their mind in a split second, a Taurus's anger is truly scary, because it has built up for at least two centuries. When it finally comes out, run!

So, if you want to listen to a Taurus talk about themselves (their favorite topic) and their rise to success, but don't have any hot-ass bulls lying around (and if it's after 7:00 p.m., they will be lying around, for sure), then try to watch a video of one online. Jack Nicholson, the quintessential Taurus, has done some interviews in his career, but fewer than you might think. As his longtime love, the Cancer Anjelica Huston (what an amazing match), has remarked, Jack Nicholson is not necessarily a fan of being on TV and has done lots in his life to avoid it. She said once, "Jack doesn't want to be that friendly guy in your living room." How ironic! There isn't a Taurus alive who isn't more themselves than in a living room. It just has to be their own.

Despite his inclination not to do interviews, somewhere online you can still find a random interview from 1982, with a stately British interviewer, where Jack Nicholson gives a mini–case study of what makes most Tauruses awesome. As the recording starts, the interviewer asks the question "Can you tell us a point in your childhood when you decided to be an actor?" To which Jack Nicholson replies: "It was a gradual thing, as it probably is with most people. . . . You know, when you're out there in New Jersey, you don't suddenly pop up in the middle of your football practice and say, 'Yes I am going to be an actor.' It sort of doesn't do it that way. I probably started really thinking about doing it after I was doing it. And vaguely when I was working at MGM in the cartoon department, a job which I got really mainly to observe moviemaking because I was so starstruck at that time. Still am."

Here Jack Nicholson exemplifies the Taurus's virtue and belief about their place in the universe. Unlike a Leo, who might think that they were born to be a star, or an Aries, who simply waits for everyone to recognize their genius, a Taurus usually stumbles upon their fate. Despite being one of the most famous American actors of his time, Nicholson explains that he started off "starstruck" and still is. As the interview goes on, Nicholson explains how he appreciates that it took him some time to figure out his calling:

> I always have felt that I was lucky because if I had been successful that early I'd be in a position where I was trying to make a comeback now. Almost all of the actors, for instance the first show that I was in, Michael Landon was the star actor in it, and while we were doing the play he got *Bonanza*. So all of my career, up until when Michael left *Bonanza*, went on while he was on *Bonanza*. And that was very good for him, you know, and everybody was envious as I would be naturally at the time. But in reality now obviously I wouldn't trade it.

Again, Nicholson shows off his skills as Taurus. While he simultaneously acts humble about his slow rise to power as an actor, he still is able to take a dig at Michael Landon, his Scorpio competitor from years ago, who seemingly had the upper hand. After all, Landon got the star role and a solid gig on a show—but also, in retrospect, was pigeonholed for life into a particular kind of good-guy role. You can feel young Jack Nicholson drip with jealousy, as he too wanted this role, but he can now see how his grand life has been shaped by not getting it.

The interview ends with the interviewer asking Jack Nicholson why he is known to call the great, sexy Aries actor Marlon Brando "the Big Man on the Hill." Jack simply replies, in that slow, methodical Taurean voice of his: "Well, he lives up the hill from me."

Saying something off-the-cuff and down-to-earth (literally) and also asserting his power, Jack gives a true earth-infused zinger. With this simple statement, he's letting everyone listening know that he lives in a good neighborhood, in a fancy house that must have cost a lot, and near a powerful movie star, because he himself is one as well. It's a sort of informal but calculated demonstration of class, status, and friendliness. A Taurus punchline through and through. For all the world to see.

Things you might want to know about Taurus

Taurus is a fixed earth sign and the second sign in the zodiac. They follow Aries on the karmic wheel and share the connection all neighboring signs share. Taurus has learned a lesson Aries has yet to learn. Like a baby, Aries will grab at anything, if it seems like fun, but Taurus builds things on more solid foundations. If Aries is all "I am," then Taurus is all "I have." Taurus carries Aries's spiritual experience of fresh starts with them (actually, Tauruses seem to carry all memories with them—forever—but more on that later). Taurus is the older baby, delighting in the tactile sense of life: the feel of the air on its skin, the sweet taste of mother's milk, the beautiful lights that go on and off when the day shifts from night until morning and back again. Still, the baby metaphor remains apt. A Taurus can endure a lot—more than might seem humanly possible—but if it doesn't get what it wants or if you take its toy (or food, God help you), you will have quite a few screams and punches coming your way.

An even more appropriate way of thinking of Taurus is, of course, as a bull. If you have ever been around bulls, you might know that they tend to do their own thing quite a bit. They like to hang out and eat and just kind of chill. That is, until you mess with them too much, or attempt to take something that belongs to them, like their food, love partner, space to lie down on, or anything else that they possess. Then you've just uncovered the biggest red flag known to humankind. And yes, they will charge. I would get out of the way now.

All signs have their own bad reputations, but Taurus does get one it doesn't always deserve. I'll just say it: a lot of people think Taurus is a boring sign. Tauruses really aren't boring at all, and if you are one of those people who finds them very exciting, I am sorry to even bring this up. If you are a Taurus and you are confused by this, pay it no mind. Just keep chewing your cud.

Why do people think of Tauruses as boring? Well, for one thing, a Taurus has a tendency to do the same thing over and over again, especially if it is something that has worked before, but even if it is something that hasn't. They like things to stay the same, and they love the depth of routine. For them, it's not really about doing the same thing, it's about what happens when you do one thing deeply.

I'll give you an example. If you have decided that every Monday you are going to take the same exact two-hour walk through the woods, and you follow through for the next forty-five years, then it's not about doing the same exact walk, it's about the depth of experience that happens as each time becomes a new sort of adventure. After year ten, you know that walk so well that you start to notice the exact day the yellow flowers on the corner of the path come out. After year fifteen, the birdsong has ceased to be random and is a melody you know deep in your psyche. So much so that you can recall it in your dreams, and then you do.

Taureans' true love is real life. The frequentative nature of everyday experience makes a life—a deep and profound life. It's this deep life that they spend their whole existence searching for.

This is not to say that a Taurus is dependable in the way a Virgo might be. Well, a Taurus is certainly dependable, if the situation is part of their larger goals, which are always lifelong. Any sort of obligation that relates to their career, such as any task deriving from a fulfilling job they have committed to, they will carry out gladly. If you are trying to decide between hiring a Taurus or hiring a Capricorn, and you want someone to actually always show up and do the task at hand, hire the Taurus. A Capricorn will work tirelessly, as long as you have hired them to be the boss, because then they can spend their time telling people what to do and hire other people to do the work for them.

A Taurus will give you none of this fuss and will show up dutifully to work, though sometimes a little sleepy or moody, or harboring a bottomless resentment over the one time you didn't remember their brother's birthday or forgot to get them that esoteric French mustard for their ham sandwich (for the evolved Taurus, let's hope that's vegan ham, although, let's face it, it probably won't be). Still, a Taurus is a safe bet to always do the job. It's a quality they master completely. Their noteworthy ability to actually follow through is something to be respected—even feared, if they are your professional adversary. If you are trying to have a contest with a Taurus to see who can last the longest (at anything), I promise you, you won't win.

This is not to say that a Taurus doesn't know how to relax. In fact, they demonstrate the same sort of steadfastness when taking their vacation. Sometimes people find them lazy, because they have seen a Taurus in "vacation" mode. You know, just really resting, sleeping, and otherwise enjoying happily every sensual experience you can dream up. As I mentioned, I almost married a Taurus, and whenever I was driving my Aries self crazy trying to pack a million tasks into two hours, he would tell me to slow down and rest for a while, like a week or so. "Sleep for a few hours," he'd say. "Then next week we will go on vacation. Resting is good for you." It's good advice, really. In this insane, twenty-four-hour-a-day, no-boundaries work environment of Apple computers and caffeine-powered late-capitalistic workplaces, remembering to rest sometimes can be hard. But that Taurus I loved was right. Resting is good for you.

A Taurus has a sense of the importance of resting because they are born equipped with a profound sense of time passing. I always joke with the Tauruses in my life that they move in geological time. It's a joke that most of them don't find funny, because it suggests slowness. But it's a compliment, really. Many of the signs, especially fire and air, can move in atemporal ways, always a bit in the moment and outside of a progression of time itself, through their associative thought patterns and ability to expand time to their will. But history and time both do actually move in a linear progression. Things do happen after one another (or at least that's what we've all agreed to believe).

A Taurus understands a linear progression very well. They understand that you don't get to point B until point A happens. Taureans move through time more deliberately than other signs, with focused persistence, because they know you must endure every point to get to the future. Their approach is refreshing in so many ways, though frustrating to an impetuous fire or air sign. It provides a dependable sense of things. It suggests that if you keep moving and progressing, the world does, too. What could be more comforting than that?

This sense of time relates to a Taurus's sense of history both on the personal and the world scale. A Taurus usually is a bit of a history buff, or has specific knowledge in a particular field of interest. Taureans, with their ruling planet in Venus, love all the arts, especially music. A Taurus will remember most of the random facts about world events that most of us forget. They are particularly good at trivia.

Related to this, Taureans have impeccable memories regarding personal histories. They really will remember everything that has ever happened to them, with an emotional depth that can shock you. A Taurus can seem calm on the surface, appearing to go with the flow. But they internalize everything and, like Scorpios, will remember any slights or compliments you've thrown their way. Luckily, if they like you, they like you, and likely will forever. They can be very sentimental about almost everything, and will keep the one time you brought them cookies at work framed in memory as a happy moment. Treat this apparent sentimentality with caution. Never get into a fight with a Taurus unless you have all your facts straight. Because they really do remember EVERYTHING and are always ready to snap back with a detail or two that no one else could be bothered to recall. Their exactitude and persistence with facts is uncanny.

It might be good to mention one other thing about Tauruses, just in passing. Yep, that's good old Mom. Although Taureans aren't obsessed with their mothers like Cancers, whose ruling planet of the moon makes moms their goddesses, moms are also really important to Taurus. The idea of domesticity and stability enlivens them, and this relates to the image of the mother. It's true for them even if their particular mother wasn't exactly this sort of figure. They will try everything they can to give her the benefit of the doubt. And if you like a Taurus, you must do the same. Also, never insult any other member of a Taurus's family. Yes, they will bite you if you do. And no, not in a hot way.

Taurus as a lover

If you are searching for a partner who will take your relationship very seriously, who will remember every early look and kiss you've ever shared, who will write poems about your kisses and pour rose petals in your bath and cook you dinner, who won't ever, EVER leave you at the altar, so to speak, or flake out once you've actually signed the lease on your new apartment together, who will hold you all night and then some, then you are in luck. A Taurus can be this person for you, and more. They will want to be your divine domestic partner and gladly will move heaven and earth for you. They've been waiting for someone who can really appreciate their assets. If that's you, then you should consider yourself truly lucky. A Taurus is a person of many riches when it comes to love. It just might take them a little while to get there. Remember always that this fixed earth sign is arguably the most fixed of any in the zodiac.

The best matches for Taurus are Capricorn, Virgo, Pisces, and Cancer. It is said that Cancer-Taurus is one of the best matches of the zodiac, because they have the same motivations to make a stable home and will cultivate a sense of family together. A Taurus will feel like the magnetic pull from the center of the earth is at play when they meet a Scorpio, and if the Scorpio doesn't stray, the love will last a lifetime. (Hell, it probably will even if the Scorpio does, although the Taurus will never forgive them.) Taurus and Libra share a love of beautiful things, but this is where the compatibility ends, as they have absolutely no way to talk to each other. Taurus and Aquarius will like each other's stubborn sides and then things will go downhill from there. Taurus will be drawn to Gemini's fun personality and endless chatter, but when the Taurus tries to pull the two of them closer, Gemini will bolt. Taurus and Leo is a common match, and nobody is too happy about it, especially them. Most Taureans will fall hard for a Sagittarius, and for a little bit (read: a maximum of eight months), the Sagittarius will get a thrill from Taurus's not so subtle determination. After that, the Sagittarius will lose the Taurus's number and the Taurus will cry for years. Aries and Taurus is a very cuddly match, but God help us all when they start fighting. Taurus will love another Taurus, but it will last only because no one wants to make the effort to get up and go to the door.

Before we get too deep, however (which, I know, is probably never possible, considering the endless amethyst depths of a Taurus), I want to give some advice for those signs who are into a Taurus and want a quick method of seduction. If you want to get with a Taurus and don't have a lot of time for courtship (the average length of Taurean courtship is at least six years from the first time you held hands), there is a quick fix, and it's called food. If you want that Taurus to fantasize about your hot bod all day at work, open your Grubhub app and start typing in two search terms: "fried" and "chocolate." I guarantee you if you send a Taurus something decadent to eat with your name attached to it when they least expect it, their workday won't go fast enough. For extra effect, drop the words "honey" and "sweetie pie" somewhere when they write to thank you. No question they will be at your door, pants-less, by 5:01 p.m.

Taureans are sexy as fuck and they know it. The sexiest thing about them is the way they hug. I still think about the one time my old Taurus boyfriend sweetly hugged me (no, that's not weird or anything). They just have a way of enveloping you in warmth and kindness. If you haven't ever escaped into a Taurus's safe arms, then you haven't really ever lived. Their embrace means acceptance, desire, protection, and vulnerability, all at once. Their arms are their own kind of foreplay. With you in their arms, they can start to believe that you are theirs. Possession excites them more than anything.

Taureans' super-sexiness doesn't always translate to the bedroom in terms of inventiveness. They believe in sex as an expression of love but also as a positive bodily function. They tend to think that if a body can do something, then it isn't a bad thing. They are nature lovers this way. Because of this, they actually can get into things like sex toys in a big way. If one can have a little pleasure, then why not a whole lot of it. Not naming names, but I've known a Taurus (or two) to drop a couple of grand on an enormous quartz dildo, bedazzled (safely, if you're wondering) with crystals and expensive gems.

When you are trying to turn a Taurus on, consider that their throat and neck are where their desire comes from. It's why many Taureans are great singers or speakers. They really love long, romantic kissing, including passionate make-out sessions that last multiple hours. (Oh, who am I kidding, everything a Taurus does lasts multiple hours.) Also, they love neck massages, with strong and gentle rubbing all over the area. And try nibbling them at the neck, good old-fashioned hickey-making style. They will go wild.

Sex aside, your Taurus lover may say sometimes they want to be alone, but frankly, that's just not true. Perhaps you hurt their feelings and you don't realize it, and they are giving you some time to figure out what you've done. Because if they aren't mad and they love you, they want you to be there with them, always, ready to go under the covers when it's time to sleep after your last adventure together. They are loyal and loving and also pretty needy. All Taureans are sort of the best kind of dogs, ready to sleep at the foot of the bed if they need to, if that's what it takes to be near you. But be near you they must. They don't want to be annoying, but they also are . . . persistent. If you shut the door, they will wait in front of it until you open it again. If they possess one quality, it's patience.

Taurus and Scorpio are opposite signs in the zodiac, which in astrological terms means that they are polar opposites yet still share deep similarities, especially when it comes to love. Comparing the way a Scorpio and a Taurus love is instructive. A Scorpio lover would like to conquer your soul and all its trappings—would like your ego to be theirs through all space and time, in a never-ending form of spiritual possession. A Taurus's desire for you is manifestly about physical possession. They want to completely be one with you in this lifetime. That can be a terrifying idea if you aren't into it. But if you are, then seriously nothing is hotter. Ask any Cancer what it's like to sleep with a Taurus, and you can see in their eyes the moon all misty with mountain air. For the right person, a Taurus love is everything they've ever dreamed of come true. In this insane world, a Taurus hug can feel like the answer to everything.

Tauruses' need for possession relates to their idea of commitment. They definitely want commitment, and lifelong commitment is their ultimate goal. This is not to say that they don't ever experience their fair share of non-monogamous sex. They are creatures of the body and they like sex, no matter who it's with. They will sleep around if it suits them and if they haven't yet made a commitment to anyone. Once they're in a relationship, they are more open than you might think, especially if the action itself involves "feeling good." They understand that we are trapped in these bodies, so we might as well enjoy ourselves. Enjoying themselves is practically their religion, after all.

However, if they've committed themselves to a monogamous thing, and you (their partner) decide that you can have some random sex or, worse yet, be into anyone else, then you might need to also be ready to sign the divorce papers. They may be slow to make up their mind, but once they have locked the door of the house, with you in it, then you damn well better be happy about it. Because once you unlock that door and decide to party at the local jumping joint for the night, then you'd better have taken with you everything you own, including your grandmother's dishes. A Taurus won't ever forgive any of your transgressions. And they certainly won't forget. Remember, they don't forget anything.

Truth is, if you've plucked the sweet rose from the bush and have gotten everything all set up in the beautiful house you share with your Taurus (and it will be beautiful), with maybe at least one good dog to sit by the fireplace, then who needs the idiots at the local bar anyway. Oh, you fuss too much, stop looking out the window and come sit in the armchair alongside your true love. There are plenty of blankets (and there always will be, even if you live in Florida and it's mid-July), a giant bowl of pasta with imported truffle oil and a little high-end basil, and someone just downloaded a lot of shit on Netflix. Are you crying? Is it out of happiness? Don't worry, whatever is wrong, your Taurus will protect you. Their soft arms will make everything bad go away. Rest your eyes a little. Sleeping will do you good. "Sleeping is the only love," the Silver Jews sing in the background.

Taurus as a friend

Taureans are as true to their friends as they are to their lovers. Taurus is very family-oriented, and they will tend to see close friends as extended family members, entitled to the same level of care and concern as any cousin. If you have ever made a friendly impression on a Taurus, and particularly if you ever did something that made them laugh, they will absolutely never forget you. Even if the two of you have been out of touch for a long time, they will still think of you as someone close, inviting you to graduations and baby showers and sending you thoughtful messages on holidays and birthdays. Your Taurus friend will definitely always want to be the one to hold your hand while you are crying or otherwise upset.

A Taurus wants to protect everyone they love, and that means you. As long as you have a Taurus on your side in the moment, they will be by your side like no other friend ever. If they commit to your friendship (and they see commitment as an important step in any relationship), you can be sure that they will protect you from the outside world forever; however, protecting you from themselves and their temper, well, that's another matter. As I mentioned earlier, Taurus seems sort of chill and low-key—that is, until you anger them.

Tauruses don't like to be bossed around or ever expected to do something just because you said so. Because friends tend to not be as demanding of them as a love partner might be, if you are one of their friends you won't always see this angry side of them. But if you do incite it, by trying to control them, taking something that is theirs, or otherwise disrespecting them, especially in public, then you will be sure to see the bull charging at you, and it won't be a pretty sight. You will barely remember that calm Taurus you saw a moment ago, as you will now see fixed earth in a rage, a pure red, like the bloodred flag a matador carries. (Unfortunately, in this metaphor, that red flag is you.)

That's the thing about Taurus anger—and any of their moods, for that matter. They just don't fuck around if they really feel something. They can literally fight all night (and the next night, and the next night . . .) if they feel like it. So it's best to avoid fights with them, if you can. They do like to be challenged, however, and will enjoy an intellectual conversation or two with you, provided you think basically the same way they do and/or are willing to change your mind to completely mirror their opinions. Luckily for many water signs, Taureans actually prefer friends who have emotional needs and outbursts, and who call them crying at odd hours. They don't like the crying part, because it upsets them so much and they feel so bad that you are really sad, but they like that you've turned to them. Plus, I lied, they secretly do like the crying, because it shows you feel, and Tauruses love people who feel lots of things and give in to the irrational in a way they themselves can't ever quite do.

The other thing about a Taurus friend is: they are an earth sign, after all. Again, they aren't snobs, but they have a tendency to think ruthlessly about personal connections and how they can get money and stability over time. If they think of you as an "important" person, they will suck up to you probably better than any Capricorn could have dreamed of. They also in these situations have a predilection to tell lies. They may be motivated to lie because you have an asset or a commodity they desire. Or they might think it's just plain good business to know you. Even so, their solid Taurus love will kick in eventually, and before they themselves know it your bond will be real. No Taurus, however professionally cunning, is likely to ever completely abandon you.

Indeed, a Taurus rarely will ever completely abandon anyone. It's just that you won't always get what you want, or what you once got from them, if they feel that associating with you has stopped being productive. At the same time, there is that one-in-a-trillion occasion where a Taurus has decided that you have done something they can't forgive, or your charm has lost its luster, or you've lost some resource they needed. And then they will cut you off, if they must. They won't like it, but they will do it. And once you are out in the cold with a Taurus, there is absolutely no turning back. Again, their fixed nature will come into play. And fixed they will be to the word "good-bye," if necessary. If this is the case with you and your Taurus buddy, I will start praying for you now. Because you will miss them if they go away!

Taurus style

Venus is a classy ruler, and Taurus does have a fabulous way of dressing. Cher aside, you usually won't find a Taurus in too flamboyant a costume, unless they are getting ready for a costume party (which, incidentally, could be every day, explains Cher, playing the lifelong role of "DIVA" in the movie of her life). Never, ever forget that Audrey Hepburn was a Taurus.

Taurus, like their earth sign kindred Virgo and Capricorn, usually likes to wear clothes that escape the immediate attention of most people and help them fit into a crowd. Although unlike the other two earth signs, Tauruses tend to look good, wearing clothes that fit them well. They don't mind spending money to get things tailored so that they look as sexy and fit as possible. They also don't mind spending some cash to get a very nice one-of-a-kind piece (or two) for their wardrobe. They will make sure it lasts a long time.

For a Taurus, clothing is a way to show status. But since they aren't snobs like Cancers can be, they will wear all of their gold watches with a bit of flair. They enjoy the attention they get from people when they look as if they have some money in the bank, but they don't like the idea of their financial security making anyone feel uncomfortable. If they have a Chanel bag, they will use the same one over and over again, and it will be in a classic shade (like very dark brown). They like brand names only if the average person can't tell that an object cost a lot. They'd rather it be an inside secret to people who can afford the same sort of thing. Conversely, they aren't one to announce that they've found a bargain.

And they kind of think fancy stuff is bullshit, if the piece won't last you for the rest of your life. They prefer good-quality items that make them feel powerful—something a Taurus needs in order to feel alive. This might explain why I have known a lot of Taureans to wear Converse sneakers, so much so that I tend to think of it as a "Taurus shoe." All those Tauruses must appreciate the look and stability of classic sneakers. I admire them for this, but it's hard for me to relate. As an Aries, I've tried to like Converse, but even in neon pink they bore me.

Taurus tends to follow earth sign patterns of favorite colors: deep yellow ocher, browns, dark greens, and midnight blue. Their go-to is an all-black outfit, and they will somehow make it look classy and not goth. They like everything on them to have a little bit of dirt tone to it, as it helps them feel grounded. They sometimes will like a burgundy dark red, like the color of wine. Aged red wine is something they hold up there in high regard with things like money, Mama, and God (however they define it). They like whites and creams and pale colors, provided they are natural-feeling and the fabric looks a bit like burlap. They will wear patterns, but not particularly loud ones, unless they are a performer and the role calls for it. If it's polka dots on their silk shirt, then it will be a black background and tiny white dots. If it's stripes, it will be navy and white and barely anything else. They usually love plaid, but never a loud plaid. They love jewels (there's that Venus ruling planet again), but only refined ones, like an understated emerald or a small gold chain. You usually won't find a Taurus in statement earrings, no matter what the situation. And if you do, then it's because they got paid to do it. You can bet the stars on that.

Texting with a Taurus

Taureans don't love texting, particularly long conversations that could more easily be had in person over a big glass of wine, while staring into the eyes of the person they are talking to. A Taurus finds texting a little too abstract, a little too technical and weird, and won't easily get the hang of it. Every text they send will be done with an air of irony, as if they can't believe they are actually typing "on this thing" and not communicating in the real world. Although they respect and love the idea of innovation, they still think the world should go back to its old-fashioned days: pre-texting, pre-phones, pre-computers, pre-TVs, pre–street signs, pre-anything. They are always wanting to escape into a reality that involves a log cabin, a dog, cheese, chocolate, and sex (in that order).

That doesn't mean they won't text you, however. If your texting communication involves something related to work, they will be prompt in getting back to you and giving you any details you need. If you have a co-worker who is a Taurus, they may get into a texting vortex with you and start expressing A LOT of pent-up opinions and emotions that seem to come out of nowhere about co-workers and how inept they are. If they think you have some sort of expertise in something that they don't, or they want to find out your opinion about something, they won't just text you once and accept one simple answer that you dashed off in a hurry. They will endlessly ask you questions that demand very specific answers and will not give up until they have exhausted you and gotten every drop of information out of you.

If they are your friend, they will enjoy texting you sporadically with emotional gestures that may seem to come out of nowhere. Again, time just doesn't move in the same way for a Taurus as it does for most people, and to them it will feel just like yesterday that the two of you shared this particular moment together (that actually happened seven years ago) that they must commemorate via text. And just as I described elsewhere, the word "sentimental" was basically developed for a Taurus. On holidays, they will text you something mushy and tell you how much you mean to them and send you pictures they took twenty years ago of you smiling. If they ever felt an intense heart stroke for you, texting is the perfect place to remind you how much they care. Trust that even if you haven't heard from a Taurus in a while, they definitely still love you and you will hear from them at some point, probably sooner than you might think.

If your amour is a Taurus, then count yourself lucky, because they will probably try to be better at texting you than they would just about anyone else. They like to keep all of their lovers close and maybe you even closer, so they will use texting as a way to keep their access to you. Oh yes, they will check up on you, at least a few times during the day if you work away from home, to make sure you still love them and haven't forgotten about them. They will write at exactly 2:32 p.m. every day to learn what you'd like for dinner so that they can start planning it for you (it had better be spaghetti). Better yet, they will probably just FaceTime. If you are away from your Taurus soulmate for too long, texting just isn't going to cut it for them. They long to touch your sweet face and will count the hours until they see you again. All it takes is a couple of "I love you, sweetie pie honey sugar pie honey face" texts during the day to make your reunion at 5:01 p.m. all that much sweeter.

Taurus: I just did your taxes, smooshy face.
Aries: Thank you!!!!!
Taurus: Will you go to the movies with me tonight?
Aries: Definitely!

Taurus 1: I've been working
Taurus 2: I've been working on something
Taurus 1: I've been working on something important
Taurus 2: I've been working on something important for you

Taurus: It's so snowy outside. I wish you were here to sit with me by the fire.
Gemini: [one week later] Have you heard of William Blake?
Taurus: Of course.
Gemini: Wanna come over and read him to me while I sleep?

Taurus: I bought you an engagement ring.
Cancer: I just made enough spaghetti for 10 people.
Taurus: [rings bell] Wanna get hitched?
Cancer: You'll have to meet Mama first.

Taurus: I read the report. The conclusions have nothing to stand on.

Leo: I read it too and I completely disagree.

Taurus: You'd disagree with life itself.

Leo: If that meant never talking to you again then sure, I would. Life, I disagree!

Taurus: Let's go to the beach today.

Virgo: Yes!

Taurus: On second thought I hate the beach.

Virgo: Me too!

Taurus: I went to the museum and thought of you.

Libra: I love the way sculpture contains all time.

Taurus: I grew the strangest lettuce.

Libra: Feed it to me on top of some lemons.

Taurus: I will never leave you.

Scorpio: I wish I could say the same.

Taurus: We are soulmates.

Scorpio: We are something.

Taurus: A car is picking you up soon for our date.

Sagittarius: Oh that's today?!

Taurus: I could just come over, if that's easier.

Sagittarius: It's not.

Taurus: You are majestic.

Capricorn: You look so complicated under the winged hearth.

Taurus: Could I fly?
Capricorn: If you want to.

Taurus: Strawberry or cherry milkshake?
Aquarius: Pickle-flavored. And I'm vegan.
Taurus: I know, but veganism is ridiculous.
Aquarius: Never contact me again.

Taurus: I can be everything you've ever wanted.
Pisces: A tiny ballerina lodged in the dashboard of my wandering
    automobile?
Taurus: Even that.
Pisces: Peace.

The Taurus imagination

If Taurus were a city, it would be London, with its deep history, sense of decorum and order, and dash of celebrity and pageantry in its political process. If Taurus were a kind of weather, it would be a moody summer rain at 3:01 p.m. that goes on until 7:45 p.m. and then brightens into a dark purple sunset. If Taurus were a punctuation mark it would be a colon, a neat and tidy place to put a list of things or to further explain a subordinate idea. If Taurus were a type of jewelry, it would be a nice gold necklace that you can wear with anything. If Taurus were a day it would be Thursday, with everyone still working hard at their jobs but ready for the weekend, and a little bit of Sunday, especially the Sunday dinner part. If Taurus were an animal, stuffed or not, it would be a bear, big and cuddly and fuzzy and warm, with the real one tearing you up and swallowing the soft parts of you and the stuffed one soothing you. If Taurus were a type of dream, it would be one you could barely remember, but would include some pink smoke over a solid mountain, and you would feel a refreshment after waking up that would be extremely kind. If Taurus were a type of exercise it would be Pilates, very graceful and overpriced in urban areas, but also simple and great. If Taurus were a type of cooking tool, it would be a cake pan for, you know, delicious cakes, savory or sweet and also maybe both. If Taurus were a plant, it would be grass, like the kind that fills an endless field, and it would beckon you to lie down on it, because why not, life is short, and you should, at least in this present moment, be happy.

A Taurus's imagination always involves building. Whether it be a career or a lifelong love, a Taurus rejoices at the idea that if you put effort into something for a long time, you will be rewarded with something strong and solid that you can hang your hat on. This extends into expectations for everyone else around them, too. You must be a solid figure, someone dependable who also is able to spark their interests, and with your own solid sense of fire and passion. A Taurus's imaginative landscape includes an endless sense of fire. Not a fire that would burn anything up, but one that brings warmth, that fuses things together, that solders pieces and melts things when necessary, that provokes and cajoles and pranks but is also good for lending itself to endless conversation and camaraderie. A real working fireplace. The imagination of a Taurus is a place where things get done, rather than happening on their own.

A Taurus's vision of heaven is one where pleasure upon pleasure is heaped. Where there is no silly sense of right or wrong, but right and wrong are implicitly understood. Instead of pearly gates, they would be a dark brown wood, and lined with giant pines and fir trees. There would be trumpets playing a song that is half dirge, half love ballad. Everyone would look very smart and sweet (and tough!) and would wear glasses. Tattooed on the hand of every lover would be a credo. "Live well," it would say.

The Famous Taurus

The perfect example of a Famous Taurus is Cher. The self-proclaimed Goddess of Pop, populating the airways for what feels like an entire century with lovesick ballads like "I Found Someone" ("to take away the heartache since you've been gone") (damn, what a burn), "If I Could Turn Back Time" (something every nostalgic Taurus wants desperately to do, so that they can live in the glorified past forever), "I Hope You Find It" (subtle burn), and "When You Find Out Where You're Goin' Let Me Know" (let all of us know, please), Cher uses the everlasting romanticism infused in these Venus-laced lyrics to show us all what it's like to really love someone. Because when a Taurus loves, that means forever. And when this forever seal is broken, the hurt goes on forever, too. Cher is the songbird of how deep this hurt can go.

Taureans love to be famous. A Scorpio will at least pretend to hate it, with their coy grin, as they backstab anyone in sight. But a Taurus will openly like being famous, because it means they get to enjoy many of the gifts of fame: luxurious clothes, brushes with more famous people, dramatic encounters, and pleasure. Once they have tasted fame, they will work very hard to keep up their status, overbooking themselves with live performances, interviews, collaborations, and projects. They will find the fast pace of making money when you're famous intoxicating, and they will enjoy being sucked up to and having an entourage around them. The exchange of power, with them at the helm, is one of Taurus's greatest turn-ons.

James Brown is another perfect example of a Famous Taurus. Working tirelessly throughout his career to bring his sweet sounds to us all, he was known as the Hardest-Working Man in Show Business for a reason. In his career of well over 35 years, he was able to place 110 songs on the charts. Songs like "Night Train" and "I Got the Feelin'" shaped at least two generations of music lovers, blending staccato oceanic beats with guttural (here's that Taurus word again) romanticism. James Brown sang plainly and wisely about love, life, and all of the important things in between. When he sang "Get Up (I Feel Like Being a) Sex Machine," he brought hordes of listeners out of their slumber, dragging his very classy glittering and loud capes behind him in his classic side step. If you've ever watched a video of the Godfather of Soul perform, or have been so lucky as to have seen him live, you can understand the sheer number of hours that went into the making of his genius. All of that Taurean hard work, sweat, and power made music that still inspires us all.

A Famous Taurus might use their fame to do something that helps the world, but generally their work is more personal. Other earth signs are more apt to be true idealists, like Virgo Bernie Sanders, but Tauruses are more likely to be artists or musicians, using their place in the world to sing us their truth. They put their beliefs in their songs. It's true, too, that a Famous Taurus will enjoy their mouthpiece as a place to seek out revenge of some sort, particularly the love-spurned variety. Think Adele's "Send My Love (to

Your New Lover)," a tongue-in-cheek love song meant to burn the whole house down, including the asshole who was stupid enough to break up with her. Bernadette Mayer's poem "You Jerk You Didn't Call Me Up" extends a similar go-fuck-yourself-dickwad message:

> I haven't seen you in so long
> You probably have a fucking tan
> & besides that instead of making love tonight
> You're drinking your parents to the airport

You can't help but almost feel sorry for this dumb jerk (probably a Pisces or a Gemini), too full of himself to bother calling the persona back, and getting dragged so ferociously in this poem. Of course, since a Taurus wrote this, the events referred to could have happened twenty-five years prior to when it was written. Like politicians Senator Cory Booker and Mayor Bill de Blasio have shown us, almost any Taurus has the ability to call up a historical fact at a moment's notice to support an argument. It's a skill they always have at the ready.

Other Famous Tauruses

1. Stevie Wonder
2. Janet Jackson
3. George Clooney
4. Barbra Streisand
5. The Rock
6. George Oppen

7. Tina Fey
8. George Washington
9. Enya
10. Ella Fitzgerald

Taurus playlist

- Adele, "Send My Love (to Your New Lover)"
- Ella Fitzgerald, "They Can't Take That Away from Me"
- James Brown, "Papa's Got a Brand New Bag"
- Cher, "If I Could Turn Back Time"
- Stevie Wonder, "Boogie On Reggae Woman"
- Billy Joel, "Scenes from an Italian Restaurant"
- Duke Ellington, "It Don't Mean a Thing (If It Ain't Got That Swing)"
- Enya, "Only Time"
- Barbra Streisand, "Memory"
- Jonathan Richman, "True Love Is Not Nice"

The Taurus (a poem)

What is time, you said when you left the ocean. You spotted the very divine settings of a linen barricade set up for a very nice supper. Hi, you thought, but you did not say it. Instead you carried a rather heavy load into the entryway, much to everyone's displeasure. If it were only about loyalty, the story might go on as it should. No, instead your highest romance descended the staircase. Well hello, you thought, and did not say it. And then you felt a gnashing at your teeth. Which left your mouth and went into your stomach. And then the pink ice began to complete its entire ring around the moon. The entire wet story of love, which, for some, flies away or is broken. *Oh shit,* said someone standing at your side. You could not even believe your luck. What a time it is to be broken. *It's not luck,* someone said, *you asked for it.*

GEMINI

May 22–June 20

My poetry is a game. My life is a game. But I am not a game.

Federico García Lorca, born June 5, 1898

The Gemini

In 1965, Bob Dylan gave a rare press conference in San Francisco. After a few basic questions, which Dylan answered begrudgingly, a reporter (probably a Virgo) asked him: "Is there anything, in addition to your songs, that you want to say to people?"

Good old Bob (almost a cuspy Gemini, and with a Taurus moon to boot, but a Gemini nonetheless) replied simply: "Good luck."

Yeah, that's all he wanted to say, to all those millions of adoring fans coming to poetry for the first time who were lucky enough to hear the siren's sweet call from someone as adept as a May-born singer. Good luck. Finding the perfect phrase, one that conveys,

with more than a hint of sarcasm, a half-sincere, half-cutting inten-
tion, is about as Gemini as it gets.

So in the spirit of the one sign that, in most situations, talks and
talks and talks and talks (and talks and talks . . .), those are the
brief words I will impart to you, dear reader, before we even begin
this chapter. Good luck. You are probably going to need it.

I say this with no malice. I am particularly attuned to Geminis
because, full disclosure: I had a triple Gemini father, have had
many more than my fair share of Gemini lovers, have been mar-
ried to a Gemini for over ten years, have a Gemini child, and have
had more Gemini friends and co-workers than you may care to
count. (I sure don't feel like counting them right now, but hey, I'm
an Aries.) If life were college, I've double-majored in poetry and
astrology, with a concentration in Gemini. I feel like I'm endlessly
writing my thesis on the twins. Goddess bless them. And help me.

It probably wasn't too hard to spot a Gemini the first time you
saw one. Were you bowled over by as much charm as there is wide-
open space in the Grand Canyon? Did you notice a person with
more sparkles in their eyes than there is in a whole gift set of Kat
Von D's Glimmer Veils? Was the person simultaneously checking
their email, texting fifty people pictures of a ladybug, organizing a
political revolution, reading Giorgio Agamben's *Homo Sacer: Sov-
ereign Power and Bare Life*, making out with your sister AND your
mother AND your grandfather's ghost AND both of your dogs AND
several inanimate objects, making a map of a "New Outer Space,"
and still all the while giving you scary eye contact and telling you
how hot your butt is? Yep. That's the one. Say hi to both of them
for me.

Things you might want to know about Gemini

If Aries are the babies of the zodiac and Tauruses are the slightly older toddlers on the karmic wheel, then Geminis are the twin three-year-olds of the bunch, ready to cross boundaries and get into trouble (but not enough trouble that you stay mad at them for very long). Like any three-year-old, they are just starting to cultivate a real love of language and the imagination. Whereas an Aries will cry out for what they need and a Taurus will scream, a Gemini will know how to ask for what they want. You will feel tempted to give them anything they've asked for, which they will appreciate in the moment but quickly forget. Their need for attention is just as intense as that of their younger sun sign neighbors, but they will have more tools at their disposal to fulfill their own desires. Geminis are mutable air signs, which means that they have the gift of easy communication. They concoct entire universes in their heads and they like to tell everyone about them with gorgeous words. Anyone who is willing to listen to them is their new best friend. That is, until they find (just like a three-year-old) a new one.

Like all signs, Geminis get their fair share of misunderstanding. Some people think of Geminis as these malleable, mercurial, fickle, restless, careless, tricky, tardy, sneaky, and flaky entities. Of course, this is all true and these people are correct. But it isn't the whole story.

If you are a Gemini, you are probably used to this truth: that sometimes people get scared when they hear you are one. They will back away s-l-o-w-l-y, like "Oh . . ." They are right to be at least a little scared. However, there is a lot more to Geminis than the trappings of their reputation.

Perhaps the great Gemini Walt Whitman summed up best what should be said by all Geminis when they first meet you, in place of their name or any other sort of typical societal marker: "Do I contradict myself? / Very well then I contradict myself, / (I am large, I contain multitudes.)" Because if there is one thing that we can all be certain about, it is that all Geminis will contradict themselves. And be contradictory. And agree and disagree with themselves constantly. And also disagree with you. For the sole reason that, most of the time, it's fun to. Remember: life is a game.

If you are trying to spot a Gemini in a crowd, you will first notice them by the quality they of all the signs have in excess—that elusive stuff of life: charm. They really have it—all that glimmering dust falling everywhere. If you know you're talking to a Gemini and they haven't charmed you yet, stick around for at least twenty more seconds. They will.

When you meet most Geminis, you will very quickly begin to see what I lovingly refer to as the Twinkle. Absolutely every Gemini has it. It's that mischievous, fun, and jolly sparkle in a Gemini's eyes that lets you know they are down for just about anything you have to offer, especially if it's a party. Geminis are tricksters, in the best and most ancient sense of that word.

That's because they are ruled by the planet Mercury. If you know anything about that dude from an ancient mythology textbook, you probably remember that he: a) had wings on his shoes; b) was the protector of poetry, luck, and thieves. That about sums up any Gemini, too. Their twinkling eyes looking at you—well, what could be better than that? Yeah, I know, it sucks: nothing.

Geminis are extremely social. Even the occasional Gemini who mischievously tells you they are introverted will sport a pair of those twinkling eyes to let you know that they love you and that they love your attention, that they want to share their ideas with you and just have a great time with you. If you know a Gemini, you will see in time how deeply this external twinkle penetrates into their psyche and soul. An air of magic and possibility extends to almost anything that they do. Likewise, if you have a Gemini as part of your intimate life and you are finding that twinkle fading, then rush them to the ER immediately. They simply aren't themselves without that zest for life—it's an everlasting fire that is quite impossible to ever stamp out completely. Be very scared if you see it gone, because something about their aura is seriously fucked up. Let's hope it's not beyond repair. With a Gemini, it hardly ever is.

Most Geminis move in a kind of bouncy, jumpy manner (resembling microwave popcorn, which they all love, by the way) that is rather adorable to watch. It's easy to notice only when they are far enough away for you to see it, which of course is a rare occurrence because they are so irresistible and are usually standing very close to you. I recently saw my Gemini friend give a poetry reading, and he was literally bouncing as he read his rhythmic words. It was a beautiful sight to see. My son is an infant Gemini and he has something sort of like a dance that he does when you talk to him. He can't speak yet, but he gets so excited at the sound of words that he will sway from side to side and bounce himself around, laughing hysterically. A tiny poet he is, no doubt. My Libra mother always tells this story about how at a party my triple Gemini father came bounding toward her like a big, bouncy ball, smiling and waving with his olive plaid 1970s leisure suit on. "I'm a Gemini, what're your hang-ups?" he asked her, still bouncing, with piles of alchemical glitter falling from his lips. I've spied my Gemini husband walking down our street on the way back from some local adventure looking like a dandelion turning its yellow head toward the wind in bliss. Gemini movements are the animation of their souls, which are lovely, happy things, infusing the energy of lemon yellow and sky blue wherever they go.

Geminis love to be anywhere and everywhere, especially if these places are new to them. They detest monotony, obligation, and duty, because all of these things are very boring. And yet, because they aim to please others, they will often be the most dutiful and committed people you know. Especially if you explain to them how much you adore them for the things that they do. Always tell your Gemini, "Thank you for being there for me. You are the best." *The best! she says*, they will whisper to themselves. *No, this is a person with good taste. I better do what I need to do to keep her around.* And thus will begin a beautiful cycle.

Still, any type of long-term commitment will entail for the Gemini a state of emotional turmoil. Because instead of being saddled with doing the dishes for five minutes, they'd really rather be in the park, at home, in the grocery store, in bed with your best friend, at work, on the road—especially if they've never been any of these places ever before and it's something new they can tell you about later, as if they were the first person in all of history to discover the open road. The way they tell it, they might as well be.

Like their fellow wanderers, their diametrically opposed sign, Sagittarius, they like their freedom almost more than anything, and the freedom to do completely new things constantly. But unlike Sagittarians, who oftentimes forget where their home is if they have been away from it for too long, Geminis will never stray too far from home. They are restless, but they also like to be rested. (Whereas Sagittarians will fight sleep if it means that they can take a train and a tiny plane to make it in time to the next great party three states away.) But Geminis need to know that they can move whether they choose to or not, even in the tiniest of ways, wherever they want, but also that they can come back to their cozy bed at a moment's notice. Many canceled plans with a Gemini can be attributed to this fact—their bed just calls to them. So don't be mad when a Gemini stands you up. If you can keep their interest, most importantly mentally, you will become that cozy bed and they will keep coming back to you, for what might as well be forever. And I do mean FOREVER. Do I mean *forever ever*, classic Gemini André 3000? Yes. Yes, I do.

Geminis do have a kind of devotion to family and especially to Mama, but not in the way a Cancer might. Mama is not exactly god to a Gemini. But they are so susceptible to a person who gives direction, and so in need of it themselves, that whoever provided that first set of directives concerning how to get dressed and perform other forms of daily living, they will follow around pretty faithfully for their entire lives.

Geminis do have a preponderance of dark moods. This is a very real side of Geminis that they will let only their most intimate friends see, and if you are talking to them for more than five minutes, this will mean you. If they get all sour with you, please don't take it personally. You really did all you could, what with making them laugh and everything. It's just that Geminis can go deep into nihilism, and you don't want to catch a Gemini on a bad day. That is, if you can't handle the sight of a sugar-coated ornament stripped of its decorations, and plunged deep into the reality of nothingness. I know I for sure can't. It's one of the saddest sights to see. Put on a show quickly, so they will momentarily forget that everything is meaningless. Start learning to juggle random fruit now, if you have to.

Ironically, it is the dark, festering side of Gemini that makes their bubbling presence at a social gathering so inviting. Infused in every Gemini joke are strong feelings of emptiness and of the absurdity of life. These sometimes get mistaken for superficial glibness, but really it is the deep knowledge that on some level existence is relatively purposeless. And that's why you will always invite them to your party. Because even though they will get flat-out drunk usually, singing songs and reciting poetry well into the early morning, dancing with anything moving, even if it's a takeout bag, this wild fun is not simply just fun. The void sure does make a damn good party song. Turn on Prince's "Let's Go Crazy" and you will know what I mean. Anyway, let's not dwell here too long. This is the Gemini chapter, after all.

Gemini as a lover

All of my longest relationships have been with Geminis. I'll say this: Geminis are kind, giving, and somewhat detached lovers. If you are the kind of person who wants to be told that the mildest touch of your fingertips makes them have stirrings in their soul, forget about it—Geminis really aren't for you. If you are the sort of person who wants to be locked in intense spiritual communion from start to finish, find yourself a Scorpio, because you will be lucky if the Gemini looks at you at all during the act. (They are probably too busy thinking about whatever book they were reading before things got hot and heavy.)

They will definitely find occasion to tell you that you are good-looking, funny, and generally very attractive, though. Over and over again, in and out of the bedroom. Some people would rather they kept their mouth shut and not be so crass, but I'm an Aries, so I love it. I love a Gemini compliment—it feels so real, even if it usually is an immense exaggeration or even a complete lie. And anyway, most Geminis won't say the actual boring words "you are hot" unless things are at fever pitch. Still, they can be very direct. You will know exactly what they think about you. Once you've been with a Gemini for a while, you can start to think you are the sexiest person ever to have lived. If the chemistry is right, Geminis just make you feel good about yourself. (And unfortunately, they're good at making you feel not so good about yourself when they want to, too.)

The best match for a Gemini is a Libra, and this connection will last for several lifetimes. They are also soulmates with Aquarius, as they can appreciate each other's weird moods and inventive syntax. Gemini-Aries is a very happy match, like two best friends who also have sex. They will surprise themselves at some point when they realize they can't live without each other. Gemini and Leo will like dressing up and going to fancy dinners, and if they can make this a lifestyle, it will work. A Gemini and a Sagittarius will always fundamentally get along and even their fights can be cute in retrospect. Geminis will appreciate Tauruses' honesty about loving creature comforts, but they will have a hard time relating after about a week. Capricorns will go after a Gemini and a Gemini will ultimately say, "Eh." Geminis and Scorpios can go either way; the sex will be great, but each will ultimately find the other one boring (but for different reasons). Geminis and Pisces like to talk about books they have read, but the attraction ends there. Geminis will like how Cancers do everything for them but then will probably resent them for it. Geminis will love other Geminis, but then who will take the lead? Geminis and Virgos really shouldn't talk to each other, but that's okay because most flirtation can be done with the eyes anyway.

Although Geminis can be extremely selfish in many areas of life, if they have done some practical and spiritual work to learn to pick up the cues of their lovers, they will be concerned with your sexual needs very acutely. They will want to do a good job, so that you will think they are the best lover you've ever had. They won't be, but please tell them they are—criticizing a Gemini in this area is not a pretty sight.

(Repeat after me: Do not criticize a Gemini. Do not criticize a Gemini. ESPECIALLY not about what kind of lover they are. Do not criticize a Gemini. Do not criticize a Gemini. Saying it over and over again might help you. Just remember, I warned you.)

If you want to get a Gemini turned on faster, you'd better be into arms. And I do mean literal arms, like the appendages hanging from one's shoulders. Because if you want to really make things start up fast, all you need to do is stroke, caress, and kiss a Gemini's sexy arms and hands to make them melt and be yours for a long time (or at least the next twenty minutes). But aside from some arm foreplay, who are we kidding, the fastest way to turn a Gemini on is to be an absolute nerd. And if you can't really go full-out nerd in your daily life, then learn to be a nerd about something during the seduction phase, and be ready to talk their freaking ears off about some obscure topic you've read at least ten books about. There is nothing that turns a Gemini on more than a person really going at an idea. As they watch you speak, the wheels will be turning elsewhere, and they will want to make you theirs forever. Or again, theirs at least for the next 17.5 minutes. (But who's counting.)

Something to mention is that sometimes (and I do mean only sometimes), they love to cuddle before, after, and during sex, in a very particular manner. Like if they are happy and really like you, they will want to hold you the way a giant grizzly might latch onto a bag of the last berries in the forest for some ungodly number of hours. Conversely, they might still really be in love with you and be totally not into cuddling on a random day and their kisses will feel like a block of ice. Again, like I said earlier, with all things Gemini, try not to take it too personally. Trust me, they don't care if you do or don't. So you are better off not caring. Also, it's a little bit like when you are having trouble with a MacBook. If you shut down and restart forty seconds later, generally a totally different experience awaits you and it's like the other thing didn't even happen.

Ding!

Most of all, Geminis are very friendly lovers. You will feel the kind of joy sleeping with them that you feel when you take a road trip with your childhood friend and then stop randomly along the way for ice cream in Ohio. The ice cream will be absolutely delicious, but on the other hand no one ever said ice cream is the kind of thing they serve you in the other world. But then again, maybe it is. Everything depends on the strength of your imagination.

Gemini as a friend

Despite their flighty reputations, Geminis are solid friends, especially if being friends involves adventures, parties, dinners, glamour, and generally having a blast.

The idea and practice of fun really is extremely important to a Gemini. As long as a Gemini is having a good time, and you are the facilitator of this good time (not necessarily in "control" of it, but making it happen), they will want you around. When Geminis feel good and are able to love life with no terms of entanglement, they are very happy. Geminis cling to the people who provide this for them. And I do mean cling, like when you grab someone who's making you laugh too hard. Laughter is their lifeline.

Geminis don't love obligation, but they understand it. Like, for example, don't expect a Gemini to help you lift heavy things. (I mean this literally: never ask a Gemini to help you move.) But if you are truly in need, they will be there for you. And if you explain why it's important for them to be there for you, they will be there even quicker. You must explain, though, because they aren't born with the occult emotional wisdom of Cancers or Pisces, and they won't figure it out on their own. In all manners of communication, they need to hear the words to know what you want from them, despite knowing better than anyone how untrue words can be.

Likewise, Geminis—although they will put up a fuss and say they hate it—somewhat thrive on routine tasks. They are truly workaholics. They like to be told they have to do something, so that they can have something to do that makes them feel important and also because work gives them something to complain about.

And complain they will! But again, being asked to do something makes them happy. The unhappiest Geminis are those who don't have a lot of friends and obligations to complain about. These sad specimens almost do not exist, but when they do, it really is heartbreaking. Almost any other sign can survive being lonely, but not a Gemini. They will do everything in their power to avoid it, even if they have to make friends with the pile of dust under their bed. Chances are, even if you aren't that fun, if you are all they have, they will keep coming back for more, just to avoid the awfulness of being alone.

Geminis are the social synthesizers of the zodiac and thrive on knowing a lot of people and making connections between them. This practice isn't all that, shall we say, deep, but Geminis have profoundly good memories when it comes to particular details about people. They love to tell you about your next-door neighbor's hobbies and how well you two might get along, and how they'd be happy to give you their phone number, etc., because you know everyone loves them and gives them their phone number, and why wouldn't your next-door neighbor love them. Are you insinuating that they don't? How would you know?

Geminis are gossips in this specific way, knowing about people not necessarily for the sake of accumulating social capital or to achieve power, the way a Capricorn might. Instead, they just like to know the lay of the land, the scope of the field, how everything fits together. It's not that it means anything—it's just that it's interesting. And they think it impresses you when they know lots of things. (And many times, they are right.)

All this to say that if you have found that your Gemini is your best friend, and you are starting to worry that maybe one day they will get up and never talk to you again, I am here to assuage your fears. That will never happen. Geminis are surprisingly loyal once they have decided they like someone, and you really do have to do a lot to send a message that you are done with the friendship. This is in part because, despite having the ability to charm the pants off of a cockroach, they can be somewhat dense about social cues. It's also almost impossible for them to hold a grudge. If you are trying to ghost on a Gemini, they will just think you are busy and come back later. If you promise any type of optimistic worldview for them, they will keep coming back for more. Think of them as the sweetest puppy you've ever met. They just want you to play fetch with them, and if you have done this once, they won't give up until they are sure all the branches and sticks and old washcloths are gone and you never, ever want to throw anything their way again. And if this happens, despite your belief that they don't have many emotions, they really will be very sad. Ever seen a puppy mope? This is how the Gemini gets you to come back to them. Every. Freaking. Time.

Yes, most Geminis will be late to meet you. They won't have the pathological lateness that involves procrastination and power plays like a Capricorn, or the pomp and circumstance of a late Sagittarius. They will be late for one simple reason: they are easily distracted. They just don't value being on time like they do being in the moment. Whatever is shiny in front of them (for instance, a mirror) will grab their attention. If they have shown up an hour late, count your blessings. Like Gemini Kanye West says, "You should be honored by my lateness / That I would even show up to this fake shit." It's true.

All the same, there is another subtype of Gemini that is exceptionally punctual, very early, even. I remember years ago a nice young poet showed up at my apartment to interview me a good twenty-five minutes earlier than he had said he would be there. When I opened the door and saw his sweet grin, I couldn't help myself. "Gemini?" I asked. "How did you know?" he replied.

I didn't answer immediately, but I knew that thirty-plus years of a triple Gemini father who was always at least forty-five minutes early to everything had prepared me well. "Poet's intuition," I finally said to that cute Gemini. And it was.

On the whole, though, if you have a new Gemini friend and want to hang out with them again, forget about time. Instead put F-U-N on your mind and invite them to go out to a bar, go to a library, take a class with them on some obscure philosophy, go to an art show, throw a party, make a meal together, get hooked on a TV series and watch every episode with them, talk until dawn about anything, talk about how smart they are and what a good person they are, make up songs, cheat on diets and lovers together, fall asleep under a blanket, hold hands.

Gemini style

Let's face it: Geminis like to look good. It's not so much because of a visual acuity or a need for aesthetic elegance—like in the case of a Libra—but because good style gives them one thing they can never get enough of. You know where I'm going, right? Yep, attention.

Geminis are mutable air signs, and so they have wild hearts (hey, Stevie) and wild minds and wild emotions, but their style is usually not all that wild. Everything else may be a little unhinged, but their style, instead of wild, will always be understatedly perfect.

Internally, they can be in a state of chaos, so they will do anything to keep their lives as controlled as possible, to counteract this chaos. But the effect of this won't be the same as it could be for a Virgo, who might organize their socks alphabetically (Geminis both love and hate this about their Virgo lovers). No, instead they will just try as much as they can to keep their life simple. And what better way than to pick one style that looks good on them, and wear it for the rest of their whole damn life. And if Mama dressed them in creams and plaids growing up, that's what you will find them in as an adult. It doesn't matter, though. They will look good in just about anything, because style is always about the expression on a person's face, not the materials or form that make the clothes. Once you see a Gemini's eyes twinkle, you couldn't care less about their lifetime collection of simple navy sweaters.

This tendency in their personal style to counteract chaos extends into just about any area of their lives. If the circumstances are correct, they will fall in love with a color quickly and obsess about it forever. Extra points if it's an earth color, navy, or straight-up the color of ice. But it could be any color. Whatever color it is, they will buy everything in that color, at least for some extended period of time. The color itself could become like a religion, and they will surround themselves with it in an odd act of devotion. Go to your Gemini's house and look in their closet. Their need for consistency in the vibes they surround themselves with will be obvious now.

If Geminis are hands-down the best-dressed people in any room, it is because of their quiet, controlled opulence. They love nice things, but not out of any sense of status, like a Cancer or a Leo might love a gold cocktail ring. They will love that gold ring simply because nice things are beautiful. Like I said, they won't have the profound elegance of a Libra, but their dressing may have a similar air. Have a party and invite a Gemini (if you're having a party you almost certainly invited at least a few Geminis anyway). The second they walk into the room, your party's look will immediately go up 100 points.

It's not exactly that when you walk into a room they're the first person you notice. They aren't fire signs. But Geminis are definitely hams, and despite their rep, they are arguably the most easily likable sign of the zodiac. Just listen for the endless babbling. Yeah, that's them.

Texting with a Gemini

Geminis are the sign of communication, so they will think any form of it is enjoyable. I've known lots of Geminis who didn't grow up texting and were confused by it at first, but as soon as they saw everyone else laughing on their phones, they learned the art of emojis very fast. As with most things they do, once you get it going, texting with a Gemini will happen at a rapid-fire pace. They are also quite capable of writing novels over the phone. If you have lots of Geminis in your life, I hope you signed up for free texting.

If you want to engage with a Gemini and keep them texting you back, the best course of action is to keep it light and have delightful discussions that involve ideas. Think of them as that cute puppy who keeps looking for the ball in your hands. They want to see when you are going to throw it their way and figure out how fast they have to run to catch it. The ball is the new idea you can share with them, like the new artist they have never heard of, the odd video of their favorite singer, a picture of an animal or child, or some random theory about space. They will enjoy your knowledge (the larger in scope the better) and will like to learn from you.

Another way to keep their interest while texting is to show your wit. Geminis become intoxicated with a person's biting humor and ability to spar. For them, verbal play is just that, a game, and they see texting as a way to play covertly throughout their day. They love this, because it keeps them from getting too bored or sad. Extra points for you if you can tell jokes at your own and their expense (be gentle with the latter, however, especially at first). Nothing is sexier to a Gemini than someone giving them a verbal jab with a wink, but you have to be careful, as their soft egos can get bruised easily. Still, a little well-placed jab to them is the highest form of texting. This is also a way to get them sexting with you quickly.

One way to end a text conversation fast with a Gemini is to share any sort of intense emotion, especially if it's about your feelings for them. They don't like that in person and they definitely don't like it over the phone. Even if they have strong feelings for you, they won't want to talk about it in a series of kiwi emojis. They will just want to tell jokes and pretend feelings don't exist. Don't text them "I love you," because if they say it back it was just because they felt that they had to. Don't text them about the kind of day you're having, unless it's a way to complain about someone you both know. Then they will be your fiercest supporter and plot revenge as well as any water sign (except they won't follow through with it like a water sign will). But save your "I'm sad"s for a Virgo. A Gemini simply won't care.

This is not to say that they won't want to share their own moods (and mood swings) with you. If you are a frequent texter with a Gemini, you will get about twenty million "I'm sad"s a day from them, except it won't actually be those words. If they like you, they will tell you about every slight they experience, how jealous they feel about that someone with the big car, how bleak the world is, and more. They will also tell you how much they love the state of Louisiana, how delicious caramel-covered raisins are, how beautiful winter trees look from the train they are on every morning at 8:03 a.m., how green the apples are at the farmers' market, and so on. They will share everything wonderful and horrible about life with you gladly. As in so many other spheres, with texting, Gemini can be surprisingly and pleasantly reliable.

Gemini: I just finished my 8th novel today. Mind taking a listen? It should only take 5 hours to read it straight through.

Aries: [no response]

Gemini: Just added 100 pages. I'll call you now and just start reading.

Aries: Ok sexy. But I can only talk for 120 seconds cause I have to catch a private jet in 10 minutes. Going on a second date with a Sag.

Gemini: I just made a beautiful cake!

Taurus: I love cake. Can I come over and eat it?

Gemini: Oh it's for my birthday party.

Taurus: [crying] I guess I'm not invited?

Gemini 1: What "sea" is like L/OV-E and

Gemini 2: Ah the complete disc set

Gemini 1: LOL

Gemini 2: 4 plus 4 is as simple as a net

Gemini: Are you free next Tuesday because I need someone to drive me to the airport

Cancer: You can count on me! What time do you need to leave?

Gemini: 6 am

Cancer: Great, I'll just come over now and live with you for a week so I won't be late.

Gemini: I got us two tickets to the opera.

Leo: Fabulous!

Gemini: It's in 5 minutes

Leo: I was born ready.

Gemini: Do you think I'm smart?

Virgo: The smartest person I've ever met.

Gemini: You have the most amazing taste.

Virgo: Can I darn your socks?

Gemini: I wrote a song for you.

Libra: I'm available to listen.

Gemini: When?

Libra: [1 min later] I just kicked my date out.

Gemini: Will you help me?

Scorpio: Do what?

Gemini: Be a better person
Scorpio: You're asking me?

Gemini: You are so friendly and irritating.
Sagittarius: Are you flirting with me?
Gemini: Obviously.
Sagittarius: I might be free later.

Gemini: Do you know anything about tax codes?
Capricorn: I'm naked.
Gemini: Can you help me with my taxes?
Capricorn: For a small fee.

Gemini: I'm a genius.
Aquarius: You're a genius.
Gemini: I think you're very smart!
Aquarius: I'm a genius.

Gemini: I'm crying.
Pisces: FINALLY!!!
Gemini: Just kidding!
Pisces: Asshole.

The Gemini imagination

If Gemini were a city, it would be Hong Kong, with its intense skyline full of modernistic buildings and icy-blue clouds. If it were a kind of weather, it would be a hurricane. For punctuation, it's the hyphen, endlessly connecting words that may or may not belong together (oh, who ever can tell, anyway). If Gemini were a vegetable, it might be asparagus, which is made even better with a spritz of lemon juice, so its sweetness can come through. If Gemini were a type of clothing, it would be a well-fit jacket, pulling any old outfit together with some grace. If Gemini were a time of day, it might be dusk, with those purple and rose undertones that make the colors of everything moody, infused with vibrations, and extra beautiful. If a Gemini were a room in your house, it would be the living room. Geminis are the space where life is, where all of your visitors come to say hi and bring you a bottle of something, or show you their silly pictures. If Geminis are a Post-it note they are the extra-big, 8×6 one, in neon orange, yellow, and pink. They are ready to take down your ideas and change the landscape of your thinking. Geminis thrive on the idea of life after death, where their bodies might be meaningless, where a soul-mate means a thing to engage in the spectral dance, where they can meet all of the beings that have driven them to spend all their lives talking. If Gemini were a meal, they would be dessert. But not like a Taurus dessert. They would be the lightest sponge cake, with a drizzle of raspberry sauce, made by a chef who just won a MacArthur fellowship. There would be mint on the plate. But it wouldn't be real. It would be made out of a hundred-dollar bill yet would still be edible. No matter how much you try to stop yourself, you will always eat the last drop of that money garnish, trust me. They are banking on that.

Of all the air signs, Gemini is in many ways the most air. Gemini blows life into things, infusing your simple thoughts with more complicated ideas, making you support your ideas for endless hours, throwing your notions about something into the clouds, to get tossed around by a ferocious storm and then spat up on the rain-soaked sands to bask for hours in the sun.

For many of us (especially our fire sign kindred), meeting a Gemini will sometimes feel like opening the window in a stuffy, dark room on a fall day. The air feels clean, crisp, inviting. You can breathe! On their best days, a Gemini feels refreshing to others, a pick-me-up. And even on their worst days, although you do require relatively thick skin and a sort of emotional coldness to deal with them during these periods, they still make life all the more exciting and worth it.

To understand how a Gemini feels in the world, it's important to understand the idea of the twins. Every Gemini you know is actually two different people (and most of them are actually more like ten people). The two must coexist, and that's difficult. The conflict inherent in that duality can be a source of Gemini angst, restlessness, and rage.

Think about it: do you know how annoying it must be to hear a potentially competing voice inside you all of the time—a voice that may challenge your thoughts and actions and make you question everything constantly? We all have this to some degree, as the forces within us are in a constant dance of conversation, and sometimes the conversation can get heated. (For example: your Scorpio moon just had ten dirty martinis and is talking to your Virgo sun, who needs to go to work tomorrow.) But for every Gemini, this other person is there all of the time. It's a hard concept to totally get your head around unless you are a Gemini yourself. The most important thing to remember is that it's real.

Like any two people, the twins who make up any given Gemini

may be similar in personality or different. That is to say, some Geminis really do deserve that nasty Dr. Jekyll and Mr. Hyde label. But other Geminis really are two very similar people, and if you don't know the Gemini well, you may not see the subtle differences between the twins that well at first.

How the twins manifest themselves depends on the Gemini, and what other planets they bring to their sign. I would say that for Geminis who have an internal struggle to do the right thing—a strong moral code—there can be some internal strife when one twin just wants to fuck a random person in a bathroom bar while the other twin wants to be pure and celibate and "good." (Please don't think that I actually think either option is bad or good—I have no judgment here about any sort of behavior that makes you happy. Remember, I'm an Aries.)

If their life constantly presents them with these scenarios, a Gemini can unknowingly create "bad" and "good" twins, with the bad twin coming out sometimes at the worst moments just to spite the other. This can hurt a lot: it's two roommates fighting over who gets the shower first, when they both needed to be somewhere important three minutes ago. That's not a pretty picture. Imagine how hard it is to be the person who reconciles that fight nearly every second. If you can, you might be getting a clearer picture of the burden of a Gemini.

All Geminis have thought a lot about morality. Some of their ideas they have taken from what they've learned from their families, as Geminis are very tied to their families—exceptionally devoted to them with what amounts to immense patience. They may also first have formed their ideas of morality from books. Geminis are all scholars, no matter what the particular Gemini's profession.

They pore over ideas, bouncing and batting them around to find the parts that stick.

In terms of ethics, most Geminis have thought long and hard about what's right and wrong, and what they feel about what's right and wrong. In fact, if you are trying to win an argument with a Gemini (which is possible, sometimes), the fastest way to make them budge is to call upon the idea of a moral code. You can say, "I see what you mean, but the right thing to do is X." It's even better if you say why and provide an example of why this was the right thing to do in another situation.

Most Geminis really don't want to hurt anyone. They are extremely gentle creatures, just little fuzzy baby animals. And when they do hurt people (which is nearly all of the time, sadly), they are always genuinely surprised, because they really didn't mean to. Or maybe they meant to, but only to have a little fun, and definitely not the way you have taken it. That little nibble was actually a bite, and was a lot more than anyone bargained for. Sometimes they just don't get how sharp their teeth are.

The Famous Gemini

The Famous Gemini is just like all of the Geminis you know, except happier. This is because without the profound attention that comes with fame, and given the boring trappings of the everyday— having to ride elevators and wash socks and, you know, show up to your friend's wedding when you are the best man and engage with all these people who don't understand that you are the greatest genius ever to have lived—Geminis' egos can get bruised easily.

It's really hard to be a non-Famous Gemini, because so few people know you really should be a Famous Gemini. But Famous Geminis don't have to worry about that. It's hard to get too upset by a slight, what with all of that endless applause.

The Geminis you know will tell you that they would never want to be famous and that they enjoy their non-famous lives just fine. Geminis lie a lot.

Famous Geminis are pretty cool famous people. A Famous Gemini will take their expertise and their skills in all things social and utilize them as a driving force in understanding something important about their field of study. They will notice this thing before everyone else, and it will be obvious once they present it to the public. For example, if they are in sales, they will have a quite obvious but as yet never-before-used marketing technique that will be brilliant once they put it into play—but again, its structure will be earth-shattering only for its simplistic brilliance. An example of this sort of Gemini businessperson is someone like Leonard Blavatnik, who founded Access Industries, an American conglomerate. Blavatnik made his millions through diversifying investments in chemicals, media, venture capital, and real estate. He knew how to synthesize resources and sell this synthesis itself, versus giving the world a particular product. Or take someone like Marilyn Monroe, who knew how to delightfully craft a persona of the classic American vixen, blond and buxom, full of giggles and quirky bravado, and sell it to both Hollywood and the whole world. A Famous Gemini will be at times shockingly verbose (Kanye West) but at other times simple and elegant: world-class, really (Kanye West).

The Famous Gemini is interested in synthesizing trends and

people into a movement, but is not necessarily interested in leading the movement (like an Aries would) or being a cult leader (like a Scorpio might). They want to be part of the action, but not in charge. Yet their genius is in understanding that a centerless universe is an exciting one, because it means that all people are threaded together into one voice. A Gemini will take this one pulsing voice (which Scorpio Sylvia Plath, referring to poetry, called a "blood jet") and make it their own. Even when it wasn't originally. This trait is most obvious in Famous Geminis whose professions are the communicative or artistic fields, but again, all Geminis work in communication, no matter what their trade. An example of this is tennis champion Venus Williams, who not only dominates the tennis court but also dominates interviews, to hilarious effect.

The classic Famous Gemini exists in a state of contradiction while performing this synthesis. In classic Gemini fashion, Walt Whitman's answer to the question "Do I contain multitudes?" boils down to "whatever." Famous Geminis are not afraid of Whitman's idea of contradiction, which is in many ways about existing free of boring, binary ideas of right or wrong, this or that, and so on (and so forth).

Famous Geminis are large and contain many voices, breathing them together and bringing them into one thing, noticing trends almost before they happen and making them swell into harmony. That's why Bob Dylan may be the quintessential Famous Gemini after all, despite all his Taurus influences. In his songs and persona, he charms you by simultaneously caring and not caring about your opinion of his contradictory nature in whatever he says. In "4th Time Around" he narrates a string of love affairs through veiled feelings of hatred and tenderness for multiple people. He seems potentially "in love" with all of them, but eventually we see that perhaps his deepest love is for the final "you" in the song, who is always there (a Libra, I'm guessing). He sings about leaving a lover's house and then finally going to the *you's* place, only to find that the *you* wants to obligate him, too:

I never asked for your crutch
Now don't ask for mine

Here, as in so much of his music, he synthesizes the work of Woody Guthrie, Allen Ginsberg, Joan Baez, and Little Richard into his own kind of folk song. He exists in a space of contradiction, presenting so eloquently the conflicting emotions he feels about this you—who took him in but maybe asked for too much from his guarded Gemini emotional landscape. (And by the way, what sort of person would ask for a Gemini's crutch? So silly, Libra.)

Kanye West has famously said that all musicians are Geminis. This isn't true. But certainly West is an important Gemini artist. In "Power" he epitomizes the classic Famous Gemini stance and synthesis of trends:

I'm living in that 21st century
Doing something mean to it
Do it better than anybody you ever seen do it

And while in his career generally he displays the Famous Gemini ego, this song actually demonstrates Gemini ambivalence to power. They all want it, because it means adoration, but once they have it, they feel almost bad about it. Partially this is because they don't know exactly what to do with it. Like all Geminis, West struggles with the chaos of personal power, while still continuing to synthesize our times exquisitely.

The contemporary American poet Nikki Giovanni is another classic Famous Gemini. In "My First Memory (of Librarians)," she writes about how important libraries are to her: "All those books—another world—just waiting / At my fingertips."

This is possibly what all Geminis, not just Famous Gemini poets, feel about the space of a library, with its intense landscape of contained imagination, with all of those wild worlds ready to be broken free and opened up into the mind, like a never-ending perfume of ideas. Even today, when it seems as if reading a book is potentially the most antiquated action ever, Giovanni reminds us of the beauty of these Thought Churches, our public libraries, where everyone is free to enter, think, and be. To go into the other world through words—that's the agency that all Geminis give us.

Famous Geminis see all the things we can't see, because we are too busy seeing the small things to notice how life all comes together in a grand pattern. They are friendly creatures, despite their foolish statements and tendency to make enemies. Their place on the creative karmic wheel is essential.

Other Famous Geminis

1. Stevie Nicks
2. Gwendolyn Brooks
3. Prince
4. Jacques Cousteau

5. Mary Anning
6. Harriet Martineau
7. W. B. Yeats
8. Lucie Brock-Broido
9. Angelina Jolie
10. Morgan Freeman

Gemini playlist

- Kanye West, "Heartless"
- Igor Stravinsky, "Funeral Song"
- Prince, "Alphabet St."
- Oscar the Grouch, "I Love Trash"
- Lana Del Rey, "Summertime Sadness"
- Notorious B.I.G., "Hypnotize"
- Blake Shelton, "I'll Name the Dogs"
- Richard Strauss, "Dance of the Seven Veils"
- Stevie Nicks, "Wild Heart"
- Bob Dylan, "Visions of Johanna"
- Lisa "Left Eye" Lopes, "Creep"

The Gemini (a poem)

You walked right in. Being entirely of yourself. You felt the words go from other minds and into your mouth. They got caught and began to choke you up. So you spit them out. Quickly. O you! People change. People grow. You do not do either. You get more settled into the chaos of it all as it envelops you. You get more sure of the sun than ever before. And time moves on. There is nothing more holy. Than the sun leaving and now you're free. Strange flamingo. If you stand still and look right into the camera. You will see your own face in the future. And you won't be scared. You will smile. No no you won't smile. Your expression will be very serious. It will be a comfort then, to know. No take that bird who wanders in the churchyards. What is it looking for? What is the point? Nothing, nothing. O nothing. Nothing is beautiful. Beauty resounds. It can see everything. It can speak.

CANCER

June 21–July 22

I believe in a heaven I'll never enter.
Pablo Neruda, born July 12, 1904

The Cancer

In 1995, on the now vintage channel MTV, there was an interview that outlines perfectly what it means to be a Cancer. It's as if it were staged by astrology itself.

The video is an interview after a concert between that steady Taurus Kurt Loder and Madonna (who we all know is a Leo). When the interview begins, it seems we can expect the banal exchange of 99 percent of celebrity interviews. Madonna, by then a total American icon, eases quickly and with a sort of leonine glee into non-witty banter with Loder. After all, the camera is on her, and what card-carrying Leo doesn't want that?

What comes next is infamous. As Madonna is speaking, some objects come flying at her head. The camera tilts down and we see Courtney Love (uh, yeah . . . she's a Cancer) now throwing her MAC compact and other items from her purse up onto the stage. After a few seconds, Kurt Loder, loving the drama and probably also feeling sorry for Courtney, invites her up on stage with them.

Courtney gets up there quickly, almost magically, and soon is doing a Cancerian dance in front of everyone. Sidestepping like a real crab and apologizing for "interrupting"—as if she hadn't intended to do just that—she asks both Kurt and Madonna if she should go. She seems to expect them to say to her fifty times over, "No, no, Courtney, we want you here." Kurt does tell her a few times, unconvincingly, to stay, while Madonna seethes, her annoyance palpable under a midwestern fake smile, her pure silk bright teal shirt gleaming under the hot lights of the cameras.

After sitting down, Courtney speaks off camera to Tabitha Soren (don't worry, I didn't know either, but it turns out she is also a Leo), explaining to everyone that she and Tabitha were in a fight because Tabitha was "mean" to her. From there she quickly jumps from topic to topic, explaining why she has a crush on Scorpio Dennis Miller (because he's "smart"—uh, yeah right), mentioning that she would like to start dating astrophysicists, crouching down awkwardly when Madonna asks if they can talk about their shoes. She even tells Madonna about a date with Kurt Cobain, early on in their relationship, when they went to see her movie, *Truth or Dare*. Madonna then abruptly leaves, reluctant to have her time on camera shared for a tiny minute, her pride wounded. (Oh, Madonna. Please get over yourself.)

Watching the exchange is a good crash course on Cancer. The video also involves a mention of Courtney's mother opening the first Birkenstock outlet (it really wouldn't be a Cancer segment without some mention of Mommy) and Courtney having sex with Sagittarian Ted Nugent. Courtney flashes that classic Cancer grin, which appears to contain the full moon lit up for a second. That is, until you see the tiny crack where the moonlight seems to spill through years of sadness, regret, and vulnerability, which inform joy so profoundly that the idea of joy might not exactly be the point. Courtney's need for attention, to dominate the stage, deceptively similar to Madonna's, is undercut by her need for approval. Years of perceived rejection by Madonna, Tabitha Soren, and perhaps the whole music business machine are displayed front and center in a glorious display of EMOTION. It's the most amazing thing to see a person unhinged like that, especially in the context of a televised show, where it is totally not expected for anyone to act that way. We should all do a little more of that.

That's what Cancers bring to us. They make us feel. They show us that emotions are not something to hide away, but that they are the very point of everything. By the end of the segment, Courtney is hugging Tabitha Soren (although be sure that she will hold a grudge against Tabitha until one of them dies, and probably after that). For a Cancer, it's not the anger, or the hug, that matters. It's the fact that as humans we do both things constantly. Except that Cancers are a little more ready than other people to do them both simultaneously, or in a few cycles, in quick succession.

So the next time you see a sexy Cancer flash that classic grin, don't just empty your pockets and disrobe as quickly as possible. Take a moment to realize the human depths that are part of everything they do. Cancers are the special ones. They have all these moods. Their moods are our gifts.

Things you might want to know about Cancer

Cancers are the fourth sign of the zodiac and are a cardinal water sign. Along the karmic wheel, Cancer has learned an important lesson from Gemini, whose motto is "I think." Cancer's motto is "I feel," and for Cancer, the turn of knowledge in the soul's progression is to go from thinking to feeling, as only with details, facts, and insight can a person totally be capable of absorbing human emotion and empathy. If Aries, Taurus, and Gemini all represent the babies, toddlers, and younger kids of the zodiac, symbolizing the soul's progression in age along the karmic wheel, then Cancers, too, definitely fit squarely in the children category. They are all around eight years old in age and have a need to be dutiful to larger familial and societal structures. Still, they are capable of out-and-out tantrums, usually at the most unexpected and worst times. They carry with them an air of knowledge, or shall we say know-it-all-ness, bossing around babies and older adults alike, ready to tell you how things go, just in case you were wondering. But just like a kid around that age, they will only partially know what the rules are and how to follow them. They will be skilled at maneuvering many crucial points of life, but they still carry with them the memories of being a baby and will at times cling to the idea of safety that one hopes all babies take as a given. They will long for these first memories of the soul and will do everything they can in their own lives to seek it out and create it for others.

Cancer is famously ruled by the moon, and there really is no better way to understand Cancer than to understand the moon. Most of the planets you need a telescope to see, but the moon and its travels are always visible. And just as the tide ebbs and flows, and the moon waxes and wanes, so too does the Cancer move. Just as the moon is the stuff of legend, a place that's real but still has a profound hold on the human imagination, a presence both inaccessible yet constant, Cancer exists vividly in the memories of everyone who has encountered them. They constantly provide light in the darkness, a stable mirror of our own feelings, a moonscape to rest our head when we are weary from the hustle and bustle of everything. In the moon we think we see a face; in every Cancer, for at least an instant, we see ourselves, as a Cancer contains the primal force of life, that sweet cave where we go to eat and rest and be our basic selves. Beautiful and open, but not free, pinned to the sky—that is where Cancers are. They are so magnificent. A pinprick of light, holding in its circle all the forces of open water.

If you are at work or at a party and want to know if someone is a Cancer, look no further than the door. No, the Cancer isn't the person who is trying to run out of it (that's probably a Sagittarius or a Leo, off to a better party). Measure the distance from the door to the center of the room, and then look a little to the side. See them? They'll probably have their eyes down. That is, until they look at you with a searing intensity. Do you feel seen? Yep, that's them.

Cancers will never be exactly in the center of the room, but they will want to be in charge of the whole room. Still, in every Cancer there is an inherent insecurity and fear that not everyone will know them or want them to be in the center, and thus they will stand uncertainly, probably shuffling their feet a bit, as they move slowly toward that vaunted place. Because even though they aren't sure if everyone wants them to be in charge, they are sure they are in charge. So, it's always a dance with a Cancer. They need for you to see that you need them.

Need. There's that word that is integral to both the Cancer's existence and their imagination. In Cancer Vladimir Mayakovsky's poem "Listen!" he writes, "Listen, / if stars are lit / it means— there is someone who needs it." These lines pretty much sum up what it means to be a Cancer. First of all, there is the need for meaning. Another sign, like a Taurus, might see the stars lit up in the night sky and think peaceful thoughts, or even stop thinking. But a Cancer will never stop searching for meaning. After all, someone put those stars up there and lit them up. Why?

"Because we need them," Cancer answers. Cancer logic is half-obvious, half-confusing, like emotions themselves. But once you think about it a little bit—all those stars up there—they're onto something.

Another important word to think about in understanding a Cancer is "power." Because Cancers are emotionally insecure and unsure of almost everything they do, they seek out stability with a ferocious intensity. And undoubtedly there is nothing more stable than being the one in charge, the one who is calling the shots and making up (and enforcing) the rules. If there is one thing Cancers can't get enough of, it's this intoxicating aspect of power. If you think someone you know might have a lot of Cancer in their chart, ask them about their relationship to power. If they are born in mid-July, they probably won't answer you immediately, but you will see a sly, almost sexual, look cross their face. Yep, you've probably got a Cancer on your hands, with a big side of power play. Power is their main crush. And it always will be.

A subset of power is working to get that power, and Cancers love this path. If you work with a Cancer, I hope you are on the, I don't know, passive side of things. Or at the very least passive-aggressive (that will excite them). You had better value the work you are doing and be ready to talk about why you value it at a moment's notice, complete with emotional nuance and hand gestures. Because you will be asked.

In a work situation, the Cancer is probably the boss. If they aren't the head boss, then they are close in line. They will be in charge soon, and are simply waiting (not actually so patiently) for their turn to tell everyone what to do. But again, this is all a formality, and they will tell you when and what to do anyway.

I've worked with lots of Cancers over the years, and it's always wonderful to do things with them. Mostly because they have a knack for understanding how systems work, both in terms of minutiae and big-picture stuff, and also because they get things done. That crab tenacity is not playing when it comes to finishing something, and they will work tirelessly, forgoing sleep or food, to see things through to the end. That is, if they aren't holding a grudge against their workplace, which is another story, because then good luck getting them to even say hello to anyone in the office.

If you work with them, they will expect the same sort of dedication to the cause from you. If you don't demonstrate this constantly, they will lose respect for you. And they will lose their tempers. If you think Cancers are just sweet, motherly forces, begging you to eat their cookies, then you probably really never have done anything with a Cancer for any extended period of time. As someone whom many of them see as a flaky Aries (by the way, I'm not flaky), I've been on the receiving end of quite a few of those mad moods. I am still scared.

Not all Cancers crave power in the public sphere. Cancers tend to be very good historians and librarians and are good at managing archives. They are loving teachers, and the educational field is a great place for them. They love old things immensely, because of the spiritual layers old things contain. They can feel these layers better than other people. And of course they are often artists— important ones. All that dreaming and feeling will amount to works of art that change their fields. If you are the family member or partner of a Cancer, that work of art could also be you.

This is a cliché you may have heard about Cancers, but their home really is their life. No matter how far their job may make them travel, nothing is as wonderful to them as getting home to a cozy space they have decorated with love and invested money in. They especially like their homes because that's where their families are. And it really is a cliché, too, but it's true, that nothing makes a Cancer happier than spending time with their families, however a specific Cancer defines that word.

Speaking of clichés, you may have around now sensed that I have been somehow avoiding a pretty big topic. I guess there is no sense in beating around the bush any longer. It's time to face the real subject head-on. Oh, I will just say it: Mommy. It's true that for Cancers, mothers are, hmm, how to say this, SUPREMELY important. This doesn't always mean that they wholeheartedly worship their mothers or even get along with them. But they will have very strong feelings about them. If you want to ask them their mother's opinions about, oh, I don't know, anything, then I would just be ready. For. A. Lot. Of. Feelings.

Cancers love their mothers so much because of the occult nature of motherhood itself. Like their water sign sisters, Pisces and Scorpio, Cancers always have one foot in real life and one foot in the transitional states of both birth and death (which are arguably the same state, but more on that some other time). Water signs just have a knack for understanding how hard it is to be here, alive and thriving, and Cancers especially understand the sacrifice mothers make to get and keep us here. To a Cancer, anyone who has kept someone alive through emotional and practical support is an eternal goddess, and they pay them the highest respects. So, to a Cancer, their own mother is completely idealized, as she is the person who has actually brought them into existence. They feel as if they owe their mother everything and they will get crazy protective of her. Even Cancers with fraught relationships with their mothers (of which there are actually more than you might think, or than might ever be revealed to you by a Cancer) will ultimately move heaven and earth to give them the love they feel they deserve.

Related to all of this mothering, a word to think about when understanding Cancer is: care. Cancers do care, despite any feelings you might have when they are being moody that they don't love you at all. Quite the opposite is likely the truth, although if you are a fire sign like me, you may never totally be able to grasp it. When I say Cancer is moody, I am speaking of a feeling that is particular to this one sign. Other signs may have fickle moods, but Cancers' changes of mood are so profound that when they change, the change feels permanent, even if it was only a second ago. Cancers' moods are similar to weather and its changeable nature—you have to go through some awful storms to get to a sunny day. The tides are ruled by the moon, too, and the ocean changes every day. If you love a Cancer, you must be willing to live through some extremely grumpy moods in order to get to the moment when they flash you their jolly and loving smile. And in terms of care, think of their moods as a lens through which the care must be seen. But like the moon under the clouds, the care is still there. A Cancer's love will always stick around.

Cancer as a lover

When falling in love with a Cancer, the most important thing to remember is that time is of the essence. A Cancer heart is always described as a blooming flower, like a big dirty rose that, at the height of its bloom, emits a scent nothing short of divine for miles. Cancers who let themselves fall in love (and they do let themselves) are one of the most beautiful sights in the world. But their falling in love is much like that flower. You want to be there right at its highest blooming or else you will have missed something important. The same goes for loving a Cancer. You want to get in there before you've missed your chance.

Tom Cruise provides a good example of the Cancer-in-love phenomenon. Think of Tom Cruise jumping on Oprah's couch in 2005 when he first fell in love with Katie Holmes. Sure, it was awkward as fuck, but I never really believed the people who thought his display of enthusiasm for his new love was staged. I have my own cynicism and distrust of the authenticity of things, but to me he just looked like a happy little crab or a big dirty rose in bloom, doing his moon dance of joy that he had found someone like Katie Holmes to love (uh, but did anyone ever tell him she is a Sagittarius, so that was doomed). On Oprah's couch he was just ready to tell everyone he was in love. What a gorgeous thing to see.

What I am trying to say is that if you meet a Cancer and they seem into you, if you have any intention of ever falling in love with them, it is better to do it right then and not wait for your feelings to evolve. It might be good for you personally to wait, but sadly, you really aren't going to ever get the same perfume. When bloom time is over, that big old flower really can't go back there again for you. And you will be sorry, I promise you.

Or translate a Cancer's love into another botanical example. Think of a Cancer-in-love stage like the ripening of an avocado. Just like the memes say, once an avocado is ripe, you have about ten seconds to eat it before it turns rotten. An avocado is a cautionary tale about a Cancer's heart. Once a Cancer has activated their purest and most romantic feelings, you probably have about one moon cycle to catch them in the best space to fall madly in love together. If you wait at all, you are going to have a rotten avocado on your hands. Ultimately, the rotting will be irreversible.

The best matches for Cancers are Scorpio and Pisces, because Cancers love not having to explain their intense watery emotions to anyone, and Scorpio and Pisces just get it. For this reason, Cancers love other Cancers and will usually end up married to one after a proper courtship. Cancers love to mother Tauruses, and Tauruses love to be smothered, so things work out well from there. Cancers and Virgos do really love each other, but they probably will criticize each other to death. Cancers will fall madly in love with Aries and also Leos, but I can't condone either match. Likewise with Sagittarius, which is just a bad idea for a Cancer in every way. Cancers and Geminis share a love of a good book, but they have different motivations for reading. Cancer and Libra will make a lot of sex tapes, but problems will arise when Libra wants to post them. Cancer and Capricorn is pretty much true love, until they start arguing about money. Cancer and Aquarius isn't even funny to joke about and it will just end in misery.

I always tell my friends that Cancers have effectively broken my heart into tiny smithereens—the one sign to have done so. I always say this because it is damn well the absolute truth. Cancers have brought me to my knees (literally) and gotten my ass on some pretty pointless and impulsively purchased flights across the country out of some knock-down, drag-out pure and blinding love just for them. They are seriously just so good at making you feel hope about love that I was willing to go just about anywhere for that rare elixir. Still, I wish they didn't have to ruin me and my sad heart each time with such joy. Oh, what am I saying—I'd obviously do it all again in a heartbeat. It's kind of an honor to have your heart broken sometimes, especially by a Cancer. (#callme)

I'll just say it: a Cancer will probably be the best lover you have ever had. Not because there is anything that exciting about the actual act itself (because there won't be). It will be as basic as lovemaking can be, but it will be all heart. Cancers can figure out your emotional weakness and turn that knowledge into seduction. Cancers intuit what you need emotionally and give that to you. What could be a better aphrodisiac than that.

Once a Cancer has some sort of hook in you (and it will feel like a hook, because it is in fact a pincer) they will start to come clean about their own emotional weakness. Which is their unabashed need for nearly constant attention every split second of every blessed day. A Cancer will get you to tell them you love them every five seconds, and this will be part of the charm. When they need love they will do everything to get it out of you, which includes manipulating you and also includes tons of criticism directed at you. If you aren't into being forthright about your feelings about them (which had better be ooey-gooey and 100 percent positive), then you are not going to keep your Cancer for long. If you are invested in keeping a relationship with a Cancer, you'd better be ready to say "I miss you" ten million times a day and to find it comforting to do so, not annoying. Because for a Cancer, hearing they mean something to you is all it takes to keep their devotion up for a lifetime. Hell, it probably doesn't even take that if they love you, but deep down it does keep them happier.

Speaking of criticism, it's true that Cancers can be very critical. They will act this way most toward the people they are closest to. That could mean a family member or a friend, but if you're their special someone, that will most definitely mean you. I once had a Cancer ask me, "When are you going to learn how to dress like a normal person?" If you could see what I am wearing right now, you would realize that's kind of a reasonable question, but I know for that Cancer, it wasn't said lightly. If you fall under a Cancer's domain and they own you (that verb was intentional), they will expect you to do things as they would have done them. This does include dress, but it also extends to most behaviors, including the ways in which you behave in your private spaces—which, if you are in a relationship with them, is also their domain, even if they don't pay a cent of the rent. Once they start becoming supercritical of your sexual skills, you have my permission to exit, stage left. Sometimes you do just really need to shut it down with them in order to survive.

If you are willing to put up with all of this for the rest of eternity, and want to get them all open in your arms for some supremely intense acts of sexual abandon and explosion, then it's good to know that basically all you need to do is to get some floral oil and be down to rub their chest (gently, please!). Cancers love some flank action and will be into a whole lot of soft (almost too soft) touches to their arms and chest. It will set them on fire, and let me tell you, water on fire is pretty interesting. Also, of course, most every sign is into nipple play, because that's just biology, but Cancers are really, really into things done to their nipples. (Think: clamps.) So, get ready to spend a lot of time giving some love to that whole area. The good news is if you get tired (they will wear you out), you can rest your head on their gorgeous chest and as they stroke your hair, the whole thing might just start back up again.

Cancer as a friend

Whatever their faults as paramours, Cancers will attempt to be your best friend. They certainly are ideal friends for the right kind of person. (Read: other water signs.) In their symbiotic friendships, they exude a sense of adventure and, simultaneously, comfort that will make you want to be around them. (However, this might just come off as a lethal combination of bossiness and extreme neediness, causing any air sign within a five-hundred-mile radius, for instance, to shy away.) They are almost always very supportive of their friends, providing a sort of "Mom-lite" figure. Although not always extroverted by nature, they love to go out with their friends and can become very brave and animated in the presence of people they trust. They will do whatever they can to help their friends professionally, most of the time because they pick friends who either have power in their chosen fields or are charity cases. If it's the latter, they will sometimes make these people their projects and try to help their careers. In the case of the former, they will show these friends off as jewels, bragging to anyone around about their friend's accomplishments, just as any good mom would.

If you are ever in need, especially emotionally, your Cancer friend will come running as fast as is humanly possible to help you. One of my best friends is a Cancer, and it's a little joke we have that when I say "I need you" he will drop almost anything to talk to me. He and my Pisces best friend (Cancer moon, Cancer rising) are part of my "water sign hotline," which I do call on in times of emotional crisis. I am so lucky to have these Cancer-infused friends, and if you have a Cancer best friend, you certainly know what I mean. A Cancer simply cannot stand the thought of someone they love suffering, especially when it's emotional suffering, which to them is the only real kind of suffering there is.

On the other hand, Cancer friends are, how shall we say this again, pretty bossy. While they will be caring and loving, they still aren't always that accepting of behaviors that to them feel counterproductive or in excess. In fact, if you are one of their friends, they may feel it's their duty to help you reform a behavior that could hurt you. This could mean helping you stop talking too much, dating too much, dressing in a way that to them seems unprofessional, eating the wrong foods, sleeping too late, or doing just about anything they themselves wouldn't do. This nagging really does come out of love. They want you to "fit in" and succeed in life. It's not always welcome advice for everyone, and it is almost always unsolicited; however, they do mean well, as infuriating as it may be to more freedom-loving signs. Some signs respond to this well, though. Have you ever met a Cancer-Virgo best friend pair? If you have, then you have seen true friendship harmony.

Cancer style

Cancers have an effortless approach to style that is actually the product of an enormous amount of effort. They like to look classy and will often purchase expensive, yet understated, pieces to wear. They like things that are tailored and that fit their bodies well. They exude sexuality, but they tend to have a classy look. They may have a fascination with old Hollywood (whatever that means anymore) and its conventions. They may not dress like an old starlet, but they will be aware of all of them and will think about them when they make their stylistic choices. They will be aware of the idea of glamour, although they themselves will not have any real interest in being glamorous for its own sake.

Most Cancers, like their water sign siblings Pisces and Scorpio, tend to appreciate dark colors. They love navy, black, forest green, and burgundy—any color the light has been banished from. They will especially enjoy wearing colors that prevent them from standing out, as most Cancers feel that people who stand out in terms of their dress are somehow offensive. They tend to avoid buying a ton of new clothes for themselves and will wear out the same pair of shoes until they fall off their feet. However, this doesn't mean they won't buy clothes for you, as they tend to spoil most people they know with all sorts of presents, most of them things no one actually wants.

Cancers also love the color purple, especially lilac. Don't ask me why, it's just something I can't help but notice. But look at the color for a while and you'll get it. It's soft and gentle, the sort of color that would infuse the sunrise above a calm beach. It expands, the way water does, and responds to atmosphere and mood. It kind of goes with everything, which is something a Cancer appreciates. Because they think of themselves as going with anything. Which can even be true.

Texting with a Cancer

At least two Cancers in my life have made me fall in love with them through text messages, and it all happened in the middle of the night. Late-night texting is a hallmark of Cancers, because for them, nighttime is the right time. The moon is out and most people are sleeping. So it's just you and them going deep into topics. And the topics usually come around to how much do you love them.

Cancers have a way of texting that makes anything they say sort of like a come-on. Or at least it seems that way to me. When they are telling a story they make a poem out of it, breaking lines in ways that give the story momentum and emotional resonance. I once was looking at some texts from a friend's Cancer ex-girlfriend. They read like some sort of millennial version of T. S. Eliot's "The Waste Land." There were windy, short bursts of description and emotion. It was a beautiful and sad poem, all about her feelings. I don't know about you, but that sort of thing is about all it takes to make me go wild with passion. I know my friend was having a hard time not texting this hot Cancer ex back. Eventually she did.

A Cancer will love to text you at night, but this is not to say they will leave you hanging all day. Oh no—in fact, they may text you more during the day than during the night. Smartphones were a great invention for Cancers, because it allows them to follow their loved ones' every second. And if your Cancer isn't writing you nearly every second, then I would be worried. In fact, I would be worried if your Cancer hasn't installed some sort of app on your phone to track your every movement. Friend finder apps were made for Cancers.

That's because when a Cancer loves, they cling. There is no such thing as too much contact to them. That is, unless they are working, in which case they will appear to ignore you completely to the point of not responding when you are sitting next to them on the couch. But even when they are too busy to respond, you had better keep them updated on where you are at all times. Otherwise they will worry about you. Oh, please don't make them worry! No, they aren't just trying to make you feel guilty when they say this, but worrying about you does give them a horrible stomachache. But it's okay, write back when you can. You have a good time.

Cancer: How much do you love me?
Aries: Are you trying to trick me again?
Cancer: Is it too much to measure?
Aries: More than that.

Cancer: I sewed your initials on my shirt
Taurus: I got a locket with your baby picture
Cancer: I tattooed your grandmother's picture on my chest
Taurus: I named a star after you

Cancer: How come you never write me back?
Gemini: Hi!

Cancer: I am hurting so much.

Gemini: Is it my fault?

Cancer #1: I know we haven't even met yet, but I've longed for this day since the moment I was born.

Cancer #2: When I was eleven I knew your name and made an altar by my bed in your image.

Cancer #1: So many people have hurt me.

Cancer #2: I will kill them all.

Cancer: I can pick up dinner.

Leo: I just want to go dancing.

Cancer: Let's stay inside tonight.

Leo: Never!

Cancer: You are the sweetest person ever.

Virgo: Thank you!

Cancer: Have you ever considered though that you annoy people when you ask so many questions?

Virgo: No. [tears]

Cancer: Hi hot stuff

Libra: Let's make a sex tape

Cancer: Of only our faces?

Libra: Sure. Whatever.

Cancer: Oh my god

Scorpio: I know

Cancer: Want to
Scorpio: Of course

Cancer: I have our wedding invitations ready.
Sagittarius: Who is this?
Cancer: Stop joking around!
Sagittarius: Um, I'm not.

Cancer: Remember when we met
Capricorn: Like it was tomorrow
Cancer: Ahhhhh
Capricorn: What are you wearing?

Cancer: I do believe in an afterlife.
Aquarius: Why?
Cancer: Everything points backwards.
Aquarius: That's interesting, but I do not agree.

Cancer: When the stars explode
Pisces: They make me
Cancer: Think of
Pisces: Our love

The Cancer imagination

If Cancer were a city, it would be Dublin, with its pulsing energy, secret and healthy green hills, and tendency toward a very cloud-infused skyscape. If Cancer were a kind of weather, it would be a torrential downpour. If Cancer were a punctuation mark, it would be a comma, just a gentle form of connection, but one that you need, is dependable, lasts, and you can always have more of. If Cancer were a type of clothing, it would be a skirt, showing off a little leg, but not too tight, please, we all need some room for more pie. If Cancer were a time of day, it would be around 10:00 a.m. You've already eaten breakfast and are ready to start the day. If a Cancer were a stuffed animal, it would be a teddy bear with a little bright red bow, and definitely a haunted one, but with good spirits. If a Cancer were a nightmare, it would be one with family dynamics in it, highly psychological; and it would pierce your thoughts the next day. If Cancer were a dance, it would be the fox-trot, with the sound of hard wood heels clicking on the floor like glass. If Cancer were a utensil, it would be the spoon, one on the bigger side, ready to hold all of the other spoons in a loving embrace in the utensil drawer, waiting to be picked up to give you just a little more jam. If Cancer were a flower, it would be the daisy.

Cancers, despite their moods and despair, tend to be idealistic and even a little bouncy. They carry some energy over from the previous stop on the karmic wheel, Gemini, and when they walk into a room, they bring with them a sense of effervescent optimism. They love the idea of possibility and chance, and they have great vision for what can be, especially because they truly understand the hard work that it takes to make an idea a reality. The happiest Cancers have some sort of profession that allows them to take charge on particular projects that help humanity. Because Cancers always want to feel like they are helping. Most of the time, they really are.

Despite these feelings of optimism, Cancers do have a core that is very pessimistic. Like their water sign kindred Scorpio and Pisces, once they see things are not working, whether that be something at work or an interaction with their roommate or in their relationship, they will go straight to the conclusion that something is very wrong and that it might not be able to be fixed. Feelings of gloom completely envelop them faster than they do other people. And if something is in fact wrong, they will feel like everyone else is to blame. They will want to make everyone else deal with "what they have done" and will be slow to (read: will never) admit that their own actions may have contributed to the problem or their own unhappiness. So if your Cancer is having a hard time finding a new job, then that is somehow your fault. And if you don't know that, they will tell you. That is, however, while they are in a dark mood. After the storm is over and the sun comes back out, they will be ready to scoop you up in their safe arms again. But before that, they will tell you how you have ruined their life. Oh, you didn't realize you ruined their life? Well, then, they are ready to tell you about it a few thousand more times until you understand.

For Cancers, family is everything, and it extends far into their imagination. They will relive their family dynamic for their entire lives and will work hard to make new families, in whatever configuration makes sense to them, wherever they go. The saddest Cancers are the ones who don't have an extended family and group of friends to make potatoes and green beans for every Sunday, the ones who leave at 7:00 p.m. so they can take a nice quiet bath alone with candles and a bottle of something. When they don't have family, they sense that life doesn't have meaning. But, no, maybe the saddest Cancers are the ones who don't have jobs. Because that's how important security is to them. A Cancer without the mutual purpose of family and building a strong career is a very, very sad Cancer.

All this talk about sad Cancers is making me sad. Oh, can't we just hug it out, water goddesses? I'm free if you are.

The Famous Cancer

One would think that a moody, shy, and caring person might not like the spotlight, but that's just not the case. Cancers like that fame means proximity to power, an abundance of money (usually), and people's adoration. They revel in the whole stuff of celebrity culture because they love gossip and the way human nature is exaggerated when a person has fame. But they also feel conflicted about it. They do not love the glitz and glam, like a Famous Libra might. They appreciate being able to make things happen easily, but they see through superficiality, longing always for depth in all its forms.

Cat Stevens is a good example of a Famous Cancer. He achieved great success and then decided to get out of the spotlight, as celebrity culture didn't match his ethics and his spirituality. Yet while he made music, it represented his caring, Cancerian nature well. His songs, especially from his heyday in the 1970s, read as a playbook for the Cancer heart. Even his titles will tell you all you need to know about what Cancers feel: "The First Cut Is the Deepest," "Don't Be Shy," "Trouble." When he says that "love is better than a song," we believe him. We all must remember that, when we get too mired in the work of life, real love is better than a passing tune. Real love stays with you, after the music has stopped. All Famous

Cancers are looking for things that have longevity, and they use their fame to achieve that.

Cat Stevens's "If You Want to Sing Out" is also a perfect Cancer song. "If you want to be free, be free," it tells you, just like the way a really good mom will tell you when you're feeling low. The song reminds us that "there's a million things to be." It promotes tolerance, with everyone doing their own thing, peacefully. Most Cancers want that, and a Famous Cancer, a good one, will try to support that in whatever they do. Remember, Cancers care. (Ex-lovers of Cancers, please keep quiet and put your hands down. I'll get to you all eventually.)

Frida Kahlo is a Famous Cancer who has changed the landscape of humanity's relationship to art. Kahlo made the self the focus, important and interesting, by infusing reality with a surreality that made the familiar elevated. She placed the emotional world, those moody oceanic crags, at the center of her work, thereby creating a space for countless artists after her to do the same. And in all of her self-portraits, you can feel the self, in her piercing dark eyes, looking out of her paintings with a higher knowledge of spirit. She used her fame to do all of these things and give us the gift of her work.

If we looked at every sign, we could of course find some examples of fame having made people worse. I won't name names here (George W. Bush), but sometimes a possessive and power-hungry streak can make Cancer an unfit ruler. Also, if a Cancer was famous but their career has dwindled, they can show signs of great sadness. To say Cancers don't get over things easily is a pretty big understatement. Now imagine that feeling played out on the international stage. If you know any Cancers who aren't getting much work anymore, check in with them often and take their emotional temperature, as they probably do need your support. Change is always hard for Cancer.

Other Famous Cancers

1. Malala Yousafzai
2. Shelley Duvall
3. Hart Crane
4. Wendy Williams
5. Meryl Streep
6. Kevin Hart
7. Robin Williams
8. Nelson Mandela
9. Patrick Stewart
10. Helen Keller

Cancer playlist

- Selena Gomez, "Hands to Myself"
- Lil' Kim, "Big Momma Thang"
- Gustav Mahler, "Symphony No. 3"
- June Carter Cash, "Ring of Fire"
- Missy Elliott, "Work It"
- M.I.A., "Borders"
- George Michael, "Father Figure"
- Linda Ronstadt, "You're No Good"
- Lena Horne, "Stormy Weather"
- Beck, "Blue Moon"

The Cancer (a poem)

A field of green. Is where you lie. With the elements. Like time, but unmasked. Where you can be anything at all. But you won't be. Signing your sign off with a tiny little *s*. *S* is for sex. And snake. An aqua map where you put an *x*. *X* marks the spot! Where your heart is beating. Come find it. So we did. Beat beat beat. It's like the starfish that enter the arena. Fighting fighting. But that's what they are here for. Everyone thinks that nothing means anything. But you don't. You loved once. It was another time. Another world. You made a scene about love. Out of words. Then set it in stained glass. A big red translucent heart. Is set up in the window. It's lit up by the sky. And everything else. Love. It hurts you still.

LEO

July 23–August 22

Proud people breed sad sorrows for themselves.
Emily Brontë, born July 30, 1818

The Leo

There's an entire chapter on fame in Andy Warhol's *The Philosophy of Andy Warhol*. You can find it among other chapters titled "Love," "Beauty," "Success," "Economics"—all of which turn out to be, more or less, also about fame. Endless rambling, name-dropping, where he went, who with, recollections of phone conversations, who's obsessed with him, who isn't, who kissed who, why he wants to open a restaurant for lonely people, how he went to therapy because he was picking up everyone's problems— and truly, what you realize not even having finished the book is that this is exactly the type of person you want to be friends with. And who you want to invite to all your parties. And someone so utterly enamored with being alive that the chapter called "Death" is only two sentences, the first being: "I don't believe in it, because you're not around to know that it's happened." Has there ever been an utterance more Leo than that? Insistent on the individual, pre-occupied with physical existence, and so seduced by the material world, even death is dismissed as (at best) a rumor? It's brilliant.

Leos live life with command and fervor. There is a mania to their appreciation of people, places, mirrors, mentions of their own name—and that mania is infectious. I've rarely been bored hanging out with a Leo. Even their self-interest is amusing because at its core, it's not nihilistic. It has soul. Its goal is building rather than taking away, and there's a genuine curiosity about the world that they bring with them everywhere, and which you can find right around their lips. Leos are optimists and advocates of opulence. They don't tire of being looked at and they don't tire of looking back. If you've ever talked with one for more than thirty seconds you'll know everything that's happened to them that day, who they're sleeping with, who they want to sleep with, where you can buy them a drink, and you'll also witness a casual but extended mention of someone powerful and important (someone they're connected to, even if loosely). Leos are hyperbolic and highly emotional. Many of their sentences begin with "I." They like to hijack conversations by relating your problems back to theirs, or just to them in general. Somehow—in your utter annoyance at this—you won't be able to look away, interrupt, or challenge them easily. They are the smoothest talkers in the zodiac. Despite their obvious narcissism (or perhaps because of it), they know exactly how to read you and get what they want. It's why so many of them are good at business.

Leos want devotion, obsession, and attention. After they have it from one person, they want it from everyone else. It was Warhol, after all, who in 1968 predicted that "in the future, everyone will be world-famous for fifteen minutes." Fifteen minutes for us, twenty-three hours and forty-five minutes for Leos. They won't settle for less. And honestly, they're probably annoyed they're not getting the full twenty-four hours as is. Warhol's famous prediction has reverberated throughout our lives since. He might as well have invented modern celebrity and internet culture. He certainly described aspects of what he couldn't have known would be social media and our fondness for selfies (remember his screen tests?). Deep down Warhol knew that all of us have some Leo in us. We're obsessed with ourselves. We're infatuated with our own boredom even. As a Leo would probably say—so what?

Things you might want to know about Leo

Leos are a fixed fire sign and the fifth sign of the zodiac. They come after Cancer and have learned an important lesson from them: emotional receptivity. They know how to connect. They're people people. Highly energetic, interested in pleasing, and incredibly seductive. Adulation and trust are two things Leos can't live without. They will go anywhere and even change who they are in order to get them. Their ruler is the sun (the one star *we* can't live without), and it isn't lost on Leos that part of that huge life force is lodged somewhere within them, making them the stars in any room, a lot like supermodels in the early '90s when they more or less ran the country (sorry, Congress).

It goes without saying that Leos are natural leaders. They're also effective motivators and their power is rooted in magnetism. The way they negotiate a deal of any kind is the same way they flirt. Playful, assertive, a little on the nose but forgivable. Every part of their body is used to bewitch. You'll likely feel like the only person in the room, bar, hotel, whatever. Just you and a pushy Leo talking about your secrets, fantasies, and deepest fears. They can get so much out of you if they want. Soon enough you'll be handing over your keys, ending your marriage, and taking them to Bermuda because you've never met anyone quite like them. It's like they got a degree in being persuasive and acting appropriately slutty enough to pass for okay. If they were a drug, they'd definitely be ecstasy.

Another thing you should know about Leos is that aesthetic perfection matters to them more than it does to most people. Beauty is their religion and they're hardest on themselves. They also love to be surrounded by attractive people. If those people are rich, even more so. Not to be tacky (but to be tacky, because Leos are)— status goes a long way with a Leo. Obviously they'll never admit that. But they don't need to. Just watch how they act around some- one who can help them. They kiss ass and they do it well. Politics is another career they excel at and one that's almost built for them. Except what gets Leos in trouble is their excess. They will do any- thing to escape how boring life can get. Over-the-top vacations, champagne at noon, a constant desire to meet (and sleep with) new people. They're thrill seekers and value the new. They believe it will be better than the past. They need to be attended to at all times, like a child, and people's opinions are more important to them than any scripture. They're ruled by public opinion. In the movie of their lives, Leos would say they want you to think they're smart, but really, they want you to want them. On a basic, primal, want-to-rip-their-clothes-off level.

Somewhere under the surface, under all that ego, is the real. Leos live there, too. The lion is a tribal creature. They're protective and loyal. If you're one of the pack, Leos will do anything for you. Their generosity, both financial and emotional, is second to none. But there's a deep existential sadness that they hide from public view. They wrestle with it alone and away from their "pride" because Leos need their friends to see them as relief from everything awful in the world. They feel responsible for the happiness of others and will mask what they're personally feeling conflicted about. They're great actors. Leos perform strength anytime they're out. That leaves little room for their very real anxieties and lack of confidence to be addressed or noticed. Basically, they don't want you to see them as anything less than stunning. A self-sufficient superhuman force that could rescue you from any drama. In short, a hero.

High standards and self-torture aside, hair is a great source of power for Leos. It's where to find their aura. It's also what gives them a superficial and real sense of self-worth. Though they're not looking to make a statement or experiment. They won't dye their hair purple on a whim or anything. What they want is to find that one style that will solidify the whole Leo package and be forever associated with them. They want to be classic. Iconic. And usually they'll have a gesture they'll use to draw your attention to their hair, reminding you of their allure and how desirable they are. How everything feels possible in their presence. How whatever happened to you in the past, it's never coming back. It's over. They're right there in front of you. Leos are the peak of the party. The moments you hardly notice happening because they feel so good and pass so fast, only later do you obsess about them and wish life could be like that all the time.

Leo as a lover

To get a Leo's attention, you don't have to be coy. You don't have to play games either. They're not a Scorpio or a Sagittarius. Start by giving them a compliment. Bring up their hair. Quote something they said, even from a minute ago. Something they tweeted or posted would be better. Yes, it's crass and desperate to do this with anyone, but Leos love this kind of pursuit. Simple, baseline obsession is what gets them to notice someone initially. Approaching them intellectually or showing off how skilled you are at something will turn them off. Leave that for later. They don't want to think of you as competition or "better" than them in any area. They want to be indulged. They want to be worshipped (from the very beginning). Acting like a stalker will actually take you to the front of the line. And yes, there's a line. Leos have many admirers who would love to be walked around on a leash, following their every move and being witness to their overperformed confidence.

Hopefully we're all familiar with the term "starfucker," because that's what Leos are. They care about who you are on paper. Fame, money, status, where you live, where you went to school— it matters to them. Sometimes when I meet a Leo's boyfriend or girlfriend I joke that they really made it, they have the Leo-approved pedigree. It's a tricky balance because, as I mentioned earlier, Leos don't like being challenged. Their partners have to be extraordinary, but not more extraordinary than them, or at least different enough for a comparison to never occur. Though Leos love to compare themselves to people. They are constantly running hierarchies in their head. Comparing exes to current lovers, lovers to those of their friends, their friends to potential friends, etc. Being with a Leo can feel a little like high school all over again.

No matter what they tell you—and they will lie so as to appear evolved—do not believe them: Leos are not capable of taking constructive criticism. Some might, but will still have a hard time interpreting it as anything but an attack on their character. This goes for love, not business. In business, where they're much more preoccupied with being the best and performing well, Leos will listen and adjust. Keep in mind that they are their own toughest critic, and that's partly why they don't like hearing even the slightest critique from anyone else. It just magnifies and fuels their list of inadequacies. It's true that people who project the greatest confidence often put too much stock in their bad reviews and too little in their good ones.

Back to romance—it comes easily for Leos. They are sweeping, attentive lovers. They'll go to great lengths to impress you. At times you'll wonder what they're really after—if it's recognition (Best Performance as Romantic Lead) or the true investment of a messy and difficult partnership. They are compatible with both of their fire sign siblings. The sex will be hotter with a Sagittarius, though it will also confuse Leos, who will want a more stable connection. A relationship with an Aries, while not stable, will last longer. And both Aries and Leo share many cliché ideas about love, so they can throw those at each other and be self-satisfied.

Of the water signs, Cancers are a Leo's best bet. Like everyone, Leos will chase Scorpios, but they're definitely too high-maintenance for them. They also won't like how Scorpios can steal attention from anyone without even trying (really just by lighting a cigarette). And a sweet and loving Pisces will certainly last for a while with a Leo, but Leos get bored of them. Leos need glamour like we need universal health care. A Pisces is way too earnest for them in the end. And this brings us to air signs. Adventure. Mystery. Maybe a little too much mystery for Leos, but they'll be endlessly entertained with Geminis and have a flirtatious rapport with Libras. Aquarians will intrigue them deeply but leave them feeling a bit cold.

I've known many Leos who are incredibly compatible with earth signs. Especially Capricorns, and at times Virgos. What Leos love about Capricorns is how dependable they are. What they appreciate in a Virgo is how nurturing they can be. Leo and Taurus are a turbulent match, with both constantly vying for attention. Taurus wins in the end because they don't compromise on principle. Their glamour is earthier and less self-conscious, too. A Taurus is more singer-songwriter than overproduced pop star dying to come off as authentic (Leos).

The erogenous zones for Leos are their back and shoulders. Playing with their hair is also a direct portal to their libido. Leos are carnal. If you aren't fucking them at least four times a week, they're definitely thinking of fucking someone else (if not doing it already). They assume everyone wants to have sex with them. If they're feeling less heat from you now than they were in the beginning (when you started dating), it will make them feel bad about themselves and they will consider cheating. Not necessarily because they want someone else but because they'll assume you want them less or "not enough," by Leo standards. To be totally fair, Leos are very loyal. They are at the top of the list of people who can have very long relationships. They're not scared of commitment. But if you cool off even just a bit, there will be drama. You should know they also like public sex, especially in a stairwell.

To be with a Leo is to know that you'll be the less visible partner—when arriving at a party, meeting up with friends, or doing just about anything together. To be with them is to accept that they're always on stage, constantly performing, even when no one's in the room. The most authentic moments for a Leo happen when all eyes are on them. They come alive among people. They have an actual need for the presence of others in order to feel real.

If you fall in love with a Leo, you'll learn how to navigate the tricky maze of their flirtatious personality. This includes their tendency to seek approval even from people they dislike. Not only do they want to make sure no one they love is angry with them—which can really ruin nights and conversations, as they'll constantly bring up things they've forgiven you for—but their enemies are of great interest to them. It's a real love-hate relationship. Leos don't like to define themselves by who doesn't like them. The paradox is, they want to be liked by people who loathe them most.

We all know that love happens suddenly. You can find some Capricorns who doubt this—and some Tauruses, too—but Leos know it better than anyone. They're ready to be destroyed or rebuilt by desire at all times. I once went on a date with a Leo who was coming straight from the airport, flying in from California, and he didn't even drop off his bags. He just showed up at the bar looking incredible and said the word "love" in the first fifteen minutes. I was terrified and completely compelled. Then he invited me over, even though we both had to be up early the next day, and let's just say I couldn't believe his stamina. And how easy everything seemed. Leos make you feel comfortable. They are warm lovers who will be forthcoming from the beginning.

Even though we think of Leos as out and about, and the true extroverts of the zodiac, their homes are very important to them. When a Leo invites you over, it always means something. They want to get close in a real way. Their fire sign brethren, Aries and Sagittarius, differ here. They could say anything from "I love you" to "I hate you" and the truth could be the opposite the next day (which isn't to say they didn't mean it in the moment). But Leos are the fixed fire sign. They're truly rooted. They're consistent in their loyalty and less impulsive. You will feel a security with a Leo that is hard to match. You'll also become addicted to it. And it's not necessarily a bad thing that you do. Leos want a romantic partner at all times. They need someone else to do things with and, let's face it, someone else to witness their existence and take their Instagram photos. They're that person who goes from one relationship to the next, sometimes making horrible mistakes, because they're afraid of being alone. For a Leo, to be alone is to be forgotten.

Something else that distinguishes Leos from their fire sign family is that they aren't bossy when it comes to love. Or at least they don't want to be. They're a boss everywhere else in life. In love, they're dying to relinquish their armor and be taken care of. They also like it when you make decisions—which restaurant, what overpriced hotel, where to get a nightcap. Leos find this way of being attended to very sexy. This isn't a Cancer who wants you to hold their hair back while they throw up and sob. They're expecting you to run a bath for them at the Ritz-Carlton. To have a table reserved and to be there waiting, before they arrive. Because even though Leos are incredibly punctual, they'll fall in love with you even more if you're five minutes early. They like to have someone already there. They like to be expected.

Leo as a friend

In my experience, few signs will stick by you like a Leo. Though as with a Pisces, they're probably sexually attracted to you (like they are to most of their friends). This comes from a deep infatuation with the people Leos let into their lives. It's not easy to be in their inner circle. It means you've averaged giving them 169 compliments a day for 169 months straight. It means you've seen them when their hair isn't perfect (probably when one strand was out of place). It means they've decided you're someone who's passionate and truly alive—they detest nihilism—and someone who is earnest at their core.

Getting over a breakup with a Leo best friend by your side is illuminating. You'll see a side of them that's rarely talked about. The generous, selfless warrior. Who *doesn't* sometimes want that friend who—no matter how much it makes sense that your ex left, no matter how much you shouldn't hate them because breakups are rarely one-sided—unequivocally and vehemently hates your ex, no matter how illogical? It's their instinct as guardians to do this. It's an energy that can also feel familiar and comforting in a paternal way. Virgos and Leos are the true caretakers of the zodiac. They look after all of us no matter how much we test them.

Leos are also exceptional gift givers. Once, one gave me a lighter with my birthstone and my initials inscribed on the back. Another thing Leos like to do is pick up the check. They love to treat friends. They're also always giving money to a cause or some charitable effort. Their devotion to the greater good is ingrained in them. They aren't after the utopia imagined by their opposite sign, Aquarius. They strive for simpler, more concrete ways to help. In other words, Leos aren't rule breakers or radicals. They understand that in order to be the leader they have to conform, to a certain degree, and in that conformity they gain power, which they use to help others.

Even in front of close friends Leos have a hard time letting their guard down. They're constantly trying to remain extraordinary, in their achievements and their looks. There's a deep fear that if they don't live up to what they know they can be, their friends will be disappointed in them. Of course, this isn't true. This is all internal Leo psychodrama. They're a particularly hard sign to give advice to. Their self-criticism is so charged, they're usually striving for more than even what's advised. This leads us to the hurt and wounded Leo. The Leo who performs strength in front of everyone but is not feeling strong. Often Leos need to be encouraged to take breaks from work and their various responsibilities. They push themselves too hard. Their ambition is boundless. And their depressive episodes go unseen, which can be dangerous. Introspective time away from everyone is actually healthy for Leos. It's what they should have more of, but they're so desperately worried they'll miss out on something, they can't fully immerse themselves in a restorative break.

Leo style

Have you ever seen a painting or a piece of furniture from the rococo period (late seventeenth and early eighteenth century)? Ornament, drama, luxury, gilding. Even if it's not your style, it's unforgettable and unmistakably itself. Leos could live in a castle of vast and open rococo rooms, each one leading to the next (or the décor of Lana Del Rey's "Born to Die" music video). They're like the castle itself, distinct and grandiose. There's something both imposing and seductive about how they choose to present who they are to the world.

A Leo truly would wear anything as long as it gets you to look at them. That isn't to say they don't have style, but they're actually quite influenced by trends. Even if they hate something that's having a moment, they'll try it. They'll do this to see how people react to them. If the reaction is favorable, they'll keep wearing it. If it's not, they'll pretend they hated it all along. Public opinion is gold to Leos, and though they may disagree with it, it's a bitter pill to swallow when it's against them.

In some ways, Leos are chameleons. They've been known to change their attire and aesthetics as a way to influence and have power over the people around them. The truth is, they're quite predictable. They're even a bit basic at their core. Sure, you'll see them in gold, silver, sequins, dark purple, black with a shimmer. But their soul's color palette is closer to something earthier and rustic. This won't be obvious when you meet them. Only once you've been accepted into a Leo's inner circle will they begin to reveal this side of themselves. And even then, they're the kind of people who always look good. Whether you find them lounging at home or run into them on the street, they'll be more than put together. Even in sweatpants, Leos like to have something on that makes them feel expensive and valuable. Sometimes they'll dress up for no one but themselves.

While Leos like to see themselves as risk-takers, they're actually closer to classic. The well-fitted blazer, the little black dress, the perfect white t-shirt and dark denim—it's what they're predisposed to. What they're banking on is their hair getting them the extra attention. They're also constantly borrowing—dare I say stealing—from how their friends dress. What they're good at is taking an original idea from someone else and pulling it off with more style. But they're not going to be the genius behind wearing a swan dress (Björk, Scorpio) or an entire garment made of meat (Lady Gaga, Aries). For Leos it's very important to come off as effortless. You can be sure they've rehearsed, planned, and personally scrutinized every look you see them in. They're the zodiac sign who's there to remind us that even before our actions, the first thing people notice is how we look. Obviously!

Something Leos don't really love is layers. They prefer the summer and anything that shows off skin. They like wearing sheer and distressed garments and can even look cheesy doing it, in that way someone who's trying to be cool does. As long as you correct them, they'll take note. Though it's hard to be honest with a Leo when it comes to fashion. There's so much theater involved on their end. They love to pretend that they're a badass—until one person in a room of a hundred says something even remotely critical. Then they'll spend hours thinking about that critique and making sure that person sees them looking flawless the next time they're in a room together. Whether or not they agree with what was said doesn't matter. Revenge in the form of perfection does. That's a Leo mantra.

Texting with a Leo

Leos are demanding communicators. They're impatient and either excessively effusive or ice-cold. It depends what mood you catch them in, but one thing's for sure—they want you to be the one reaching out to them. They also want you to respond immediately if they reach out to you. Anything that isn't in person already gives them anxiety, since they're masters at reading body language and tone. Remember: if you want things to go smoothly with a Leo, be transparent, kind, and overly sincere. This will be especially hard for Geminis. In fact, air signs—I'm looking at you.

Leo sext

Leo: So you're really into my hair.
You: Is that . . . a question?
Leo: No.

Leo anxiety

Leo: Can you go on Insta and like my photo? Only a thousand and four people have liked it.

Leo making plans

Leo: I think it's best if we show up after 7:00 p.m., because the humidity is very high until then and my hair will just look better after.

Leo nostalgia

Leo: Remember when the checkout guy at 7-Eleven said I was the most beautiful person he had ever seen omfg. A moment.

Leo glamour

You: Are you coming? We're waiting inside for you.
Leo: I'm so sorry, I'm right outside. But my Lyft driver keeps giving me compliments. I can't leave.

Existential Leo

Leo: You know my hair guy? The one I've been going to forever!?
You: Yeah, why.
Leo: He quit. Like to go to graduate school. The world is a dark place!

Leo in love

Leo: I'd give you the shirt off my back.
You: Oh no, it's ok.
Leo: TAKE IT.
You: I'm ok, really.
Leo: Take the shirt!! I look really hot without it.
You: Ok omg I'll take it.

The Leo imagination

If a Leo were a city, they'd be Los Angeles. Glitzy, famous, less exciting than the myth. If they were punctuation they'd be quotation marks. Always name-dropping, quoting someone they know, and probably themselves. If they were a type of weather: heat wave. Movie: romantic comedy and horror both. Leos are more traditional than you think. They want a lifetime partner. A big family, kids, and a career that would terrify anyone with its accomplishments.

In short, Leos want the American Dream. Except it's the Leo Dream. The worst mistake you can make with a Leo is to ask them to compromise when it comes to their ambition. Many Leos become artists. They possess a natural talent for the arts and crave the spotlight. Taking chances and putting themselves out there gives them a will to live. Leos make great writers, actors, musicians, painters, and any sort of entertainer, really. They more or less invented Hollywood, and Leo star power is unrivaled by any other sign.

It may sound contradictory, but in an effort to know themselves,

Leos will take on many disguises. Or perhaps it's better to think of it as continuous change. They'll try various social groups, living in different cities, pivoting from one career to the next, changing their hair and style of dress—the one thing that will remain constant is their core group of friends. As with Aquarians, it will appear that they have many. An Aquarius actually does. With a Leo it only seems that way. They can count the number of close friends on one hand. These are people who have witnessed their changes yet still recognize who they are. Leos yearn to be known. For all their performing and masquerading, trying to impress strangers and lovers alike, they want to be around people who can see through their bullshit, people who are probably kinder to them than Leos are to themselves.

Leos are gentle felines. They preside over their kingdom with compassion and empathy rather than power. While they like knowing they possess power, they aren't turned on by it for its own sake, like a Capricorn for example. This makes them excel at any task having to do with teaching and leading others. And it steers them toward responsibility and away from ego. Another way to say this is: they make great parents and obsessive pet owners. If you ever need someone to cat-sit for you, ask a Leo.

I always think of Leos during those sepia-tinged days in the middle of summer. The longest days of the year, when even the nights feel brighter. Out on some roof or a terrace. In a park or close to a lake. Anywhere that's full of people, none of who want to go home. That's really the heart of the Leo imagination. Being drunk on the sun. Being drunk on yourself. Being surrounded by everyone. And under the glare of some streetlight, sometime after the sun has set, a Leo is surely leading their pack to the next bar, the next stop, the next glass of wine. Leos are so stunned to be here. They feel tremendously lucky to be who they are. No one would love to live twice more than them.

The Famous Leo

"This is crazy," says Warren Beatty, an Aries. "Nobody talks about this on film?" He's talking to his then-girlfriend, Madonna, who's suddenly lost her voice while on tour. A doctor sits in front of her, examining her throat while cameras and a lights crew circle around, recording the entire thing. "Talk about what," she says, somehow able to speak now that she's annoyed. He's referring to the spectacle. The documentary being filmed about her and her sold-out tour, a documentary she refuses to pause even while being on vocal rest. The show must go on because she is the show. She knows this. "But this is a serious matter, your throat," Beatty says, sounding a lot like a parent. And again, Madonna halts his questioning. "Why should I stop here?" She's stern and cheeky, rolling her eyes while performing vulnerability. It's fairly obvious she isn't waiting for Beatty to answer. What she wants is to assert herself. To let him know that she's still in charge, not sick or vulnerable in the least. It's 1990. More than a decade before social media. Before every aspect of our lives is available for public consumption and we, too, may let the entire world witness our most intimate details at a doctor's office, at home, or in bed. Madonna is already there. In the future. She's let the cameras in everywhere. Even down her own throat.

"Do you want to talk at all off camera?" the doctor asks. Madonna, queen of Leos, is wearing a silk robe with her hair up in a towel. She shakes her head no and then mouths the word as well, for the sake of theatrics, just so the cameras catch it. "She doesn't want to live off camera," Beatty says. "There's nothing to say off camera. Why would you say something if it's off camera? What point is there of . . . existing?" He and everyone else in the room know what she's doing by refusing to press pause. Even without talking, a Leo commands attention through their presence and aura alone. Nothing can keep the cameras off them.

There's no shortage of Leos throughout history who've loved the camera and the stage. Whitney Houston, Mick Jagger, Julia Child, Sean Penn—who married Madonna on her birthday, August 16 (a day before his—talk about a Leo season wedding). The bigger the spectacle and the higher the drama, the more Leo it is. Andy Warhol showed up to Madonna and Penn's wedding with a canvas he painted with the artist Keith Haring (Taurus), of a headline from the *New York Post* that read: "Madonna on Nude Pix: So What!" So what, indeed. There's little that Leos will allow to derail them. What the world throws at them as obstacle is often the very thing they use to attract attention and regain their footing. They are skilled and entertaining fighters. They don't quit and they don't allow you to see them bothered.

Leos lead themselves out of trouble by their charisma and grit. Very often they'll take charge and do that for their friends, too. If they have to, they'll do it for the whole country. Bill Clinton and Barack Obama are both Leos. Regardless of what's written about their respective presidencies, they had sex appeal and people loved them. Both Bushes were boring as fuck, let's just say it. At their most attacked, Leos call on their legendary confidence. They go on the offensive and it feels like you're up against two people (or two thousand), not one. And even while accomplishing what they aren't expected to, what no one saw coming—like being the first to walk on the moon (Neil Armstrong)—Leos are rarely satisfied. To get our applause they'll think up another trick, another project with which to dazzle, proving everyone who doubted them wrong. There's no one more cunning. No one more determined to be remembered and last.

Other Famous Leos

1. Yves Saint Laurent
2. Kylie Jenner
3. JLo
4. J. K. Rowling
5. Meghan Markle
6. Lucille Ball
7. Amelia Earhart
8. Alfred Hitchcock
9. Halle Berry
10. Robert De Niro

Leo playlist

- Madonna, "Bitch, I'm Madonna"
- Claude Debussy, "Prélude à l'Après-Midi d'un Faune"
- JLo, "I Luh Ya Papi"

- The Rolling Stones, "Time Is on My Side"
- Kate Bush, "Hounds of Love"
- Coolio, "Gangsta's Paradise"
- Charli XCX, "Babygirl"
- Elliott Smith, "Between the Bars"
- Whitney Houston, "I Wanna Dance with Somebody"
- Tori Amos, "Crucify"

The Leo (a poem)

In the endless summer where you live
and the sea you turn to fire,
you are more than mirrors
and vast golden rooms,
you are more than echoes.
A wild light outside of
storms and gods, a once
remembered place returning
to the future. If you could,
you'd live for every longest day.
You'd live into forever.

VIRGO

August 23–September 22

The house, too, was like this,
over painted, over lovely—
the world is like this.

H. D., born September 10, 1886

The Virgo

On a hot summer night in Montreal, in the middle of her song "Halo," Beyoncé—in a glittering silver top and leopard print belt—floated down the stage and into the crowd for a rare moment of intimacy. Knowing Virgos, this was likely carefully choreographed, down to the casual hand gestures and head turns. The arena erupted. Even people in the back and nowhere near her found reason to scream. Being easily the biggest pop star of her generation, Beyoncé has used aspects of her privacy to maintain her allure, making any nod toward the personal a real moment to witness. It goes without saying that there's plenty of personal history in her music, but she's kept her distance: rarely giving interviews, communicating only through visuals on social media, and operating through the notion of surprise—the way she drops a record, without any fanfare, for example. This classic type of Virgo reserve is genius. It adds another level of intimidation to what is already her immaculately crafted empire—one manifestation of which is her live performance.

I've never seen Beyoncé give a bad live performance. She's in the echelon of entertainers like Madonna and Britney Spears, pop stars who know how to create meaningful and provocative spectacle, transcending even their fame and bringing us something mythical each time. More than that, I've never seen Beyoncé miss a step or a cue. On this night in Montreal, a few strands of her hair catch in an oscillating fan as she walks down the stage and toward the audience (the video is online if you want to give yourself a panic attack). At first, no one but Beyoncé is aware of this. There's no panic or wincing. She keeps singing, her long blond mane getting eaten by the whirring machine. Danger aside, the fact that this happens in front of thousands of people and Beyoncé continues performing, while guards and various helpers whirl around her, is truly Herculean. And it's almost a full minute before one of the guards is handed a pair of scissors (from god knows where) and frees her, Beyoncé moving again toward the audience as if nothing had happened, though surely she must have felt something, if only her own terror. Handled. Survived. Not even slightly derailed from the plan, from the schedule. You won't find anyone tougher than a Virgo.

Things you might want to know about Virgo

Virgos are a mutable earth sign and the sixth sign of the zodiac. They come after Leo and have inherited their big heart but also learned about the trappings of the ego. In almost all cases, a Virgo would rather talk about you than themselves. This is most obvious when it comes to feelings. They hate talking about their own. That's because it's actually all they think about, but they view feelings as uncontrollable, minefields of desire. They like systems, logic, and problem-solving. Feelings are an area where those things obviously don't work. Virgos are also the kind of people who can make it through the day with a bullet in them if they had to. They don't do much complaining. They're enduring, almost to a fault.

What drives a Virgo? Keeping things going. Keeping the world functioning. Virgos are often committed to something larger than themselves and achieve self-worth from being needed. They love sustaining things. Gardens, people, long-lost languages. They're the ones who know exactly what organic remedy to try and which herb will heal you. Their help is not self-serving either. They offer a specific type of kindness: personal, involved, and far-reaching. Even if they're mostly stoic, there's plenty of empathy behind that stoicism.

All this can be hard to see at first. If you have Virgos in your life, you know they often come off as harsh. Their criticism is usually phrased in the form of a question, one that's passive-aggressive and usually bringing up the past. Something you may no longer remember or think would bother them at all. Virgos hold on to things. They have a great memory and can keep grudges, which they view as practical and protective rather than mean-spirited. They're also incredibly precise. Their own precision holds them hostage and they're aware they can be read as overwhelming, which they try to make up for by being self-deprecating.

The Virgo surface is polished and brilliant. If you compare yourself to them, it's intimidating. The standards Virgos hold themselves to are impossible. It depresses me to see their schedules, houses, and color-coded dry-cleaned lives. You should know they don't expect anyone else to live like this. In fact, they're mostly ready to be disappointed by others. For those of us who are far from perfect (everyone except the Leos about to look in a mirror after they finish this sentence), this is good news. But it weighs heavy on Virgos that they are constantly performing at a level no one can match. They're prone to feeling used or taken advantage of. From their friends, they tolerate mistakes they'd never make themselves. Blowing off plans (air signs), showing up late (fire signs), not being able to leave the house without a scheduled therapy appointment (water signs). And even a Capricorn or Taurus can let Virgos down with how brusque they can be (Virgos are not that kind of earth sign).

Personally, I'm always about ten minutes late. This tends to work in a city like New York, where everyone runs behind. When I show up to a meeting or date with a Virgo, I know those ten minutes are thirty in their eyes. And actually, they like to show up early. Once, I was meeting a Virgo for coffee, and he assumed I wouldn't show up when I wasn't on time so he left, ran an errand, and came back. They're resourceful that way and hate wasting time. The remainder of our coffee date was full of passive-aggressive jabs about his plans for the rest of the day. A frustrating thing about Virgos is that they pretend they aren't upset when they really are. As a fire sign, I can't understand this. Especially because their inability to express themselves over small things (like being late, which they wouldn't consider a small thing at all) can lead to deep rage later on. And Virgo rage is rare and terrifying. The government should send out an alert whenever it's happening.

Follow-up texts. Reminder emails. Advice you didn't really ask for. All of these are part of the Virgo arsenal. The good news is, Virgos don't have a diva complex (they've learned a lesson from Leos). They aren't doing any of these things in a manipulative sense (Cancers, I'm sorry, but this is you). In fact, the opposite is true. They're the healers of the zodiac. Their ego is tied to measurable achievement and they're often happy to relieve you of some dull practicality in an effort to be useful and demonstrate their skills. Sound like someone you'd hire for a job? Someone you'd want as a colleague? Someone who has a big heart and might also be . . . a little boring?

Virgos have certainly been accused of being boring. In college I knew a Virgo who was the designated "responsible friend" at parties. He certainly was always hydrated. And I did imagine him waking up early in his immaculately clean apartment, then reading for pleasure after checking his finances. Something to aspire to maybe, but as the queen of Libras, Oscar Wilde, once said: "Everything in moderation, including moderation." Please write this down on one of your many lists, Virgos.

The greatest of Virgos is perhaps Astraea, who in Greek mythology was the last of the immortals to abandon the earth. Her purity and innocence allowed her to be faithful to humanity and withstand a lot. And I bet you know about that one planet, the one that always seems in retrograde. The great messenger. The constant communicator. I'm talking about Mercury, of course. Virgos are ruled by it and it shouldn't come as a shock to anyone. They're the best sign at sorting and organizing information, and the systems they invent are devised to communicate things clearly and consistently. Like that feeling when Mercury's not in retrograde and the world somehow feels lighter, and more reasonable to deal with. Since Mercury also rules over the mind, Virgos will approach problems through the intellect rather than the heart. This is why they might be perceived as cold, and why their silence can be misinterpreted as indifference (Aquarians are like this, too). Trust me, indifference is not something Virgos employ in any aspect of life. They care. They might even care too much. Hence the building of their symmetrical lives—a pursuit that masks their existential panic.

Virgo as a lover

Virgos are secretly kinky. They're ready for nipple clamps after one glass of wine. So much for that famous self-control. Their perfectionism throws them into a state of unrestrained ecstasy. The catch is, that's half the Virgo population. One in two Virgos will act out their fantasies with you. The rest will be more or less vanilla. Their wild side is there, but you'll have to coax it out of them (sort of like sex after marriage?). The key with Virgos is always making it seem like you're the one who's curious about . . . handcuffs, whips, dildos, restraints, etc. I'm a Sagittarius, so take it from me—if you want to see how hydrated your Virgo really is, and how long they can go, come home with a sex toy (size matters to them), make sure it's beautifully wrapped (the way they'd wrap something), then suddenly let them notice there's a butt plug in the room. Naturally they'll resist and find this embarrassing. Part of getting Virgos to loosen up is withstanding their initial dismissals (and butt plugs do get you to loosen up). Virgos can be harsh. They need to reject things quite emphatically before changing their minds. If you think they need something other than a butt plug, feel free to experiment. I think anal beads would be too much for them. Though a gag might be perfect. It would get them to shut up and stop reminding you where not to put your hands on the bed so you don't spill any lube.

If we're talking earth signs, Virgos are more compatible with a Taurus than a Capricorn, but both have great potential. A Taurus will be more glamorous and indulge a Virgo. A Capricorn will make them feel safe and taken care of. The truth is, the classic earth sign match is Taurus-Capricorn, and by classic I mean the one that will last forever. So Virgos might feel a little left out. (I can't tell you how many Taurus-Capricorn matches I know. It's almost like those signs have a GPS on each other.) As far as hottest sex, Virgos and any fire sign, but especially Sagittarius, because they will give Virgos the most attitude. And secretly, they like that. They like the trouble and running around. Virgos and their opposite, Pisces, can also be a strong match, but other than the fish, water signs are not a long-term match for Virgos. They'll want to control them and rearrange their lives, which no Scorpio will let you do (though a Cancer might because they're a pushover). Of the air signs, Geminis will drive Virgos crazy and have a similar effect on them as a Sagittarius. They're both so different from earth signs that there's a lot of opportunity for sexual tension. Virgos and Aquarians are a big no. In fact, don't ever watch Virgo and Aquarius porn. It's about as exciting as flossing.

The erogenous zones for Virgos are their stomach and waistline. Pulling them toward you by their belt loops will turn them on. Putting your head on their stomach before and after sex will make them feel cared for. Anything below their nipples and above their hips is a big yes. Sneaking in a hug from behind (or anything else from behind) is also something they'll respond to. As someone who's had sex with several Virgos (all in a row too—it was a rough time in my life), I can tell you that they act like big tops in life (and they are), but lean more bottom in bed. Obviously, there are tops who are Virgos. I'm aware. But just know that it's not easy being a bossy, anal-retentive bitch all day, so being submissive in bed is hot to them.

I often say that sex with Virgos is like going to a casino. A gamble. It could be the best sex of your life, but don't expect anything. What you can count on is a long courtship. Virgos are quite traditional. They enjoy elaborate and antiquated ways of communicating. Letters, stationery, personalized notes, the whole thing. And very long texts and emails too. They are thorough! As you sit there reading their texts, you may wonder why they're telling you about naming their plants, or how they love cooking meals that take an entire day to make. You may wonder where the actual romance is—the urgency, the fire, the fucking feelings. At some point you'll be tempted to ask your Virgo if they've ever actually expressed a feeling (don't ask them that), or if they need a vacation more than anyone in the world (yes, that's them). If you put up with their emotional masquerade long enough, they'll know you're in. And they'll give a lot back to you.

If a Virgo is being restrained but also texting you about mundane things that don't really matter, they're full-on obsessed with you. No disrespect to Virgos, but their stories, anecdotes, and pickup lines—they're not exactly fireworks in the night sky. A Virgo's seduction is fairly typical. Sharing recipes. Taking you somewhere outdoors. Playing you their favorite record on vinyl and thinking it's super-edgy. It's all very charming, of course. Virgos are not game players. You don't have to second-guess what you share with them or ask your friends how to respond when they text. What you see is really what you get. That's the good news and the bad news. Once, a Virgo I met online bought me a plane ticket to come see him and basically spend a weekend having sex and drinking wine. I won't say where, but I thought this was quite creative for a Virgo. And it was smart; luring a Sagittarius with a trip usually works. Until I decided not to get on the plane because I had a huge meltdown and texted him 46 times in a row just to see how he'd respond. Well . . . he was terrified (but still wanted me to come). I don't like anyone who's scared of intensity. Sorry. And sometimes no matter how much you plan, life changes on you. Your Virgo lovers don't want to know that, but they'll learn. And I guess if I had to give another reason why I didn't get on that plane . . . the ticket wasn't to Paris exactly. If he was an Aries or Scorpio, it would have been.

Another thing to know about Virgos when it comes to love is that they have clear boundaries. They're compartmentalizers. They already know how they want to include you in their life—which friends you'll meet first, which friends you won't meet, when they'll introduce you to family, etc. Virgos know a lot of people, mostly because they've helped them with something. Their loyalty to their tribe is immense. You'll be introduced to your Virgo's important people progressively. Nothing will happen fast. If you protest this initiation, things won't go well. They'll be thrown off and stew, silently. They'll be insulted. Remember that despite their anti-effusive nature, Virgos are service-oriented. They need someone else to take pleasure in the plans they've put forth in order for them to feel pleasure as well. Everything people say and do matters greatly to Virgos, despite their steely exterior.

A secret: most thoughtful and sweet gestures (even if they don't go according to plan) will make Virgos fall for you. They just want to know you care and that you're genuine. If you choose a bar they hate, forget one of their allergies, spill something in their pristine house—it's all about the intention and the energy that went into it. Virgos are already prime date planners. They kind of expect other people not to do as well, and maybe even relish that because it makes them feel better about themselves. You should try to take the initiative despite how particular your Virgo is. Initiative goes a long way with Virgos.

So what about commitment? Naturally earth signs are hard to scare off. Capricorns may argue with the intensity of a dictator, a Taurus may never compromise, but neither is going to ghost you. They won't flee no matter how complicated the problem is. Virgos share this quality. Although if they begin to identify problems they determine are "irresolvable" or "problematic in the long term," you're in trouble. And they'll do this without even consulting or confronting you about it (confrontation scares them, another difference between them and other earth signs). The Virgo mind is constantly computing the viability of relationships. Gestures small and large, silences, your way of being in the world even when they aren't there (which they have their way of discerning)—it all matters. Virgos are loyal, but if they see a relationship isn't working, they'll be smart and dismantle it. Not in a direct way, but incrementally—pointing to various small things they've calculated as adding up to a big thing. There will rarely be a big fight that puts them over the edge. Think the opposite of a Sagittarius. Virgos won't burn down the house at once, but certain rooms will be on fire along the way until it's obvious one of you needs to check into a hotel. And yes, they'll have plenty of well-researched options for hotels along their escape route.

Love with a Virgo can be intensely powerful over time. It is a bond that deepens and changes. Perhaps you're thinking— shouldn't that be love with anyone? Well, sure, it would be great. But Virgos are willing to put in the work. They're willing to get to know you slowly and thoroughly. There's a lot to be said about that. And there are many signs in the zodiac that struggle with this kind of pursuit (Aries, Gemini, Libra, Scorpio, Sagittarius, Aquarius, just to name about half). So enjoy your Virgo love affair. It's possible no one will look at you with that kind of devotion ever again.

Virgo as a friend

Maybe you have a fantasy of a friend you can totally lose it in front of? Someone you don't need to perform for. A friend who handles your tantrums and mood swings. A friend who sees you at your absolute worst without blinking. Virgos are more or less the canonized saints of friendship. Their empathy is limitless and comes with action. They don't just listen. They're your one call after you've been arrested. They're better than a lawyer. And calling them for help is more useful than calling 911 because they're at their best in a crisis and won't send you a bill.

Crisis aside, Virgos are constantly taking you places and signing you up for things—book clubs, weekend trips, going over the FBI report of your future boyfriend. They're not a wild card. Your secrets and obsessions are safe with them. Though you'll feel like they divulge fewer personal details than you do. That's because Virgos are strategic, even in friendship, which is one reason they can be read as cold. They'll follow your lead and confide in you with time. If you think a Taurus takes an eternity to open up, well, you haven't been in a cabin in the middle of nowhere with a Virgo like I once was. Perfect meals. Endless drinks. And still I couldn't find out anything about this Virgo's fears or fuck-ups. In part, this is because Virgos maintain an appearance of invincibility in all relationships. Not because they don't trust you but because they're just wired that way. To show the cracks seems impolite to them. Like they're asking you for empathy (which they have a hard time with even when given). They're always thinking, "I don't want to burden this person with anything about myself."

Something frustrating about Virgos, which you probably already know, is that they're the least likely to believe in astrology or magic. Basically, everything that actually runs the universe. This is because they're faithful to "facts" and "logic" (as if magic doesn't have its own mysterious logic). I mean, these people likely have three life insurance plans by the time they're twenty-five. They've probably picked out their burial plot. Their wardrobes are coordinated by season and their bookshelves are alphabetized and accounted for. Everything is chronicled. It's no wonder that the mystical feels uncontainable and terrifying to them.

What Virgo friends will teach you is how to be a good friend yourself. They're ready to take care of you without asking for a lot in return, but they do need something back. They can be the strong friend, yes. Still they need your calls and attention or they'll reach a place so internal, the levels of repression there are on another level. Remember that being able to navigate the world with a plan doesn't mean you're prepared for your emotional life. Virgos are, at all times, a little lost. If you can get them to have more than three drinks in one night (good luck!), maybe they'll admit to needing help, or at least to not having all the answers without it translating to failure.

How to be a good friend to a Virgo? Be nosy, even annoying. Constantly check up on them and ask personal questions they'll find shocking but will secretly love. I think of Virgos like cats in public and dogs in private. All they want is to be invited everywhere. To be known for their nerdy alter egos. Unless you're one-on-one with them, this will be hard to see. They come off as overly discriminating and too particular—the result of their public shield, one they've taken years to engineer, and which is tattooed on their body and can be softened only if you approach them with radical vulnerability.

Even Virgo strangers can feel like friends in very real ways. Once, in New York, I was on the A train and going uptown to look at an apartment I was thinking of renting. A woman went into labor in my train car. For several stops she had her head against the window. Something was wrong and all of us kept an eye on her. I know people talk about how rude New Yorkers can be, but really the city makes everyone into Virgos. Stoic, stern, great in a crisis. So imagine a semi-crowded train, middle of the day, with the A/C blasting but it hardly matters because it's the end of August. The woman finally puts her head down in pain and that's the cue for the guy next to me to bolt up and kneel in front of her. He asks if anyone is a nurse or doctor and most of us shake our heads no, a bit terrified. Then he opens the train door and hops into the next car, and the next, and it feels like an action movie at this point. He returns with a doctor, who looks like the rest of us, a bit shaken. He sits with the woman, offers her water, and talks her through breathing. At the next stop, a team of three EMTs come into the train and wheels her out. This all takes forever and everyone is late no matter where they're going, but for once, we don't care. Or at least I don't. We make eye contact with one another in that *can you believe this* way, and somehow everyone looks a bit more human. The doctor is chatting with the guy who made it his job to look for him, saying he just turned fifty-three a few days ago and is still a runner. I'm quite sure he was a Virgo. The two of them got off somewhere after that, still talking, maybe not friends exactly, but not strangers either. I always tell people that Virgos are rarely strangers. You'll know it when you need one.

Virgo style

If there's one word to describe the style of Virgos it's *intricate*. They love layers, vintage pieces, and subtle but elaborate design.

Everything about their look is coordinated and considered. Sometimes they'll dedicate months to finding the right brooch or a piece of jewelry they'll see as the final, pull-it-together part of an ensemble. It's a process. And "process" is another good word for how they think about their wardrobe. Virgos are never quite satisfied with anything, so they'll constantly remind you that such-and-such piece would look better if they'd found it in dark green, or if the material was silk instead of cotton. The friends of mine who have the most clothes are Virgos. The most jewelry, also Virgos. The most eclectic taste given their supposedly practical personality, it's them again. Virgos.

An earth sign will always wear something that reminds you of luxury. Even if a Virgo is going for a simple look, they'll have one piece of bling on, or maybe vintage Gucci frames and a piece of onyx or jasper next to a more precious stone. They love crystals. They also love knowing the history of their pieces and will tell you about them if you ask. Virgos are addicted to context and understanding where everything came from and why. The history they've infused their garments with is important to them. They'll know when they last wore a shirt, whose birthday it was, what was going on in their life at the time, if you and them were fighting, etc. They're both secretly nostalgic and personal historians. They love lifestyle blogs, apartment therapy features, and anything to do with aesthetic origins.

Buying clothes for Virgos is hard because they're actively crafting their style and have done so their entire life. You might think you know what they like but their taste is so esoteric, it's difficult to pin down. Of course, they'll never let you know they don't like something you've bought them. They're too polite and guarded for that. If you do want to test your luck, go with a high-quality basic. Use value is important to them. So are commanding boots, anything handmade, the greenest green, expensive eyewear, precious and non-precious metals, and romantic capes and shawls.

Texting with a Virgo

Impeccable grammar. Immaculate punctuation. Intense clarity. Virgos should receive an award for texting. Unless, of course, you're fighting with them and it feels like you're in court. I'm not always in the mood for banter about their latest self-improvement, either. Usually they'll drop this in on the sly, which is your cue to congratulate them, since their self-validation is nonexistent. They're their own taskmaster and trainer. The terrifying day will come when you, too, get called on to make plans with a Virgo. Just say yes, then tell them you're going into a meeting so they can stop with the follow-ups.

Virgo sext

Virgo: If I finish work by 7, we could have sex by 8:15.
You [scared]: Ok!

Existential Virgo

Virgo: Even if nothing matters, it's still important to dust the top of the kitchen cabinets twice a week. It changes something.
You: Can you come do mine?

Virgo nostalgia

Virgo: I was just thinking about that time I came with you to get your hair cut and you didn't know it but I saved a piece of your hair and put it in my "Memories from 2015" folder, color-coded blue for beautiful and labeled 3:15, the time of your haircut.

You [confused]: Oh. That's so . . . sweet.

Virgo making plans

Virgo: I'm just following up on my follow-up text from yesterday about dinner in 2074, on Monday at 8pm. I've sent you an invite for your calendar. Please let me know! Xo

You [alarmed]: Got it!!

Glamorous Virgo

Virgo: I'm about to charge 69 organic cleaning products on my card right now. I deserve it!!!

You: Are you okay?

Passive-aggressive Virgo

Virgo: Per my last text, I'll be in your neighborhood later tonight. I'm inquiring whether or not you'll be free to see me, even if briefly.

You: Honestly, I was just in the shower omg.

Intellectual Virgo

Virgo: This week's New Yorker poem reminds me of you. I cut it
   out. I'll give it to you next time.

You: Send me the link??

The Virgo imagination

If a Virgo were a city they'd be Portland. Hip, progressive, and an-
noying. If they were punctuation they'd be a period. Final, authori-
tative, and at times hard to read. Type of weather? A long, boring
August day. Type of sheets? The most expensive linen. Probably
in oatmeal. Or perhaps a natural beige (and here they'll tell you
what the difference is, since I also think this color palette sounds
the same).

Room type? Well, they wouldn't be a room at all. They'd be a
closet. Clean, ordered, and in one dark corner something sharp
resembling a secret. A secret about someone and a Virgo's fear
they've disappointed them no matter what. Virgos live in a personal
torture chamber. Not a video game or sex dungeon, more like a
long hallway with a flickering light and a red door at the end. Be-
yond it is the world, which very much needs them and runs with
great efficiency because of who they are. Most days they make it
through the door. Some days they don't.

Though who are Virgos, really? And when's the time they're
most Virgo of all? They're actually vast fields of mint in the middle
of the afternoon. They're small leaves circling the window, hav-
ing made their way inside after the rain. Virgos are vintage clocks

that can only be repaired by one person in a city of eleven million. They arrive many minutes early (before anyone has opened) and wait long after everyone has left. Virgos are mountains and iron and green tents. Virgos are that one friend who stays up past midnight, watching the fire and watching you sleep, writing something so true in their journal, even they won't look back to read it. Even they are scared of what it says.

Virgos are letters in cursive. Virgos are always not getting enough sleep. Virgos are keeping records of all of your records. Virgos are playing records that make you close your eyes and see trees. Virgos are typewriters from the twenties. Virgos are being in your twenties and not loving them because you worry too much. Virgos are luxurious. Virgos are local and organic. Virgos are vintage leather because buying it new makes them feel too much guilt. And guilt is a Virgo-run business. And business is what Virgos do well.

The Famous Virgo

No matter what their profession, Virgos are humanitarians at heart. They excel at medicine, politics, and business. On their own, applause and adulation aren't meaningful to them. They won't be why Virgos pursue one path over another. Virgos derive purpose from bringing values and principles to their work. Beyoncé and the cultural discussions she starts, Claudette Colvin and her work in the civil rights movement, Bernie Sanders and his platform for workers' rights and financial equity. Virgos like to champion big causes. They also care most about results.

In the Virgo mind, there's a strong belief that everything alive must be sustained. Even if the one suffering most is them, they'll fight for the greater good and resist asking for help. It was Marsha P. Johnson, a truly resilient Virgo, who along with other trans women of color ushered in gay liberation on the streets of New York. The Virgo sacrifice is a true one. Nothing is done halfheartedly or halfway. And they aren't looking for credit either. Though as their friends know, they deserve it and are often overlooked.

A lot of public attention can actually be detrimental to a Virgo's well-being. Fame and money bring in factors that are impossible to control—new people, partnerships, cultural attitudes and opinions. Virgos need their tribe of stability—the people around them who have learned to check in on them when nothing appears to be wrong. If they don't have that, they suffer. River Phoenix, Macaulay Culkin, Fiona Apple. These are all Virgos who have learned this lesson.

Aside from a deep need for balance and order, Virgos have a lot of soul and are wild in a pure way. The trouble for them often resides in feeling like they're responsible for everything and everyone, and that they need to keep attending to whatever they've committed to, even if it begins to cause them harm. They are steadfast and loyal. They can obsess about you forever (the classic love songs of Leonard Cohen); think about the big picture with brutal realism (Leo Tolstoy's *War and Peace*); and, somehow, with the whole world on their shoulders, entertain. Regardless of pain.

Amy Winehouse embodies almost all of these qualities. When I think about Virgos, I often think about a voicemail she left her first manager (you can look it up on YouTube). Unrestrained, straight from the heart, breaking every Virgo cliché you can think of—except that of unconditional love—"Nicky boy, it's Amy, your favorite Jewish girl, apart from your mum. I don't know what you're playing at, but I miss you very, very much. And love you. The love I have for you . . . the burning love I have for you, will not be dampened by the fact that you don't answer the phone to me ever. It simply won't. I don't care. I don't care if you never answer the phone to me again, I will continue to love you unconditionally until the day that my heart fails and I fall down dead. So please call me whenever. I'm not going anywhere."

Other Famous Virgos

1. Elizabeth I
2. Ludacris
3. Freddie Mercury
4. Kobe Bryant
5. Mary Shelley
6. B. B. King
7. Bill Murray
8. Prince Harry
9. Rose McGowan
10. Mother Teresa

Virgo playlist

- Aimee Mann, "Save Me"
- John Cage, "4'33""
- Ludacris, "Move Bitch"

- Buddy Holly, "Raining in My Heart"
- Patsy Cline, "I Fall to Pieces"
- Foxy Brown, "Get Me Home"
- Amy Winehouse, "Just Friends"
- LeAnn Rimes, "Blue"
- Nick Jonas, "Jealous"
- Beyoncé, "Upgrade U"

The Virgo (a poem)

Wouldn't it be you, with true precision
who won't let the season go?

Waiting for the perfect field
in which you'll hide

your message for the Earth:
a wild green thread

tied loosely
around everyone you love

and wildly so
and wildly here

(although you'll seldom say it).
Say it to the wind. The sun.

This moon who's your companion.

LIBRA

September 23–October 23

You can never be overdressed or overeducated.

Oscar Wilde, born October 16, 1854

The Libra

In his famous essay "A Beautiful Child," Truman Capote, a Libra if ever there was one, describes spending a day in New York with Marilyn Monroe. They attend a funeral, drink champagne, and by day's end, somehow find themselves by the water, talking about the afterlife and how misunderstood they are. Given that both were air signs (Monroe one of the most famous Geminis), this wild trajectory—from despair to frivolity, romance to existential dread—is hardly surprising. Air signs are unpredictable. They're interested in living as variously as possible, and often find comfort in a detour. Moving through the material world, they're in awe of material itself, yet constantly looking for something more. Something to occupy their short attention spans, which often get them in trouble and leave them confused and indecisive. This can be chaotic (friends of air signs can attest). It can also feel childlike, new, and full of possibility—like good art.

Libras are the most refined air sign. They are predisposed to being graceful, highly concerned with aesthetics, and deeply philosophical about anything from a song on the radio to the origins of desire. This is evident with Capote, who guides Monroe throughout their entire journey—checking in on her when she disappears into a bathroom to have a mini-meltdown (Gemini-style), paying for a cab to go downtown on a whim and feed seagulls by the pier, and reassuring her about her potentially fraught future while simultaneously indulging her drama. Libras love drama. They are theatrical creatures. They see drama as entertaining rather than serious. They're also dependable and nurturing, even if not effusive or recognizably warm. What you have to understand is that Libras prove their loyalty through action and through style. Drinking champagne with a friend is appropriate at all times. Decadence is proof that people don't regret life. And what Monroe finds slightly unreadable and also alluring about Capote is his dark humor and wit. Two things Libras charm with, and two things they use to cover up pain (most of which gets coded in their creative endeavors or the furniture they buy).

For much of their day together Monroe talks and talks about herself, as Geminis are known to do. She doesn't say anything important, but it's all very captivating. And while Capote often interrupts her with a joke or some provocative observation about her love life, he chooses not to reveal anything personal about himself, or let her in on the fact that he knows she's sleeping with the playwright Arthur Miller (another Libra), the very thing she's trying to hide from the press. Capote leaves the spotlight on her. He studies her, coming off guarded but polite. This is one way of saying that Libras do not need to be the center of attention. Being discreet and tactful is more important to them. Yet they have this way of delivering the truth, in their artfully phrased Libra obscurity, attempting not to hurt your feelings while being unable to lie at the same time. And so as the day ends and Capote has satisfied all of Monroe's whims, he finds her to be beautiful, but a child. A beautiful child. It's hardly meant as a critique, but it isn't exactly praise, either. If anything, his judgment is a faithful representation of the complexity of her character and demonstrates how perceptive Libras are. While they may never kiss your ass, they're great at kissing. And they'll always tell you how they see you, which turns out to be very close to what you are. You just have to be someone who appreciates that kind of honesty.

Things you might want to know about Libra

Libras are a cardinal air sign and the seventh sign of the zodiac. They follow Virgo on the karmic wheel and have learned important lessons about restraint and keeping their cards close to their chest. Despite this, they're ruled by their emotions and have a hard time managing their expectations (they haven't learned Scorpio's ability to mask and deflect, though maybe for the better).

"By being too sensitive I have wasted my life," the poet Arthur

Rimbaud once wrote. If you need a Libra-to-English translation of that, what he means is: "By overthinking I have driven everyone crazy, including myself." Often what Libras see as their sensitivity is actually their intellect at work. They can seem cold and distant (another thing they've picked up from Virgos), but in truth, they're just a slow reveal. They take their time with their loyalty and are highly discerning. They've also been known to radically change their minds about people, making them appear inconsistent, when truly, what they're responding to is their Libra intuition. There's also the Libra shutdown (and those of you with Libra friends and family will know what I'm talking about), when they stop communicating for no apparent reason, causing you great anxiety until you find out they're just shopping, reorganizing their closet, or planning some social event. Yes, Libras love the everyday. They love basic pleasures paired with intellectual pursuits. Surely there's a Libra somewhere right now reading Proust on a picnic blanket, content with their curated cheese plate and performance of nonchalance. The picnic blanket is probably designer and they're definitely on the last book of Proust.

On the inside, Libras are obsessed with control. They're bossy people. But the inside is somewhere different for each sign—the Cancer heart, the Scorpio soul, the Capricorn side eye. Libras live inside their minds. Analysis, analysis, analysis. It's what makes their engines go. But unlike Virgo analysis, which is rational and fact-based, what they're actually analyzing is their emotions. They're in a 24/7 therapy session. At work, the bar, having sex, watching Netflix. Libras are interested in the nature of reality. They're like emotional scientists.

This leads me to their second-favorite activity (after analyzing), which is torturing themselves. The Libra scales are constantly in flux. Balance is the goal, but their reality is indecision, torment, and a constant feeling that they're disappointing someone. They're very hard on themselves and will go to great lengths to assure you they're fine even when they aren't. So when you come across a Libra, really look them in the eye and ask them how they're doing. They'll probably make a joke or tell some odd anecdote. Ask them a second time then. Ask them with the intention of being engaged.

Libra as a lover

Libras are ruled by Venus, the planet of love. A planet with influence over pleasure, allure, and beauty (if you ever wondered why aesthetics figure so prominently in the Libra imagination). Partnership is a deliberate and important investment for Libras. They're compatible with Sagittarius of the fire signs, Gemini of the air signs, hardly anyone in the water family (except Scorpios, who won't bore them), and Capricorn of the earth signs (though they hate taking orders and Capricorns love to give them).

Sagittarius and Libra are a classic match because Libras are willing to put up with a lot of shit and can tolerate someone disappearing (and reappearing as suddenly) without holding a grudge. They can smooth over conflict in a way that a Sagittarius can't, giving them an edge with all fire signs, a subset of the population that likes verbal confrontation and can often come off as rude and aggressive. Full disclosure: once in New York at Cafe Cluny a Libra walked out on me in the middle of dinner because I started an argument with the waiter. The conversation quickly escalated and I almost got kicked out for trying to light a cigarette in the restaurant. Drunk as I was, I decided against it and ordered another drink. Minutes later I got a text from the Libra telling me they were waiting across the street at another bar. I was quite charmed by this. I'm grateful for all my Libra lovers and one-night stands because without them I would have probably found more ways to incite controversy and appear, from a distance, like I'm auditioning for *King Lear*. On many occasions Libras have been the mirror I've needed to see how hysterical I am. Somehow they pull this off with a cool indifference and without any obvious judgment (though who really knows what's going on in that little head of theirs).

Libras and Geminis have the possibility for real longevity. They enable the other's curiosity and are willing to do just about anything together. It's a dynamic match full of real surprises. You can always spot them at a party because the Geminis are entertaining and the Libras are trying to walk back something their partner just said. As you can maybe tell by now, they have a tendency to do that with many signs. They're quite tolerant. One thing Libras won't tolerate is vanity, which is why Leos aren't compatible with them. There's a certain frivolity to the Libra spirit, having to do with not taking oneself too seriously. Leo vanity lacks an irony that Libras find unforgivable and boring. There isn't enough mystery to Leos. They can be tacky, we all know. And tacky is a Libra's worst nightmare; it embarrasses them more than anything. This is perhaps why Libras do quite well with earth signs, who won't be embarrassing but are at times rigid. The sense of stability Virgos and Capricorns provide is attractive to Libras. They also appreciate how thorough both of these signs are. Taurus and Libra are a total wild card. They'll either never stop vacationing together, or they'll burn down everything because they have a hard time compromising. (I mean, have you tried to compromise with a Taurus? It's like talking to a brick wall, but a hot brick wall.)

No matter what sign their partner is—even if it's a bad astrological match—Libras will go to great lengths to make it work. They are people who seek resolution and value equilibrium. They're great at starting dialogue and keeping it going but often have trouble sticking up for themselves. One reason for this is their high tolerance for discomfort. Another is the fact that they hate making a scene. They're all about social grace and espousing a veneer of perfection, something they believe is disrupted by conflict. If you ask a Libra, anything can be solved by reading a great novel and perfect lighting. And if you're sleeping with one, definitely let them redecorate your place and help you with your wardrobe. Cut is the most important thing to them when it comes to fashion. And you should aim to be on top of your game with all of your looks because they will be—no matter the occasion.

The erogenous zone for Libras is their lower back. It's exactly where to put your hand when kissing them. It's also where you want to touch them while they're riding you or when you're on your knees in front of them. This makes them feel wanted. It also brings out their inner exhibitionist, which is a rare occurrence. In the bedroom you'll likely have to take the lead with Libras. You'll have to be the freak first. Remember that they're the kind of person who needs permission to be messy or wild enough to use parts of a chandelier as a dildo, which one of my Libra friends once tried in France.

While they talk a big game about being flirts, Libras are actually quite traditional in how they approach romance. We can define traditional in different ways, and it might as well be a ridiculous term, but what I'm saying is they're not hiding handcuffs under their pillows like Virgos (who probably also have a list of emergency contacts for what to do in case someone loses the key). The real truth is, Libras want to lock it down with their lover. They want to show off how great they are at being domestic, throwing parties, and their varied taste in art. Libras are a catch. They know that but they'll never say it, so they'll show you.

Beauty and pleasure make life worth living for a Libra (remember they share a ruling planet with Taurus, the sign of earthly pleasure). They're thoughtful gift givers and pay close to attention to your tastes and preferences. Date nights will be considered. Dark and lavish bars, a night at the opera, and almost anything at the theater. Their predisposition leans toward what's classic rather than what's hip. And they're definitely an old soul, so you'll find yourself talking about philosophy or some obscure poetic form just as often as they engage you in pop culture, which interests them tremendously. If there's one thing Libras are obsessed with, it's people and how they live their lives.

Another charming thing about Libras is that they have a knack for remembering important dates and moments. Anniversaries, birthdays, that time you looked at them and they knew you were lying. Their emotional intelligence is high. It's almost impossible trying to hide things from a Libra. Keep in mind that while the home and domesticity are important to them, they don't see their bedroom like a Taurus (never wanting to leave) or the kitchen like a Cancer (thinking that any problem can be solved there). Libras love going out and they're terrified of being alone. Maybe because they know they're quite good at being alone and can get stuck there (at home with all their books and ideas). What a Libra really wants is for you to take charge and take them out. What they require is one compliment so well observed and emphatic, they know you truly mean it because it has required your attention. Don't throw the easy stuff at them. They're not Leos. Libras want something more than adulation. They want something almost unendurable when it comes to love.

Libra as a friend

Libras stay out and drink with me and never want to go home. I appreciate them because I can be repeating the same idiotic narrative for the hundredth time—how some fuckboy never texted or that I don't make money as a poet—and they'll absorb it, cool and discerning, asking if I want another drink. Even if they find someone ridiculous they won't say it directly. They're not cruel like Capricorns. Libras critique their friends through anecdotes, analogies, metaphors, book recommendations (once a Libra recommended a book on the sociocultural history of silence, which was more or less his way of telling me to shut up). They're also great peacemakers. They remain impartial the longest and put value into considering various points of view. A Libra does not like doing anything fast. If they're going to show up for you, they're going to really show up for you, having thought through whatever dilemma is at stake a great deal.

Ironically, Libras are not like this in their personal lives, where their scales are constantly tipping toward one extreme or the other. They're so private most of the time, hardly anyone sees their inner chaos manifesting. But it does. And if you're close with a Libra you'll know that after months, years, decades of knowing them, they'll feel comfortable enough to send you a long text, 70 percent of which will be them apologizing for sending it, and 30 percent telling you about some problem, usually one they're exaggerating because they've thought about it for too long. This will spiral into drinks, where they'll jump from one topic to another, and every five minutes or so, they'll circle back to what's really bothering them before once again changing gears to talk about your new shoes. As a friend, it's hard to know if you've ever really helped a Libra. They have no problem saying thank you, but they're the type of person who would say it even if you didn't help them. A part of them has resigned itself to knowing that the human condition is unknowable, with most things posing as answers while not being so.

One thing you'll notice is that Libras have more acquaintances than almost anyone, except maybe Aquarians. That fashion person they ran into on the street? Someone they once slept with and still keep in touch with. Their connection at the *New York Times*? A classmate from college they usually send a birthday note to. And most Libras have one or two bartenders who are obsessed with them. Libras like to be regulars and have several places. They love their little rituals and live for getting personal with the people who orbit them. Don't be surprised if they know everything about their bartenders—exes, family history, psychic dramas—but the bartenders know little about them. That's how they like to do things. For Libras it's not so much about being mysterious as it is about appearing understated and tasteful. In terms of taste, with Libras less is more. That goes for talking and divulging secrets, and it applies to fashion too.

Most Libras are not opportunistic, although they're interested in building a life where they stay loosely connected to everyone they've come in contact with and whom they've found to be a source of pleasure. It's stunning watching them work a room. There's more authenticity and empathy in their gestures than the term "work a room" connotes. But let's just say they're great at it. They're so obsessed with other people, and how the people close to them live their lives, that they're one of the first signs in the zodiac who would line up to marry their friends. (Air signs all fantasize about doing this, and earth signs are actually the ones who do.)

The trouble with having many acquaintances and being socially savvy is that Libras often feel depressed about not going deep enough in their friendships. They're the perfect candidate for depth. Their reservoir for processing and listening is immense. Since they're so perceptive, they'll often identify how a person will fit into their life very early on, and they'll make a decision right then about whether or not they'll stay an acquaintance, or if that person has the capability to be a real friend to them. This thought process is not revealed to anyone, of course. A Libra doesn't want to hurt the feelings of even people they dislike. Just know that you're quite lucky if a Libra invites you over, cooks for you, and tells you something about their childhood after a long speech about some rare Matisse painting they saw.

Libra style

Say you're going to the most important dinner of your life or have a long-awaited date. Or maybe it's your first time at a sex party. Absolutely let a Libra dress you. At the very least, talk to one beforehand. Libras know how to dress for any occasion. Their wardrobes reflect that. While they generally fall into two categories—flawless, slightly conservative, classy (a lot of black, pinstripe, clean cuts, black leather) or over-the-top, indulgent, and attention-grabbing ('80s prints, neon goth too-cool-for-school aesthetic)—Libras have range. They are versatile. They like to switch it up, even if they've committed to being refined or edgy. They also take great interest in the personal style of others, and are inspired by anyone who builds a sense of self through their aesthetic choices (because naturally they do the same). Libras are curators. Of everything really—from the hangover outfit you see them in at 7-Eleven, to what they're wearing when they "spontaneously" run into you while working on their screenplay at a coffee shop (vintage Marc Jacobs while everyone else looks like a run-over rat).

That a garment is well made is the most important thing to Libras when it comes to fashion. They will rarely spend money on anything cheap. They also won't compromise and will wait for exactly what they want, whether that means endlessly shopping for the perfect white tee or looking for the right grain of leather in a biker jacket. You can be sure they know what they want too. They have a vision for how they want to look, even if they sometimes lack the resources. Their "ugly" choices are part of this. Okay, I hate to say it, but I've known Libras who wear socks with sandals as a fashion statement. In that hip, monochromatic, slightly alien way. I think they're brave, though I wouldn't do it.

Libras are obsessed with textiles. Anything rare and sought after. Unlike their opposite, Aries, they hate shock value and cheapness. Rarely will they wear something for the sole purpose of turning heads. They also like to repeat their good looks and establish a kind of signature style—something they'll be remembered by. There's a real French and Italian flair to Libras. All of them have a signature scent. One they've matched to their sensibility over time. It's likely floral with a hint of something darker underneath. Shoes are a big weakness for them too. They absolutely believe that spending a lot on footwear is a good investment (like it's real estate or something). I know Libras with massive shoe collections who struggle to pay their rent but don't care to change their ways. They're big spenders and proud of their frivolity. It makes them fun shopping partners but maybe not the friends to go to for financial advice.

Texting with a Libra

Is it an invitation or a statement? A check-in or a passive-aggressive jab? What exactly do all the "okay"s mean? And must Libras really oscillate from a strict use of punctuation to unpredictable and fulsome exclamation points? Libras are confusing, but they don't mean to be. You're not texting a Scorpio. What you may interpret as manipulation is Libras being Libras—indecisive, perpetually overthinking, and prone to outbursts of emotion they'll feel embarrassed about and follow up with months of silence and restraint.

I have two good Libra friends and they're both always in the act of typing. You know that dreaded text bubble you see when you're holding your phone waiting for someone to say something. After ten minutes of me staring, waiting for what I assume to be a love letter or a manifesto, I'll get a text that says "ok!" or "I'd like that." The Libra brain really is like a Pedro Almodóvar movie. There's an internal circus hovering over everything, but they can't betray that, so they cover it up with brevity and camp.

Existential Libra

You: Wanna get dinner?

Libra: [45 minutes later] The trees are so ominous today. I'd like to, but I'm not sure if I can.

Bad idea Libra

Libra: I know it's a weeknight but I just went into debt for these Gucci rain boots and I want to wear them out immediately!

You: Okay but it's not raining and it's definitely the weekend.

Passive-aggressive Libra

You: Are you mad about earlier?

Libra: I wouldn't say that. I'm just going to stay in and watch this French film where a girl murders her friends by mistake. It premiered at Cannes!

Intellectual Libra

Libra: One must have a mind of winter / To regard the frost and the boughs

You: Um wtf is everything ok??

Libra: Reading some Wallace Stevens. Divine!

A Libra in love

Libra: I'm ready to book two tickets to Italy and throw away my phone. All I need is my man and a vegan option.

You: But yesterday you said being with him was like watching the Titanic sink?

Libra: Sometimes I'm just so horny for drama!

Depressed Libra

You: What are you doing this weekend?

Libra: But really what are any of us doing, we're on this planet for less than a hundred years, probably already halfway through our lives and there's no real guarantee anyone will find true love, and if we do, how do we even know it's what we want, or that it isn't an illusion we've projected on another person? I'm not doing anything. You?

Glamorous Libra

You: ETA?
Libra: I shall arrive in 4 minutes in an Uber XL which I ordered for my anxiety and in the name of world peace.

The Libra imagination

If Libra were a city, they'd be Paris. The moodiness of the Seine is more or less a portrait of their inner life. If they were a punctuation mark, they'd be an ellipsis—dragging everything out, afraid to make a decision. Type of weather: overcast October day. Right on the edge of something turning, like an important realization. And if they were a flower they'd be white tulips. Understated and elegant, placed in a simple but expensive vase, adding just the right touch of splendor to a room.

There's true spontaneity in a Libra's arsenal. You could even say they enjoy being flashy and campy when it comes to luxury. If you want to vacation well, go with a Libra. For them it's not about indulgence. Libras are already born glamorous. They believe glamour is proof that life is worthwhile and they embody that proof. Walk into the office of any fashion magazine and you'll be surrounded by Libras who gravitate toward visual allure and well-

made things. Ralph Lauren, Donna Karan, André Leon Talley—
all Libras.

Other realms where Libras excel are literature and philoso-
phy. Perhaps it makes sense as they're thwarted romantics. They
have the urge to make big gestures and pronouncements but are
too fearful of rejection and their own inner critic. It's important
to be gentle with Libras because they've already berated them-
selves enough about whatever problem you're going to bring up.
It's not that they can't take criticism. They can. They're not Leos.
But whereas a Leo will defensively dismiss your criticism, Libras
will internalize it. They won't be able to forget it. They'll constantly
wonder if the negative thing you said was true, even if they know
it wasn't.

Libra self-awareness is crippling, but it makes them fantastic
writers (F. Scott Fitzgerald and Cervantes, just to name two). You
could even say that Libras are better at imagining and writing
about love than being in love. This is what makes them exquisite
dinner partners. The most thought-provoking dinners I've had
have been with Libras. There's little they don't have an opinion
on. And they've always read the latest gossip. They love to gossip.
They love pretending to be irreverent. And they'll never admit
doing either.

The Famous Libra

"In love and art, one plus one equals three." Bruce Springsteen, a
Libra who was born to run, has said this many times over the years.

What it means is there's a mystery ingredient to the best things in life. Something that can't be taught or seen. Like a certain energy you can't describe but are attracted to in someone. Libras tend to think of this as style. Not necessarily how you dress but a way of being in the world, how you think and interact, the aura a person brings to everything they do. An art of living, so to speak. This is a pursuit Libras undertake and an outcome they aspire to.

This quest to get from one to three (whatever magic three represents for you) has brought us many important and fascinating Libras who have changed how we live. John Lennon and Gandhi obviously. For them equilibrium meant justice, idealism rooted in reality, and a refusal to accept the limitations imposed on the human imagination. Since Libras are creatures of the mind, they have faith it will prevail and find a way out. Cue some black-and-white French film with frustrated intellectuals wearing Prada and protesting the government for world peace. Libras also have the common good in mind and are flamboyant. For all their brooding, they're calculated extroverts. There will never be another Oscar Wilde. Controversial and entertaining, entirely unafraid of public opinion if it means defending taste.

Cinema would lack heart and humor without Pedro Almodóvar. Painting would miss the emotional depth of Mark Rothko. And for Springsteen, one of rock's most humble gods, it isn't surprising that the one-plus-one equation relies on people and bringing them together. His legendary shows are known to go on for hours, with multiple encores. And he usually performs in the same blue jeans and white shirt uniform that has become classically American. Until that last hour, when the shirt comes off and he's at his most visceral and uninhibited. Inviting the audience to go back to their lives with the same rawness. A Libra victory over the mind.

Other Famous Libras

1. Alexandria Ocasio-Cortez
2. Snoop Dogg
3. T. S. Eliot
4. Lil Wayne
5. Eleanor Roosevelt
6. Virgil
7. Avril Lavigne
8. Serena Williams
9. Kim Kardashian
10. Friedrich Nietzsche

Libra playlist

- A$AP Rocky, "L$D"
- Verdi, "Di Provenza il mar, il suol," aria from *La Traviata*, act II, scene 1
- Usher, "You Make Me Wanna . . ."
- Meat Loaf, "I'd Do Anything for Love (But I Won't Do That)"
- Cardi B, "Best Life"
- John Lennon, "Imagine"

- Ja Rule, "Always on Time," featuring Ashanti
- Marina and the Diamonds, "Primadonna"
- Nico, "These Days"
- Dizzy Gillespie, "Ow!"

The Libra (a poem)

On the perfect day of your life
you've woken up early
and gone to the city.
Sat on the same bench
with all your white flowers,
obsessions from years ago
and possibly farther.
Even entirely still
with your eyes on the water,
you can almost admit
how much longer you'll wait.
How you're very much made of waiting.
How no one waits like you do.

SCORPIO

October 24–November 21

> How easily I could be in love with you,
>   who do not like to be touched,
> And yet I do not want to be in love with you
>   nor you with me
>
> *James Schuyler, born November 9, 1923*

The Scorpio

On an Instagram post in the first week of November 2018, Drake posted a picture of himself sitting alongside a fan in a hospital room, wiping tears from his eyes, his fan looking content and joyful in his presence. Under the photo, he wrote the following words:

Gonna miss you a whole lot. We met through make a wish and we built a genuine bond you would text me and check on me while I was on tour and tell me positive things and share your dreams and goals. . . . I am sorry I missed your text on my birthday that's eating my soul right now but you know how much I loved you . . . I don't know why I am writing this on IG I just need to get it out cause it's sitting heavy on my heart. Will remember you forever K! [crying emoji, blue heart emoji] @the .kaydiaries

After clicking through the link and googling around a bit, it's easy to find a little more about the powerful story behind the post. A fan Drake had met through the Make-a-Wish Foundation had recently died. Online you can find some articles explaining how Drake also embroidered one of his stage shirts with a gold *K* in honor of his friend, known as Kay the Queen.

When you stop to think about it, his post is quite shocking in the context of most celebrity social media posts. Drake has always been known to bare his heart and soul in his song lyrics, but most of the time, his persona on social media is more polished. He maintains a thick veneer of icy professionalism in most of the things that he does and interacts with his public in rather bombastic ways. A post like this—not even he is exactly sure why he is "writing this on IG," except that he just needs "to get it out cause it's sitting heavy on my heart"—feels unpolished, raw, and super-emotional. The post represents everything that draws us to Drake and makes us feel a deep intimacy with him, despite his immense fame. By "us" I mean at the very least myself. (For me, Drake is everything.)

Drake's post about Kay the Queen underlines the complexity of a Scorpio. It's not always clear that they feel, but when they do, they feel a whole hell of a lot, more than they can keep to themselves. Whereas another sign, like a Gemini, might have posted about their friend to demonstrate to others that they do in fact have feelings sometimes, a Scorpio like Drake did it out of a sheer need to get overwhelming feelings off his chest. Drake wasn't really trying to score points by being part of the Make-a-Wish Foundation, or to show he cared about his fan. He just really, really cared. If a Scorpio cares about something, this care supersedes all.

Another part of the IG post that is so Scorpio is Drake's admission that he didn't write her back when she wrote on his birthday: "that's eating my soul right now." For all of us who have ever known a Scorpio, we know that sometimes they can be lax in responding to text messages, and that when they do respond, it might be with no more than a "hey." Sometimes that's all we need from them to get by for a while, but other times their reticence can get annoying.

Part of the reason they can be slow to get back to us is that they are so intense that whatever they are doing at the moment has their full attention, and they aren't necessarily able to switch off their intensity to respond to people on their phones. If a Scorpio wants to, they'll get back to you. They'll have no problem finding you, even if you change your number out of frustration at your own longing for them. Oh, they'll find you. You can count on that. Despite what they say when they are feeling coy, Scorpios aren't shy.

Still, that burning guilt of not responding to someone and then losing the ability to ever respond again is something that would eat any Scorpio up alive inside. Scorpios drive themselves crazy thinking about missed opportunities, and the idea of things or people once within their circle of possession now being inaccessible to them forever does torture them. If you listen to Drake's music closely, you can see how upset he gets when it seems one of his lovers has found someone new and might not belong to him any-more. But it doesn't take a careful listener to understand that a Scorpio will never get over not being there for a friend in need, especially when there isn't time left to make it up to them.

All this is to say that when Scorpios say they love you, they really mean it. Some signs just say things or feel things in the mo-ment. Leos love the drama of emotions but not necessarily the work that goes into empathizing with other people. Tauruses have the deepest emotions of anyone, but you rarely ever see them. Capri-corns sure do love to know everything you feel, but the jury is still out if they really understand what the word "emotion" means. But Scorpios feel everything. Even as they sit there stone-faced, un-readable as the ocean calmly doing its thing for all of time, while you tell them your life story. When Scorpios love, they love. That's the good news for all Scorpio friends and lovers: when you're in it, you're in it for the long haul with these sexy arachnids. Lucky you!

Things you might want to know about Scorpio

Scorpio progresses along the karmic wheel following Libra and is a fixed water sign. If Libra is all "I harmonize," then Scorpio is very "I want." Because on the karmic wheel, only after you have put objects neatly on the scales of justice and created an equal division of thoughts and feelings can you consider really desiring some-thing completely, with absolute abandon. With Scorpio, however, this depthless longing is mature. As the signs' ages progress along the wheel, you can think of Scorpio's place on it as in a perpetual Saturn return of the human soul. A Scorpio is forever thirty, old enough to know a lot yet still young enough to both change course completely and lay down a foundation and make a life. Scorpio is endlessly at a vital point of existence, and there is a tendency in all of them to embrace life (and death) passionately. This knowledge of the cycles of life is a never-ending source of strength for them.

Arguably, the number-one reason people want to learn about astrology is because they have been in love with a Scorpio. No sign is more tied to the art and science of astrology in our present-day culture than Scorpio. Heck, even this book is a Scorpio. With its moody, occult, rainy-day black-light black-nail-polish essence, in some ways Scorpio and astrology go hand in hand. Come to think of it, so do Scorpios and poetry. But more on that later.

Because Scorpio is a water sign, they can be highly emotional, determined, and stuck in their ways (notice I didn't say stubborn). But to go deeper, the biggest thing to remember is that they are ruled by two planets, Pluto and Mars. Yeah, that's right— a sign with as much power as Scorpio can't get just one planet. C'mon, now.

You might remember something about Mars from old high school classes in mythology: there was this big, sexy, violent hunk of a god who ruled war. Yes, that's the same guy, and he rules Scorpio's actions, too. He rules Aries solely, but rules Scorpio in tandem with Pluto. He gives Scorpios that otherworldly drive they have, that shrewd ability to suss out a situation and figure out how power is distributed in groups and social situations.

In fact, it's that word—power—that excites a Scorpio like no other. Power-hungry, warring Mars is part of the reason Scorpios have a reputation for vengeance (and why people are so scared of that side of them). Because can you imagine a giant god of war backing down from anything? Me neither. Fighting for (one hopes) what's right isn't easy. And it's not for the folks who are weak in the knees and who don't plan their attacks in advance.

The other planet that rules Scorpio's drives is of course the guardian of the underworld—that pretty important place people don't talk about too much these days: hell. If you know a Scorpio, it isn't exactly a big shocker that they'd be tied to the underworld. (Most Scorpios think about death at least once or twice every three minutes.) But lest you think that Scorpios are the devil incarnate, it's not really that simple. Pluto is less fire and brimstone and spiky red tail (although they've been known to sport a spiky tail once or twice, and not on Halloween), and more like the ruler of the things that are under the earth. And I mean this quite literally. Like the things that reside there, such as the seeds that we plant to grow our food and trees that give us bounty. And also, yeah, dead people.

This planetary influence is important, because it rules a major aspect of what's so lovely about Scorpios—that is, that they're fucking psychic. Pluto's dominion over them is a good explanation for this ability they have of knowing things that are yet to be or maybe just happening in the moment. If you think of planetary influence in this way, Scorpios have the underground knowledge of what will be (the seed that will one day become a tree) and the things that have come before and are transforming into new things (like the corpses that have broken down and regenerated into new properties). Because they are in tune with life, death, pre-birth, and post-death, and emotionally exist within these states at all times, Scorpios really can sense the emotional motivations of people at all times and predict the future course of things. Because what are people, if not a bunch of emotional motivations packaged together, struggling to be? You wouldn't need to ask a Scorpio this question twice. They already figured out the answer. Light-years ago.

If you are a Scorpio reading this, maybe I scared you a bit when I mentioned your love of power, and you thought it meant that you might have to run for office or something, or take a job as a CEO. Not that some of you would be above these activities, of course, but no, that's not exactly what I meant. I was thinking of the idea that a Scorpio loves power the way a Taurus loves creature comforts— they just can't help how drawn they are to it.

But don't be confused if you don't see them up on stage. Scorpios like most to be in the back room of power, pulling the strings and watching what happens. If they work in the political arena, one might find them not giving speeches but behind the curtain, writing the speeches, planning the events, and plotting the course of action needed to actually win. They're more SVP than CEO, best buddies with the boss, and orchestrating the moves of their friend in charge from behind the scenes.

Part of their drive to be the silent leader of all things is their perverse (sorry/not sorry to use that term when it comes to a Scorpio) need to hide their personal power from others. This stems from an insecurity that if they made their need to win obvious, then other people might know what makes their engine run and could use that against them. Scorpios detest the idea of ever being overpowered. And if there is another thing Scorpios do not like, it's to be caught off guard. Especially when it comes to something so dear to them: winning. So they spend most of their days obsessively analyzing the power dynamics of any situation and figuring out how to somehow top everyone else without any of them knowing that was their main goal all along. It may sound exhausting, but it's also . . . so fucking hot.

If there's a single word that almost everyone associates with Scorpios, it's "revenge." It's one of the reasons Scorpios often get that look of immense fear/respect from people when they tell them their birth date. *Oh, wow, you're a Scorpio!* they exclaim, as they both dart away and unbutton their shirt. Revenge is scary, and people really are scared of this side of them.

If you've ever had an encounter with an actual scorpion, you have seen its spiky tail. Those guys really don't have any problem stinging people. And why should they? After all, they are the ones just sleeping and doing their thing in a nice, warm, dark place— like your slippers (!!!)—and we are the ones with the gall to actually put our slippers on. Who can blame them for giving us a little what-for?

But have you ever looked at a scorpion? Sure, maybe they look a little freaky (although many people would just use the words "sublimely elegant"), but if you look at them closely you can see that their stingers are the only protection they have from being crushed in your palm. The same goes for Scorpios and the motivation behind their striking. Most of the time, they are forced into striking someone not because they want to but because of their deep fear that someone will see their vulnerabilities and crush them first. And then the Scorpio won't have won. Sometimes their only option to win is to strike, and hard.

One of the biggest misconceptions about Scorpios is their relationship to sex. (It's another thing people mean when they say, "Oh, wow, you're a Scorpio.") Most people go around thinking that all

Scorpios are nymphomaniacs. I might take this opportunity to possibly dissuade these people and make any Scorpio feel completely seen. The issue of sex for a Scorpio goes beyond the mere category of love. It's all tied to that under/otherworldly planetary influence I discussed above: Pluto. They are simply connected to what makes life hum, and this, of course, includes sex.

They do have powerful urges to connect with their partner-for-life once, twice, or thrice daily, on a deep level. (And trust me, they'd prefer this to a random hookup any day of the week.) For Scorpios this doesn't mean chatting about their day; it means getting down and dirty. They also have some dark urges connected to sex, and if they don't have a partner-for-life right now, they can get into intense sex scenarios that aren't for the faint of heart. But, again, who can blame them? They are searching for that timeless depth, and all humans have it. Scorpios are just the only ones who really go after this holy human quality at full throttle. It's what makes them so damn special.

Scorpio as a lover

There's a reason Scorpios have both the best and the worst reputation as lovers. They really put their lovers through their paces at times and can be both relentlessly kind and relentlessly cruel. If a Scorpio has decided that they are interested in you, then you really are in for what will be, at first, a wild fucking ride (emphasis on fucking, of course). Scorpios do change their mind about their lovers sometimes, but "fickle" is not the best description of their affairs of the heart. They are strong and solid lovers who will never do anything to hurt an "innocent" love interest, especially one they are courting. Sure, they think of everything in this moral way—that lovers (and people) are either innocent or guilty. (Their thinking is extremely polarized about everything.) So if you've just met a truly hot Scorpio and they are interested in you, you can take solace in the fact that they won't do anything to hurt you during their long testing period (which could last a lifetime). But if the test is over, and you fail, then yes, they will do anything in their power to destroy you. This is where their bad reputation comes from.

The best match for Scorpio is a Pisces, as the two can together be totally weird and watery all at once. They really can just communicate without even looking at each other. They don't even have to actually know each other to do so. Scorpio loves the wild domesticity of Cancer and will eat every bite of a Cancer's home-cooked meal. Scorpio will long for the consistency of a Taurus lover, but when they actually get it they will dream of their freedom. Leo-Scorpio will start with a bite and end with one, too. Sagittarius will love Scorpio, but Scorpio will keep their distance, always. Scorpio will love all of the money Capricorn saves. Scorpio and Virgo will make a real family, and they will be better off for knowing each other. Scorpio will get excited when Gemini speaks, until they realize no Gemini is actually saying anything of substance. Scorpios might love other Scorpios but will always be looking for something better. Scorpio will like how much an Aries likes them, but they won't like the Aries quite so much. Scorpio and Aquarius won't last long, but while it lasts it will stimulate both of them spiritually. Scorpio will like when Libra is jolly under the covers, but when they start whining, Scorpio will run for the door.

You can understand a Scorpio's loyal side if you know one who truly loves their partner. There is about zero their partner can do that will get them to leave them. In fact, Scorpios are often the partners of serial cheaters, as once they've decided to take a chance on someone, they will find it nearly impossible to leave them, no matter what they do. They'd rather live in a state of morbid denial for the rest of their days, even as their significant other walks in the door every night at 4:45 a.m., smelling distinctly of hay and Chanel No. 5, than admit that they devoted their actual soul past death to a big old asshole.

That being said, there is still that testing period. This will involve a lot of types of communication, usually in person. Scorpios are great people to talk to, if you like talking to your therapist. They are perfectly capable of sitting quietly while you bare your soul to them. Yes, that's exactly what they'd like to have happen in the earlier phases of dating—during their testing period, they are listening closely to everything you say. They will ask you for your life story, and they will ask pointed questions, probing for any deep emotional responses or traumas. Oh, they love when you spill those, because when you make yourself vulnerable to them, it not only helps them decide if you are worth pursuing past a few dates, but it also gives them the upper hand. Remember, power is the most important aspect of anything to them. And as you cry to them in those early days, telling them your deepest fears, they generally will say exactly nothing substantial about themselves. How many people have dated Scorpios for many months without knowing anything about them really? (Raises hand.)

What are they listening for as you tell them everything about yourself, you might wonder. It's not really the details of your life, although they will remember those with terrifying clarity for years.

They are listening for whatever you may disclose that might not make you a safe bet to fall in love with. They guard their exquisite heart as their best-kept secret, and they are not about to give it over to you if you are not pure enough to handle it. As they test you out, they will listen very closely, take notes, and begin to sum you up. At night while you are fast asleep, they will take out an ancient abacus, making diagrams of your inner mind and spirit, writing you love letters they will absolutely never show anyone, let alone you. If at any point during this inquiry, they decide that you are not worthy of their heart, their presence will turn very swiftly into an absence. It will be brutal when they exit the scene without warning. But trust me, better they leave you quickly in one piece than stick around and sadistically play with your emotions for a while. The latter the most sadistic Scorpios will do, just for the fun of it.

If you are one of the lucky ones and your Scorpio does decide to pursue you, then let's just say: game on. Remember, Scorpios are water signs, so they do appreciate a fair amount of clinginess in others. If they've decided you're the one, they won't so much cling to you as sit on your couch and never leave. And though many pretend to be, they aren't demure. They will have no problem making the first move, seducing you on multiple levels, and then carrying you into the spiritual love den they have been preparing since they were a fetus, where they will hold you safely in a state of perpetual coitus for all eternity. If you are the chosen lover of a Scorpio, I'd just like to state right now how much I hate you.

I guess what I am getting at is sex. As I mentioned earlier, Scorpio's ruler Pluto means that the sign is concerned with all things underground (like hell), and so the sign of Scorpio tends to rule the genitals (and anus, too, if you were wondering). This salient fact, along with Scorpio's healthy dose of brute force, means that Scorpio is not a docile flower in the bedroom. This is also where they get their reputation. And it's also why, if you want to really get things going in a totally extra way in the sack (which it will totally be anyway, because hello, you are having sex with a Scorpio), you should spend some extra time giving their genitals some love. Now this might seem silly to some (hi, Sagittarians), since obviously everyone's erogenous zone is their genitals, and caressing anyone's love bunch could cause a big commotion. But with Scorpio, it is just that much more a thing. So give some love where love is due. Your Scorpio will thank you for it. And they will repay it twice over, at least.

However, don't get confused and think that all this Scorpio sex-and-genitals talk means anything about how weird things might get in the actual act. Save that for Aquarian sex, because Scorpios tend to be quite conservative when they are having sex, and are not known for a lot of variety. When they are in a committed relationship, they are heavy on substance, as they say, but maybe not a lot on style, except of course when it comes to a little subtle, playful S&M, which they are down to try time and again. (Just make sure you are using feathers, not weights, and that you don't let them get too into it.) In fact, if they are experimenting with a lot of things, like even sexy underwear, then I'd be worried something was amiss. You want your Scorpio nice and boring in the sack. It means they really love you.

Everybody knows Scorpios are hands down the hottest sign, and when you meet one, you may think you absolutely need to have one for all eternity. But do make sure it's what you want. Because once they've decided on you, and they think you've decided on them, any sort of decision by you to walk away at any point until you die will be met by an overwhelming response that will haunt you forever: their sense of absolute rejection and betrayal. And not only will they feel the need to strike back, but they will crumble inside and sometimes wither completely. So don't play around with a Scorpio heart. You could literally be playing with fire and also crushing a truly gentle soul. A gentle soul armed with some pretty sharp pincers.

Scorpio as a friend

If you are looking for a friend who will be true to you, who will help you endure some awful emotional upheaval, will help you move out of your apartment (after said upheaval), lend you fifty bucks to help you get by and eventually let you move into their studio apartment, borrow their best clothes, help you get a job, and check on you for all of your life to make sure you are okay, then you are looking for a Scorpio. I hope by this point I've dissuaded you from thinking of a Scorpio simply as what they have a reputation for being: vengeful characters. Of course, they are as vengeful as a person can possibly be, but they are also the kindest humans that could possibly exist. If you are friends with a Scorpio, then you, like their lovers, are among the lucky ones. Scorpios are great friends and are caring, sweet souls to those they are closest to.

Now for the fun part. Scorpios are absolutely a blast to hang out with. That is, if for you hanging out involves someone giving you complete attention, going along with whatever you want to do, and being a walking history textbook about almost everything. Although a little stuck in their ways and slightly conservative about what they might try at first, Scorpios do love the thrill of something new and will jump out of a plane with you if you make it sound good enough. They like friends who exhibit passion and energy, and will supply their own tenfold. They can be chameleons, and if they really like a friend will start to act, dress, and talk just like them. (A creepy trait you just have to be ready for.)

If you want to try to get a Scorpio to be your friend, the first rule is to be sort of intense and to suggest intense activities. I mentioned plane jumping above, but if this isn't your style, you could opt for something intense spiritually or mentally. Scorpios love museums, especially ones that are very old, and they will accompany you to any of these with an excited glare in their eyes, reading up beforehand on exactly what's being exhibited. They will enjoy going with you to esoteric music shows and will respect that you know things they don't, as they love to learn new things. They can think of themselves as rather nerdy, although I personally wouldn't call them that. They are much too informed by their instincts to have the heady glamour of a Libra or a Gemini, but they do appreciate knowledge, and will appreciate hanging out with you in ways that give them more of it (even if it's not book knowledge). They also love going to the movies with their friends, although they are much too sensitive to handle gory horror movies (despite being walking horror movies themselves).

For every deeply loyal Scorpio in your friend group, beware of the possible reversal when you decide to do something to piss them the fuck off. Scorpios aren't really known for letting shit go, and if there is some perceived slight they have endured at your hands (like if you've forgotten to meet them for coffee or haven't called them back at Mach 3 speed when they are crying), you might have a Scorpio ex-friend on your hands. Because if a Scorpio dares to love you like a sister, and then you do something they perceive as disloyal, not only will you be cut off swiftly and appropriately but they will also do their best to make sure your life and livelihood are ruined forever. They will talk so much shit about you behind your back that your ears will be ringing for decades, and you will probably just fucking crumble from the amount of shade and negativity being thrown your way daily. My advice: keep your Scorpio friend content. Because Scorpios don't play around. About anything.

Scorpio style

Even if you don't know astrology, you know that hallmark sign that someone has a late October/early to mid-November birthday. Yeah, that's right, it's usually that person who has a bit of goth vibe going on and is likely dressed head to toe in dark colors. And by dark, I do mean black. If Scorpio needs to go out somewhere (that is, if they aren't lying in bed naked all day), they will try to make sure almost every item is black. If they want to dye their hair, they will most likely choose black as the color, too (that is, if the salon doesn't have a nice rich eggplant), and the same goes for any jewelry or accessories that they wear. They will all be dark and slightly dramatic as well.

Aside from the color, and in terms of form, Scorpios wear clothes that make them—uh, how do we say it—look hot. That means different things to different Scorpios, but most of the time, it means that when you meet a Pluto person, they just look a little extra va-va-voom. They definitely know how to find clothing that really highlights their bodily assets. Part of the reason is their shy knack for doing things that have a hypnotic effect on people; this extends to clothing. At the end of the day, Scorpios want to move through the world seamlessly—making an effect without causing a fuss, so that they can focus on long-term winning versus short-term applause. Hot-looking, however subtle, is just how they do this best.

Now, as you are reading all of this, you are asking the obvious question: But what about Björk? After all, a dress made of a giant stuffed swan doesn't look like an all-black tight ensemble designed to make her ooze with sex appeal. Well, yes, I see your point, kind of, but Björk is another great example of how we are both right. After all, Scorpios are intense in whatever they do, and for Björk, being a fucking genius in both fashion and music is just an intense endeavor. For Björk, wearing gorgeously loud colors and forms is a way for her to both put on a sort of uniform and win the game in the long term. (And yes, that does mean a swan dress.) If you are a Scorpio reading this, know you don't have to dress any one way—there are so many options to be you in the world. The key element is making sure people don't forget you. But I probably don't need to give you advice on that.

Texting with a Scorpio

I hate to be the one to say this, but texting with a Scorpio can be one of the most frustrating experiences of your life. After all, Scorpios tend to see things in very definitive terms. A person is either a friend or a foe. To flow well, texting sometimes involves nuance and more than short, staccato bursts of emotional admission. Speaking from the Aries side here, while I myself am not a big fan of text-ing, I understand that it takes momentum and energy and random thoughts to make it work. In our world, where we definitely aren't present with one another in person very often, a texting conversa-tion can be a space to "hang out" virtually with someone, all the while never having to spend actual time with them.

This can annoy a Scorpio, who thrives on intense eye contact and visceral expansions of soul through the body. If a Scorpio isn't conveying concrete information about your plans with them, they will only be good at texting two things: aggressive proposals and emotional utterances. That's because during the day (or night), de-spite their cool demeanor, a Scorpio's emotions can really get the best of them. Even if they haven't texted you in about four years, you may get an "I can't live without you" in the middle of the night one random Tuesday. Oh, they just couldn't help themselves. They do sincerely love you and will until the end of time. But also don't expect to get another text from them until hell freezes over.

On the flip side, if you think you can behave this way in the texting arena, you will quickly be so sorely mistaken. Whereas they can get back to you when they are good and ready, you had better write them the second they even thought about typing your name into their contacts. As with all rules applying to interactions with Scorpio, everything is a fierce double standard. You should expect to write your Scorpio back immediately, even if it is 4:00 a.m. and you weren't expecting it, and you should in no way ever leave them hanging for more than ten seconds. They won't remember how they kept you home every Friday night for two years, wait-ing to hear from them even once. They will only remember they just wrote you half of a word three minutes ago and they haven't heard back from you yet. Especially if they are in their "let's do this" mood, you are so screwed if you are actually doing something and can't text them back quickly. About one minute after the initial text they will start sweating, wishing they'd never put themselves out there to begin with. If they double-text you, they are really desperate and are probably madly in love with you. Anyway, if this is the case, what are you doing here reading this book? TEXT THEM BACK IMMEDIATELY. Again, just want to state: I hate you.

Related to this, ghosting a Scorpio is something you should do only if you are a really mean person. You have to really hate a Scorpio or be a Scorpio yourself to do that. Or probably another Scorpio wouldn't actually do that to their fellow Scorpio, but someone with their moon in Scorpio might. Anyway, if you stop writing them completely, you will actually drive them bananas as they struggle to understand how you could do this to them. They won't remember how deeply they broke your heart, or that you would have moved to hell itself if it meant you could wake up next to them every day. They will only see that you are silent in the little window of time they have given you to be a specimen they desire to communicate with, and will start going wild wondering what happened. This could work to your advantage if your goal is to ensnare them for a short bit. They will wonder who on earth could be so bold as to disrespect them like that. Your independence will turn them on, but I warn you, they will remember how rude you were, and eventually it will probably all end badly because of your foolish actions. I mean, texting or not, it's all going to end badly anyway—this is a Scorpio we are talking about.

Scorpio: Can you help me with something?
Aries: Ok
Scorpio: Never mind
Aries: I love you

Scorpio: We could start to build a life
Taurus: This is my dream
Scorpio: Want to move in?
Taurus: Tomorrow?

Scorpio: [silence]
Gemini: I feel like you're into me
Scorpio: I might be
Gemini: No one can ever resist me

Scorpio: I feel like you're into me
Cancer: I might be
Scorpio: You'd never be able to resist me
Cancer: I couldn't

Scorpio: U up?
Leo: Only for you
Scorpio: I'll be right over
Leo: Sorry I'm out

Scorpio: You make me feel otherworldly things
Virgo: You must say that to everyone
Scorpio: I never say it to anyone
Virgo: Awwww

Scorpio: Dinner in an hour?

Libra: I'm out of town.

Scorpio: I can see your light is on from the street.

Libra: Who is this?

Scorpio #1: They never understood.

Scorpio #2: They weren't meant to.

Scorpio #1: Was I meant for you?

Scorpio #2: Hardly.

Scorpio: I know you're into me

Sagittarius: Don't be so sure

Scorpio: You're not?

Sagittarius: Of course I am!

Scorpio: Snakeskin

Capricorn: Every day baby

Scorpio: You get me

Capricorn: Do I?

Scorpio: The circumference of what?

Aquarius: Oh never mind you didn't read the book.

Scorpio: You like me

Aquarius: Do I?

Scorpio: Finally

Pisces: A heart

Scorpio: To

Pisces: Win

The Scorpio imagination

If Scorpio were a city it would be Rio de Janeiro, with its close proximity to water and its furiously bright beaches and costumes, the statue of Christ the Redeemer overlooking all those hills and mountains. If Scorpio were weather it would be "as hot as hell," because what else could it be. If Scorpio were a punctuation mark it wouldn't be any one of them. Scorpio would just break off the sentence mid-phrase, never to return, except in five hundred years to check in to see if you still missed them. If Scorpio were a pair of earrings they'd be morbid, like a bronze cast of dead spiders, and they would somehow involve real bleeding, conjured from the inanimate metal spiders at will. If Scorpio were a vacation, it definitely wouldn't be summer vacation, because all of that space where nothing is going on would annoy them—they would just like to get things going, thank you very much. If Scorpio were a period of day, it would be the hot light of noon, where the sun is at its highest. The devil's hour, we call it.

Have you ever seen an eagle fly freely from tree to tree, in the open blue sky, and felt a profound sense of peace? Me too. And no, this isn't some corny Americana image I am going for. I am trying to paint, at least in part, the picture of a Scorpio soul's essence, and how it relates to an immortal sense of the everyday. The true essence of Scorpio is this lone bird, flying without a pack, circling the sky with its sublime calm. Eventually it will find other birds.

Scorpio as a loner is key to understanding this sign's energy. Because whereas they do need bulletproof ties to family and a life-long lover, they also need absolute freedom to pursue who they are, and their own projects and goals, without the nagging influence of others. Part of this comes from their need to be themselves without anyone else seeing this self completely, lest they try to overpower them. It also has to do with Scorpio creativity. Scorpios need to make new things and ideas in order to be happy. It's hard to do that sometimes when there is anyone else around. So this is why they need to be that lone eagle soaring from the trees time and again.

Keeping this in mind, Scorpios need to organize their lives so that they have enough alone time. No matter how much they protest, a Scorpio should always have enough time to venture out on their own (at least for an hour or two) to go see a new exhibit at the local natural history museum or read a book about an artist who works with jellyfish. Without this time, they can get resentful. Worse yet, for all of those people who do want them around all of the time (read: everyone), without this time, they really can just walk away in order to get it. You can only hope that, when a Scorpio gets to be their own eagle and can acknowledge their basest drives, they learn to carve out time for themselves and don't leave a bunch of people brokenhearted.

The Famous Scorpio

While there are plenty of famous Scorpios in the history books, the most important thing to realize about all of them is that they are usually not the people who are front and center. They tend to be second in command (think Joe Biden), where they can pull the strings and manipulate the situation but never have to fully be the face of power. This allows them all kinds of actual power, and they will conserve their energy in ways a front-facing Leo never can. They will sit on their throne in the shadows, building momentum, so that when it is time to move and strike, they are always ready. Sure, this keeps them from getting all of the credit they deserve sometimes, but it keeps them from taking too much of the blame, too.

Scorpios will pretend they hate fame. The biggest liars among them (and believe me, there is a competition for the biggest Scorpio liar, and it's hard to say who wins, because everyone involved is lying) will say that they hate the spotlight, and that the hot glare of the paparazzi is not what drives them. And while cuspy Libra-Scorpios like Kim Kardashian never even pretend to say this, this has to do with her considerable airy energy. Just remember that Kim's momager, Kris Jenner, is a full-fledged Scorpio. Scorpios love to secretly influence the person in power to do the things they want to do, without having the full limelight. Whereas a fire sign always excels on the stage, a Scorpio is a better fit behind the curtain, pulling the strings of the operation and telling everyone where to go with just the immense power of their eyes.

It's truly amazing to consider how many Scorpio poets there are. The list is endless. Most poets who "make it" into our collective consciousness tend to be born around Halloween. It totally makes sense: Who better to tap into the language of the dead and the undead than those who are themselves both dead and undead? Scorpios are born knowing a lot about the underbelly of life.

If we think of Scorpio poets, we can't help but think of two big ones: Sylvia Plath and Anne Sexton. These American women from the middle of the last century are often unfairly linked in the historical imagination. Driven to succeed, they became as famous and widely respected as poets as is possible. Although these two

Scorpio poetic geniuses did know each other, like a lot of Scorpio-Scorpio combinations, they maybe weren't what we might consider "friends." Both women wrote poems that are perfect portrayals of the imagination, getting deep into the collective psyche of what it means to be a feeling human being, which is just so Scorpio. Other Scorpio poets include Nathaniel Mackey, Marianne Moore, and Dylan Thomas. We are glad that so many Scorpios go on to become famous poets. We need them.

Pablo Picasso was a force of sheer creativity, making art that challenged convention throughout his life. Like any good Scorpio, he tested himself and the boundaries of the field with his ability to create out of strong instincts, influencing cubism and surrealism. His life is a metaphor for any famous Scorpio, artist or otherwise, or really any Scorpio at all. He lived without fear of what others might think of his work. Through a rigorous and almost religious devotion to it, he had faith in its immense worth. Like all famous Scorpios, just by being himself he changed the world in the process.

Other Famous Scorpios

1. Whoopi Goldberg
2. Winona Ryder
3. Ted Berrigan
4. Bill Gates
5. Diddy
6. Tracee Ellis Ross
7. Chloë Sevigny

8. Howard Dean
9. Alice Notley
10. Carl Sagan

Scorpio playlist

- Frank Ocean, "Thinkin Bout You"
- Katy Perry, "Legendary Lovers"
- Drake, "Nice for What"
- Mahalia Jackson, "Trouble of the World"
- Aaron Copland, "Quiet City"
- Lorde, "Green Light"
- Espinoza Paz, "Perdí la Pose"
- Lyle Lovett, "If I Had a Boat"
- Sigala, "Sweet Lovin'"
- Joni Mitchell, "Blue"

The Scorpio (a poem)

A wild acre of entirely palm trees. Blown over by rain? No, rain only falls. The wind makes sheets of invisible momentum. Do you mean that the entire landscape was flooded with debris? No, I mean to say that the whole world was heavy with intention. Asking questions. Silently. Going in and going out, in a rather methodical fashion. Making everyone bleed. Soft and worn-out shirts giving way to sheets of soft and worn-out linen giving way to soft and subtle naked bodies. Giving way to what. Going in and going out. Of the underworld. Planting spring shoots with potatoes. But were they orange? The potatoes? Oh what a fool you are! All that very bitter wheat. With which you made your supper. No, but what about the wild rush. What about all of those things you promised to the moon? Oh forget everything. You won't, but. Oh go on. Live life as you wish. Without me.

SAGITTARIUS

November 22–December 21

I dwell in Possibility—
A fairer House than Prose—
More numerous of Windows—
Superior—for Doors—

Emily Dickinson, born December 10, 1830

The Sagittarius

I remember exactly what I was doing when Britney Spears shaved her head. Painting my nails black and ignoring my Cancer boyfriend. Somehow we'd lasted through three years of college and in February of 2007, during our last semester, I was starting to get sick of him. All those texts and Cancer check-ins, constantly wanting to be reassured about everything, and getting so comfortable in our relationship that he stopped looking hot. It felt pathetic and needy. I was twenty-two and that was not going to be my life. He also had this way of suffocating me with plans. On this particular Friday, I didn't want to see him for dinner. Like any Sagittarius, I wanted to go out and flirt. I wanted to be a little selfish and reckless too.

Waiting for my nails to dry and staring at my laptop, I saw a photo of Britney Spears with half her head shaved. Immediately I clicked on the article and saw others. Britney with an umbrella, about to smash a car window. Britney holding a pair of clippers in a gray hoodie. She was in some random California hair salon and everyone around her looked terrified, not sure if they should be helping her or not. Maybe that's why she more or less had to do it herself, half laughing while staring in the mirror, half indulging some pit of despair that would grow more and more familiar to me as I got older (even though I'd never be that known or understand her life at all).

Britney Spears was the most famous teenager in American culture. Every straight boy I knew jerked off to her. Gay boys idolized her. And girls studied her shamelessly because they wanted to look like her. I remember grocery shopping with my mother sometime in middle school and seeing her David LaChapelle *Rolling Stone* cover—Britney on a hot-pink bedspread in a satin black bra, holding a landline phone in one hand (relic of the '90s) and a purple Teletubby (the gay one) in the other. I begged my mother to buy it. Of course she obliged because she probably hoped I was straight (the irony), and on the car ride home I didn't read a single word of the article. I stared at the photos and decided Britney Spears was a saint. She was a good girl. She was Lolita. She was your gay best friend and a fantasy too. That was her genius. She was communicating with nearly everyone. Those of us who grew up with

Britney have a fondness for her that borders on parental protection. Even though she was the popular girl, you wanted to help her. You knew something under the surface was deeply wrong and she was troubled, like everyone else.

That February incident would lead to an entire summer where the paparazzi would not leave Britney Spears alone. She was seen using a fake British accent at a gas station, crying in public often, and going through countless wigs while wearing sunglasses almost at all times. She suddenly became human (though of course she'd always been) while looking her most surreal. That's the thing about a Sagittarius: we seem larger than life and unapproachable on the outside. Few people will ask if we're okay because we're great entertainers. Even in the midst of a breakdown, a Sagittarius is mesmerizing and magnetic. We appear in control because we want even the drama to be beautiful. There's an effortlessness about the archer that translates to irreverence—half heart, half I-don't-care. Britney Spears is the quintessential Sagittarius. Rebellious but sweet. Looking for everyone to love her while demanding her freedom (and how free can you be if you want that). A total paradox. A cunning wild card. This is why your Sagittarius friends won't bore you. This is why you love them and find them impossible too.

Things you might want to know about Sagittarius

Sagittarius is a mutable fire sign and the ninth sign of the zodiac (a charged number associated with idealism but also judgment).

It comes after Scorpio and has inherited their passion and intensity but learned from their struggle with obsession and freedom. In fact, personal freedom is the most important thing to the archer. They will go to any length to achieve it. Spontaneously quitting a job, shaving their head, sleeping with someone they shouldn't—in other words, anything that gives the *illusion* of freedom more than freedom itself. You'll also notice that a Sagittarius may often take the position of a contrarian, whether or not they're arguing for something they actually believe in. This counterintuitive behavior is linked to their preoccupation with freedom as well. They tend to see any mode of resistance as asserting their independence.

Not surprisingly, "rebellious" is a word often used to describe Sagittarians. Another is "rude." They don't mince words and they're straight shooters. If you ask them, they're just "being honest" and "telling it like it is." If they made someone cry, well, it's not their fault. That person just "needed to hear the truth." In the long run, you'll come to appreciate this about them. Their advice and love come with no ornamentation. It's the same with their distaste. Unlike Leos, they couldn't care less if they're talking to the queen of England and telling her she's looked better, or a one-night stand they won't see again (more on their fear of commitment later).

Sagittarians don't subscribe to a blueprint. They aren't followers, though they aren't exactly leaders, either. They can be, but it's not ingrained in them. They don't need it for ego purposes. What they'd prefer is to be left alone to pursue their obsessions, making their own choices at all times and as they see fit. Sagittarians believe everyone else should be granted the same, too. There's a true idealism in their nature. A sense that the human experiment could work if we all just got out of each other's way. They'll never admit it, but they're secret optimists, no matter how goth they appear. Don't be surprised if, after reading this, you see a Sagittarius smoking a cigarette alone in the rain, only to later see them at a party, vying to be the center of attention.

If an Aries is great at initiating action (starting the party) and a Leo is the person who can sustain it (entertain), a Sagittarius is the friend who comes an hour late, flirts with everyone, says something incredibly controversial, and leaves (likely without saying good-bye—and I can't tell you how many times I've done this, since good-byes are full of unnecessary sentiment). This will get them talked about. They know it and love it. It's half the reason why they act this way. Almost every Sagittarius I've been friends with loves a French exit. Decorum and social norms feel oppressive to my people. If you want to party with us, get on our level and don't expect us to behave like we're in a Jane Austen novel. And if you should be so brave as to try and get us to do what you want, suggest the opposite—be a little ironic about it. We're not a basic bitch. We're not dying to marry you.

Sagittarius as a lover

The way to get a Sagittarius is not to try, while also hiring three private detectives to attend to their thirty-three secret lives, allowing you to know 3 percent of who they are. Everyone has probably had that one Sagittarius lover who disappeared on them like their favorite pair of jeans and made them feel unsustainable passion. What I mean is, act interested but don't be predictable or over-the-top. You aren't trying to get a Pisces or a Cancer. A Sagittarius values subtlety in romantic approach. Even if you play your cards right, you might not get them to stay. It's truly not you and abso-lutely them. That cliché holds true for a Sagittarius more than any other sign. Their commitment issues are infamous. They're con-stantly looking for something better, like a New Yorker with real estate. We just know there's a better apartment out there. And even when we get that apartment, it could be rent-controlled, closer to the train, with better light—it doesn't matter. Life, my friends, is con-stantly being unsatisfied with what you have, and maybe didn't even want that badly. For a Sagittarius, at least. They have a hard time sticking it out with anyone. They don't lie to others or themselves.

It's confusing dating the archer. They're prone to grand roman-tic gestures but can also ghost you minutes later. They change their minds constantly and are prone to acting out. They don't stew like a water sign, either. They shoot from the hip. In 2004, our Sagit-tarius queen Britney got married for fifty-five hours in Las Vegas. Of course at the fifty-sixth hour she decided to get divorced. It's not that she didn't mean to get married. She probably really felt it in the moment. And then . . . she didn't. Welcome to Sagittarius Psych 101. Innocent people have lost years trying to figure out what they did wrong or why they didn't get a text back after being promised eternity.

Being lured by a Sagittarius is easy. They are magnetic. For all their brooding and self-criticism, they know how to turn it on. This gets everyone in trouble. A Sagittarius is essentially always trying to steal someone's man. Even people they know they won't sleep with. They just want to be wanted. They require a devotional attention at all times. And since they know how to get it, they end up upsetting a lot of people who actually feel a real connection with them (though it might not be reciprocated, since a Sag is likely flirting just for fun). This makes it sound like Sagittarius lovers are cruel and heartless, when really they just don't want to be accountable for anyone's feelings about them. Unless those feelings are hot and light. Hot and light is something they can commit to. Ask a Sagittarius about marriage or long-term plans and they'll probably go to the bar and order a double of what they were having.

The erogenous zones for Sagittarius are the hips and thighs. They like to be pulled in and they like pulling you in. A lot of sexual energy resides around their waist. Just touching them there will get them going. Though maybe less so if you're an earth sign. Good luck to Capricorns and Virgos trying to bang a Sagittarius. Say good-bye to all your rules, schedules, and anal-retentive demands. Not only will a Sagittarius not care, they'll actively tell you off. Taurus is the earth sign with the greatest chance for love with a mutable fire. That's because they enjoy glamour and decadence. It's also because they have the most style. A Taurus is confident but can be understated. They know how to indulge their lovers when needed. Of course, the arguments between a Sagittarius and a Taurus will be huge. Neither sign will budge. The Taurus will worship them endlessly and eventually the Sagittarius will get bored. Which is to say, every Sagittarius appreciates a romantic challenge. The chase is what turns them on the most, so things can stay hot for a minute if you play hard-to-get well.

Aries and Leo are great matches for a Sagittarius. Hot sex, wandering conversations, arguments that feel intense for five minutes and then are forgotten. Fire signs are not ones to hold a grudge. They have more important things to worry about. Like how to get famous or have another affair. Ambition is what drives them, not retaliation. Though, speaking of retaliation, I have to warn every Sagittarius reading this about water signs. You'll want them the most. Because you know they're terrible for you and shouldn't have them. Cancers will be too clingy and domestic (definitely not glamorous enough). And a Pisces-Sagittarius match is dreamy, full of idealism and great sex—until the Pisces bogs you down with their self-analysis and insecurities. Speaking as someone who's had three Pisces boyfriends and two long-term Cancer relationships, Sagittarians are just too exciting for water signs. Catch up! Though I'll hand it to Scorpios: playing mind games does get them attention from a Sagittarius (I hate admitting this). Scorpio manipulation can be kind of hot. Except that Scorpios love to spy on everyone. They like keeping tabs. So ultimately, no thanks! I'd rather just fuck the FBI, not date them.

It's glorious to see a Gemini and a Sagittarius flirting. If you have, it will restore your faith in spontaneity. There's something so youthful and adventurous about it. These two signs can last a long time and make everyone jealous of the fun they're having. Libras are so in their heads, they'll immediately be attracted to Sagittarians—who say what they think and do what they want. And a Sagittarius will appreciate the aesthetic pains Libras go to in every aspect of their lives, making sure things are beautiful and thoughtful. The most challenging air sign for a Sagittarius is Aquarius. Both are rebels. Although you'll always know how a Sagittarius feels about you, while an Aquarius may come off as cold and unreadable. Their emotional temperaments don't match, which might actually be the cause of the initial attraction. I broke up with an Aquarius once (well, it was mutual, I suppose) because he said I yelled at him too much. They're kind of afraid of feelings. Especially any high-pitched romantic feelings. And yeah, I also slammed a few doors and maybe cheated on him. Fair warning: if you're not ready to go from 0 to 100 in a matter of seconds, or 100 to 0, for that matter—don't date a Sagittarius. They're here to feel everything. And maybe they won't tell you about it, since they're afraid to come off as vulnerable, but they'll act on it. They'll act up, more likely.

Sagittarius as a friend

A Sagittarius is the friend who gets you closer to your dreams by example. They're always hustling. Self-actualization is important to them. They see it as a way to get to their ideal life of total freedom—not having to answer to anyone, not worrying about money, and certainly not having to account for their time. So naturally, trying to get a word in when you're with a Sagittarius is difficult. It may seem like they're always talking about themselves and their plans for the future. But unlike a Leo, they're not fishing for compliments. They're hyped up. They're obsessed with possibility. And they want to get you hyped up, too, taking you with them on some spontaneous vacation, or starting a business venture you'd never think up without them.

A Sagittarius is not the friend who is constantly texting and checking up on you. If you want that, find a Virgo or a Cancer. It doesn't mean they don't care. It means they're in their own little Sagittarius world, buying plane tickets to some place they googled ten minutes ago and finding unavailable romantic prospects to obsess over. (A Sagittarius adage: if they're unavailable, you can't lose; they can't hurt you—you weren't ever going to keep them anyway.) Sagittarians will show up when you need them most and they're also great in a crisis. No one would assume so, since they have a "bad-kid" reputation. The truth is, they want to see their friends thriving. They're the kind of person who does you a favor, and never mentions it after.

Many Sagittarians have a hard time getting help and showing vulnerability. From afar, they may appear untouchable. If there's one way to be a good friend to them, it's to reach out even when everything about their energy exudes confidence (perhaps especially then). They use confidence as a defense mechanism. Mostly this has to do with the fact that dependency in any form—whether on a person, place, or anything else in the material world—scares them. They want to know they'll be okay if everything is stripped away from them and they're left with nothing on a desert island (more of a Sagittarius fantasy than a nightmare, to be honest). The more forthcoming and revealing you are as a friend, the more they'll want to take you to that island (while continuing to remind you they'd be fine on their own).

Although a Sagittarius is charming and exuberant in a crowd, it exhausts them. It may look like they have many friends, but the truth is, their intuition leads them to put their trust in a select few. One reason for this is because they value deep friendships.

At times they may even seem like non-normative friendships that feel more like marriages. If your best friend is a Sagittarius, you know how often it feels like you're married to them. And probably every other week you're thinking of getting divorced, because they've acted out, been aloof, or pushed your buttons on some issue they know not to. But life with a Sagittarius is complicated and never boring. They don't hold your mistakes against you. They aren't earth signs. A big misstep can be forgotten in minutes if you're someone who has proved your loyalty to them. And the way to prove your loyalty is to be consistent. To keep showing up, and putting up with their wild behavior and strange tantrums. They're the type of sign who will try to push you away, though what they're really doing is seeing who will stick around.

Sagittarius style

Sagittarians have more leather jackets than anyone in the zodiac. Or they have just one, which they wear constantly, to the point where seeing them without it is noteworthy and you should ask if they're okay. Jackets are their favorite garment. They like anything resembling armor. Anything that feels like protection and projects a tough exterior. Bomber jackets, military jackets, jackets that are part of uniforms. Uniforms excite Sagittarians (though not an entire uniform, because they're nonconformists). They like to wear uniform pieces in a tongue-in-cheek way, fully aware that they're going to break your rules. Remember the first time we saw Britney Spears in her Catholic schoolgirl getup? That's the perfect example.

And yes, I keep referencing her, because she's truly the mother of all Sagittarius people.

In terms of color palette, a Sagittarius gravitates toward dark colors and especially black. However, they also love tie-dye and patterns. If you married the '60s with the goth/grunge '90s, you'd have an important snapshot of Sagittarius culture. Grunge in an East Coast rather than West Coast way, which is to say a bit more put-together and groomed. Yes, Sags have been called inauthentic or overly performative because of their fashion. As if they're trying to showcase their never-ending teenage rebellion too obviously. And they are. That's actually what makes them more authentic than not. Sags are attracted to the '60s and '90s because both of those were times when there was significant pushback against norms, which was reflected quite notably in people's style.

But let's talk shoes. A Sagittarius loves Doc Martens and Vans. You'll see them in one of these (or some similar combat boot or sneaker) more than any other shoe. What you'll notice is that Sags aren't the typical rough-around-the-edges rebel, but they aren't trend followers either. They're not wearing those Doc Martens to seem like the cool kid. Intrinsically, they already think they're the cool kid based on their existential views and experimental, do-anything-at-any-moment nature. They want to be noticed, but they definitely care more about enjoying their own attire than getting compliments. This might be the Sagittarius mantra when it comes to many things.

Something nerdy and perhaps a bit embarrassing is that Sags love patches. Pins. Any outward display that spells out their values and what they find important (band t-shirts are big for them too).

They will incorporate this in their living space and their wardrobe. Mostly they do it as a conversation starter. They can talk endlessly about all the things they're "protesting" and why you should be as well. It can feel a bit new agey or like they never left college. Just let them do it. It's more entertaining than annoying.

Texting with a Sagittarius

One night I was out with a Sagittarius friend of mine and somewhere in the middle of our drinks my friend forgot they were dating someone. We had talked about their boyfriend earlier but suddenly, and seemingly out of nowhere, they decided to text a Scorpio ex who I knew was more or less the love of their life. When the Scorpio didn't respond in less than thirty seconds, my friend texted another ex, a Taurus. It was like watching myself. Exactly what I would do when drunk on a weekend, with a boyfriend who made me feel tied down.

I tried telling my friend they might regret this in the morning, but, as a Sagittarius, I knew that they wouldn't. I knew that what was happening wasn't reckless but true. They weren't in love and they wanted a way out, even if it meant dipping into the past. After ten minutes, when neither ex responded, a third person got the same sloppy text. Someone my friend had hooked up with, and cheated on their boyfriend with just the week before. Again, I wasn't surprised. And again, I didn't try to stop them. Another drink later, all three fuckboys responded. Now there were options for how the night could end and I jokingly suggested that maybe I should sleep with one of them too. All jokes aside, that's exactly what happened. My friend slept with the Scorpio, I slept with the Taurus, and the new fuckboy never was texted back. We saved him for later. The motto of this story being, a Sagittarius always gets what they want. And they're happy to help out another Sag while they're at it.

Unprompted daily Sagittarius text

You:

Sagittarius: Before you're dead you can always get on a plane, sleep with a stranger, read a poem smoking a cigarette in your kitchen alone.

Sagittarius mass text

If you enjoy being friends with me please venmo me a million dollars by tonight. Thanks!

Sagittarius happiness

You: So are you okay? I haven't heard from you in over a month.

Sagittarius: I had a great month without a boyfriend. Let's rage.

Sagittarius drama

You: I'm not asking you to write a novel but like, can you tell me why you did that??

Sagittarius: A literary genre I excel at is emotional texting in cabs. To be brief: Fuck you.

Spiritual Sagittarius

You: See you at the party tonight!

Sagittarius: I don't party with people who only believe in the physical world.

You: Okay??

Horny Sagittarius

You: Hey, what's up?

Sagittarius: Browsing the OED to improve my sexts

Sunday Sagittarius

Sagittarius: Any new ideas on why we're here or nah? Lol

You: Are you day drunk again?

The Sagittarius imagination

If a Sagittarius were a city they'd be Las Vegas. Flashy, dark, with the illusion that you could be anywhere. Las Vegas is the promise that life can change instantly if you're lucky, that your wildest fantasies are closer than farther, and that all you have to do to get them is take a risk. Remember that Sagittarius is ruled by Jupiter, the planet of luck. It's in their nature to test that luck and gamble. If a Sagittarius were a punctuation mark, they'd be the em dash. Bold, somewhat severe, and clearly noticeable. If they were a type of weather they'd be fog. Mysterious, haunting, curiously handsome. And if a Sagittarius were a landscape they'd definitely be the desert. The desert at night. And through that desert a car passes once every hour, stirring up the air and fading from view. Sometimes a Sagittarius will look up and think about flagging the car down, meeting the stranger, going wherever they're going. Mostly, they'll keep walking ahead, stopping every so often to study the sky and tighten their boots.

A Sagittarius is that girl at prom who showed up in fishnets and her dad's leather jacket. She's not sure why she's there. She doesn't have a date. Not because she couldn't find one but because she didn't try. She didn't want to ask anyone and everyone who asked her never heard back. In fact, all signs pointed to her not going to prom, but in the end something convinced her to leave her room. Right now she's in the corner, nonchalantly staring at everyone and pretending she's not staring at all. If you go up and talk to her, she'll definitely make a joke. Something morbid. Something about how she wishes they were playing The Smiths. She's not a bitch exactly. But maybe she sort of looks like one. Talking to her you'll find out about the angsty novel she's writing, how she feels like an only child even though she isn't one, and how, under all her posturing, she believes that anything is possible, even if it's not exactly cool to say that.

Maybe you're thinking you want to be friends with this person. Maybe she's exactly that road trip you go on that changes something so elemental, it's impossible to return to your life as it was. She's that stranger you have a long conversation with, in some town you'll never go back to, somewhere where you're just passing through. And she gets it. She really does. Even in her silence she understands why you want to start over, do painting instead of finance, never get married, call back someone you once loved and shouldn't have at all.

Maybe all this is true but now she's gone. You took your eye off her for a second and she found another corner from which to brood. At another party, not this one. Somewhere like here, where everyone looks at her but doesn't quite know what to say. She's not going to stay long anyway. She's already thinking of leaving. Maybe another country, maybe the moon. She's dyeing her hair black, finishing that novel in which, no, it's not you exactly, but you think you recognize something of yourself there. Because she's a dropped coin on the sidewalk. The park after midnight. She's exactly the person you wish was calling when it's surely someone else. Okay, so nothing's ever quite simple or probably enough for this girl but who cares. You're definitely obsessed. She's who you've always wanted to know. And the thing is, you don't even end up getting her name.

The Famous Sagittarius

There are two paths Sagittarians have been known to follow. The first is mass adulation, fame, and fortune: Taylor Swift, Walt Disney, Joan Didion, Nicki Minaj. The second is retreating from the world in order to make their own world, a kind of dropping out in order to fully live on their terms. These types of Sagittarians aren't as famous as the other. Although I bet you recognize Emily Dickinson's name. The goddess of American poetry, Dickinson famously never married, never had children, and she never published the majority of her poems. She wrote her entire life and lived in her family home, wearing white and guarding her independence.

The poet Robert Lax followed a similar path after he graduated from Columbia University. If you've never heard of him, you're not alone. He probably didn't want you to. He decided to spend most of his time on Patmos, a distant Greek island closer to the Middle East than Europe. There he wrote poems and lived with many cats in an all white apartment where he occasionally had visitors. His life was spent in service to his art and contemplation. If they could have met, Lax and Dickinson might have seen each other once every six months for tea. They're probably doing that now, on whatever moon they ended up on.

The artist Marina Abramovic (who actually shares Lax's birthday and mine) also decided to go down an unorthodox path. In her early years, she and her life partner, Ulay (himself a Sagittarius), traveled from place to place in a van. They cooked, made art, and did everything else in that van. It was more or less a shabby existence, but it allowed them to be artists. The van was their home. Two Sagittarians wandering the world in pursuit of their spiritual and artistic visions. As with Lax and Dickinson, contact with the outside world was on their terms. Eventually, though, Marina hit it big and gained representation by famous galleries and institutions. She was on her way to somewhere the van couldn't take her. Somewhere bigger. And plenty of people resented her for going there (but who cares). Abramovic is considered one of the founders of performance art. In a sense, she experienced both paths, pivoting toward the more public one in the end. She's a Sagittarius representative of the impulse to rebel and create her own life, and the yearning to be recognized with accolades, money, and fame. Maybe the people who blame her never had either.

Living on the edge as a Sagittarius has its dark side too. Jimi Hendrix and Jim Morrison are proof of that. Both of them were trailblazers and burned out young. Though no one can really say they didn't follow their bliss. When I worked at a poetry nonprofit, a Sagittarius co-worker of mine would always say: Follow your bliss, dude. Just follow your bliss. Dickinson did it. Lax did it. Morrison did it too. One day in New York he heard a voice telling him to move to Venice Beach and start a band. He knew he'd make it. He'd made it on another plane already. That voice was proof of it. So he went to California and started The Doors. If you're terrified of dying, write poetry or start a band. There's nothing else.

Other Famous Sagittarians

1. Beethoven
2. Shirley Chisholm
3. Bruce Lee
4. Billie Jean King
5. Jay-Z
6. William Blake
7. Brad Pitt
8. Tina Turner
9. Noam Chomsky
10. Tyra Banks

Sagittarius playlist

- Trina, "Da Baddest B***h"
- Frank Sinatra, "Fly Me to the Moon"
- The Doors, "Love Me Two Times"
- Nicki Minaj, "Super Bass"
- Ozzy Osbourne, "See You on the Other Side"
- Britney Spears, "Gimme More"
- Jay-Z, "Young Forever"
- Billy Idol, "Dancing with Myself"
- Sinéad O'Connor, "Nothing Compares 2 U"
- Mos Def, "Ms. Fat Booty"

The Sagittarius (a poem)

And who have you convinced
that midnight's truly where
you live and all of spring
is winter. It isn't true
and more than that
it's only midnight
when you're traveling nowhere.
The sky. The sky.
And all of earth,
they'll never seem to you
quite new or big enough.
You'll be a fog of birds.
You'll dress and then undress
the days. It really happened.
Fire by the water.
Arrows by the trees.

CAPRICORN

December 22–January 19

at what point after it enters
the mouth is it no longer in the
mouth but the throat the colon
making sumptuous death of the world
this is what crossing the line gains

CAConrad, born January 1, 1966

The Capricorn

Dolly Parton is the quintessential Capricorn. She's the ultimate performer, and there is obviously nothing she likes better than sitting in front of a crowd, holding court with millions of people, telling her rags-to-riches stories and tales of hurt love to the "peanut-crunching crowd" (as Scorpio Sylvia Plath would say) who have paid hundreds of dollars a head just to sit there. The key moral of all of her songs is that a Capricorn will overcome any-thing. It's not only Capricorn's favorite kind of tale, it's also true.

A Capricorn will endure, conquer, and overcome any obstacle in their path, and it is the one sign in the zodiac that no one will ever beat. Not even the fire-breathing Aries, who, if you look at them funny at the wrong moment when they haven't napped that day, will come murderously charging at you in utter coldness within a millisecond. No, not even the cunning Libra, who will invent an entire world just to entrap you and then overwhelm your will to live so much that you can't help but submit forever. And no, not even the base-driven Scorpio, who lies in wait sometimes for several lifetimes, only to strike back at the hurts you have so stupidly inflicted upon them before you were born. No, no other sign has the grit to dig into existence the way a Capricorn does. And even if you disagree, it really doesn't matter, because you are wrong and will undoubtedly suffer the consequences. If you ever choose to not acknowledge Capricorn's dominance, they will walk around the corner to let you know how foolish you've been. If you know a Capricorn, you know that absolutely no one other than them will get the last laugh.

Because she's such an icon, it's not hard to find a whole host of recordings of key Dolly Parton quips in the zeitgeist, especially taken from her live shows, where she is arguably the most herself and at her best. Dolly Parton has a lot of beloved songs, but one of her most famous is "Jolene."

"Jolene" is a song about betrayal, and it couldn't be a more classic tale of what happens when you fuck with a Capricorn. My favorite version is from a two-disc recording of Dolly's 2002 *Halos & Horns* tour. The whole live album really is fantastic, not just for the electricity and rawness of her live performances but for what she is willing to say to get a laugh (and a whole bunch of tears) out of the crowd.

What makes her "Jolene" performance from the tour so amazing is her honesty in the beginning. She starts off by saying, "This song is about another woman trying to steal another woman's man," which of course contains in one phrase all of the classic Capricorn fears about betrayal. But then before you get too sad for her, she says, "Of course, if somebody tried to steal the guys I've been out with, it might seem more like petty theft." The crowd then roars, as her self-deprecating nature is both disarming and funny. It charms the audience into a sense that the Capricorn will always insult themselves before they insult anyone else. They might be right, but what they probably don't realize just yet is that this is part of a Capricorn's trap to conquer any competitor entirely.

In the show, Dolly goes on to explain:

Anyway this is a song about an old redheaded gal who tried to steal my husband when we first got married. Oh, she was absolutely beautiful. She was tall and skinny, redheaded, long legs, everything I wanted and didn't have. She was a knockout. She didn't get him. But I look at him every once in a while, and I think, oh, I wish she had.

Again, the crowd then loses their minds. They scream and holler, completely in the palm of her hand, eagerly waiting for the song to begin and for them to get the solace and catharsis of revenge, played out perfectly in a Capricorn's psyche. It's important, though, to point out that the way Dolly chooses to portray what makes Jolene better than her is just so classic Capricorn. Of course, Dolly doesn't worry about the spiritual nature of Jolene's connection to her husband. Instead her focus is on Jolene's physical beauty, as that is what is most threatening to her. Capricorns live in a physical world.

Jolene must have been something like a wistful Aquarius, sharp and definitely very charming. Maybe Jolene in the midst of all that beauty was sort of ready to put up a little fight for something. Oh, but she had none of the staying power of a Capricorn. She didn't get Dolly's man. And maybe more importantly, she never could conquer the world like Dolly did. After all, we don't see people making pilgrimages today to Jolenewood, now do we? But we do see Jolene's foolish action brilliantly turned into a commodity for profit. Because Jolene doesn't even own her own name anymore. Nope, every time we say it, at least a couple of bucks get deposited into Dolly's checking account. (Better pay up. Capricorns don't do layaway.) Whoever that young and foolish Jolene was really doesn't matter anymore, because in our imagination, she will always be the beautiful loser. That's the Capricorn hard at work.

It would be silly if it wasn't so frightening, that moment you realize that the song really isn't a love story, it is a story of war, sung by the victor. It's the winner's parade, a ruler's party, with the bleeding corpse of the enemy being dragged through the town square as the victor smiles a little with coy indifference. It's the fierce hawk, with the rodent's teeth in its mouth, dangling that poor rat's body and entrails in the wind like a bunch of party streamers.

"Jolene, Jolene, oh I'm begging of you, please don't take my man," Dolly very sweetly sings. And then the song goes under like a forest fire.

Oh please. Jolene never even had a chance.

Things you might want to know about Capricorn

Capricorn is the tenth sign of the zodiac and a cardinal earth sign. Effectively the leader of all earth signs (and arguably everyone else alive), Capricorn comes into the karmic scene after the wild events of Sagittarius. Sagittarius spends their life thinking "I behold," only for Capricorn to think afterwards, "I avail." Capricorn learns this important lesson from Sagittarius, which is to be free. Except that for Capricorn, there is nothing carefree here. They internalize this as a sort of heavy lesson in determined independence. While a Sagittarius must have no obligations, a Capricorn must have no one to answer to. They can do absolutely anything on their own, and they will do it all by themselves excellently, thank you very much. (Although if you are asking to assist, you can find the to-do list by the door and please finish it all by this afternoon, thanks again.)

Simply put, Capricorns just don't need you or anyone else in particular in this damn green world to survive. Virgo Gloria Gaynor's disco hit "I Will Survive" is practically their anthem. Part of their strength of purpose has to do with the age of their soul on the karmic wheel. If Scorpio is around thirty and Sagittarius is in their forties, then Capricorn is distinctly middle-aged, in their fifties, making their way to sixty. This gravitas also has to do with their planetary ruler, Saturn. Just as Saturn return has a sobering effect on any person, asking them to start to consider adulthood more seriously and get their shit together, Saturn as a ruler sobers up Capricorn constantly. For this reason, Capricorns move conservatively, planning always toward a stable and thriving future—one with plenty of creature comforts and loads of capital (whether that be social or actual money, although it's usually both).

Much has been made throughout history of Capricorn's animal symbol, the sea goat. The sea goat is a mythical beast, with the bottom half of its body a mermaid tail. The goat is a good way to understand Capricorn. Because just as a goat will climb the side of a very steep mountain, despite inclement weather, or a virtual apocalypse, for as long as is necessary to achieve its goals, so too will Capricorns do absolutely anything and endure just about anything to get what they want. This is a trait that you must remember when you engage with them, because while they can be gentle and sweet and sometimes somewhat unassuming in their demeanor at first, they are never to be underestimated.

Like the way the goat needs to know their mountain in order to know how to climb it, so too will the Capricorn sense where the power is and court it. They have an understanding of authority and social order, and a deep respect for both that not everyone else has. To better understand their relationship to power, you can compare them again to Sagittarians, who will be irreverent to power if they feel they have not achieved their due or if a person or structure in power appears to limit their freedom. Capricorns don't dirty their hands with all of this mess. They will simply find a way to become said system of power and circumvent these sorts of embattled and absolutely sloppy discussions.

This is not to say that every Capricorn's goal is to completely dominate you at every turn. Capricorns' favorite people are actually those who are more powerful than they are and can dominate them. I always say that I know things are looking up in my career when I see a bunch of Capricorns trying to contact me. Hell, even one Capricorn in my inbox is pretty exciting. If you have a Capricorn in your life, chances are it's either a family member or someone who has taken note of how successful you've been lately.

When you go to a party you can see this in action. Capricorns will visibly swoop in to talk to the person in the room who has the most power. Their proximity to it just feels right to them. Like lots of other signs, they are turned on by power. But unlike Scorpio, who likes to live in the shadows of it as the grand puppet master with their whip and lube kit, or Cancer, who loves power's proximity to wealth and thus security but still might prefer a more auxiliary role, Capricorns aren't afraid to go on stage and do the dance for the cash all by themselves. No, it's not exactly power that gets them, it's ambition. Whenever you are trying very hard for the goal, a Capricorn will take notice. They will see promise in you and will find your motivation interesting and noteworthy. They will want to get in there before everyone else does, to claim you as a coveted prize for a very long time. Or at least until the next prize comes along.

This all probably sounds like an extended dig, and I guess it is. Full disclosure is that while I have been loved deeply and slept soundly next to a cuddly Capricorn in my day, I've also been profoundly burned by them. Some Capricorns have taken the time to understand me like no other sign can, and while in the light of their glorious love I have felt a lot less existentially lonely and afraid, I have also paid the price. This isn't every Capricorn I've ever met, because right now I can think of at least three Capricorn friends who have never done anything except show me the utmost kindness and protection. But a brash, party-loving Aries like me is no match for a cunning Capricorn. They will outsmart and outplay an Aries any day of the week. Because while an Aries is busy getting mad or happy, expounding on the good of nature and humanity to anyone who will listen, a Capricorn is busy in the back room, collecting the spoils. I'll be perfectly honest—I am scared of them.

Yes, the goat is a good image for understanding Capricorns, because of their steadfastness and ability to withstand anything. A Capricorn will hang on for dear life to the rocky bluff, if that's the only way to ensure they will see another day. Capricorns are never afraid to get in there and do the work. In fact, doing the work is what motivates them the most. They tend to be total workaholics and leaders in their professions. (They are cardinal signs, after all.) When there is something to be done and it means enduring pain to do it, they will do it with a profound sense of happiness. There is a truly masochistic streak in every Capricorn.

Another animal I like to think of when I think of a Capricorn is a peacock. A peacock is obviously gorgeous and no matter what it does it looks luxurious and fancy, just by the natural rich essence of its feathers. In practice it's a relatively kind animal; many people have peacocks as pets. While it may not be entirely fair to the birds to live with humans, it seems like a rather harmonious partnership. There is a church near my apartment that houses a few peacocks, and when the weather is nice, they run around and come up sweetly to adults and children alike to say hi in their bird-like way. They are stunning, strong animals and everyone wants them around. Of course the church takes care of them; throughout time, people have thought of peacocks as holy. Still, as appealing as these particular peacocks are, they are shy and rather reserved. They walk up to everyone graciously but cautiously. They have a sense of social order and don't want to cause a fuss. Like peacocks, Capricorns hold court through social sublimation.

But it's the feathers that most make me think peacocks are like Capricorns. When they thrust those feathers up in a ring around them, it is likely an evolutionary instinct to ward off a predator. After all, what animal hunting them wouldn't be a little put off by all those shimmering eyes coming at them, appearing to peer into the soul and eat them. This instinct is actually a little sad— the beauty of the feathers is tied so completely to the peacock's survival. The feathers ward off any creature that may think the peacock isn't looking. A Capricorn is always looking at you, with a hundred eyes. And while it can be hard to find the real ones, you must know that they're peering at you warily. They want to know you, and they desperately want you to know them. If you stick around long enough, they will do everything in their power to make sure that they will know you truly, for an eternity or more. Every Capricorn goat-peacock is in it for the long haul.

Capricorn as a lover

Capricorns generally are interested in lots of people sexually and will likely be attracted to physical beauty first and foremost. This is not to say that they are in fact superficial, or that what any particular Capricorn finds superficially attractive is a classic look, by any means. But like their earth sign sisters Virgo and Taurus, they tend to connect love with the way physical beauty makes them feel versus the way they feel about a particular person. It's a distinction that can be hard for people other than Capricorns, or other earth signs, to completely understand, which is why, when it comes to love and sexual attraction, Capricorns tend to gravitate toward coupling with other Capricorns. They can be very happy together in the long term.

Capricorns do also get along splendidly with Virgos and Tauruses, and they will look to Scorpios to be their lifelong soulmates. When Pisces start going inward to write their strange music, Capricorn will jump right in there with them. They will be fiercely attracted to Aries, but it will be a horrible match. Ditto with Leos, except they won't be as attracted to them. Geminis will be their playthings and Geminis will be okay with that. What starts off as friendship with a Sagittarius may turn into something meaningful—that is, until Capricorn cheats or Sagittarius runs away. Cancer will be the very thing they've been looking for, and they will want it to last a lifetime. Capricorns may be impressed by an Aquarius or a Libra, but once they start seeing the bill, that impression will quickly turn negative.

In love, as in all arenas, Capricorns value status. That is to say, they like to have a person on their arm who makes them feel proud. If you are their main squeeze, they will love to show you off and parade you around as their #1 (even if #2–#99 are somewhere in the wings). If they love you, they will love to shower you with everything money can buy. Depending on the specific budget of any specific Capricorn, this could mean different things, of course, but generally speaking, all Capricorns like to take their special someone out to dinner at least once a week to a very fancy restaurant (again, everything is relative, depending on their budget). Although people accuse Capricorns of being cheap, they are quite the opposite when it comes to spoiling a soulmate. Part of the reason is that they see a relationship as an endless stage of courting.

They will want to make sure that they entice their partner forever and that no one will come in to steal them away.

Capricorns absolutely love to be obsessed with someone and will thrive in endless and unrequited crushes. If through sheer willpower or whatever stroke of luck the Capricorn turns one of these crushes into a real relationship, the Capricorn will hold this person in the same ultimate reverence that they held them in before they belonged to them. They will see them as a rare and valuable jewel and will do everything in their power to make sure that they keep them as their own. If that means selling their friends, or even their own mother, up the river, well then so be it. They will do all of this and more in a heartbeat, if it means they can keep their prized lover as their one and only forever.

Like other earth signs and some water signs, Capricorns are pretty possessive when they are into someone, and also extremely controlling. When a Capricorn sees you as theirs, that's exactly the only role you are allowed to play. I once slept over at a Capricorn's apartment, and before we turned off the lights to go to sleep, I explained I'd probably be getting up early to go running, maybe around 5:45 a.m. Well, that majestic peacock looked at me like I had just both lost my mind and asked them to murder my cat, all in one sentence. "I don't get up until about 1:00 p.m.," they said incredulously, "so we can just get up then and I'll make you some delicious biscuits for breakfast." It sounds kind of nice right about now because I am feeling a little hungry, but for anyone who knows an Aries and their fear of being trapped, I don't have to tell you how that scenario played out in that moment. Let's just say that it ended with me leaving in a fiery huff about twenty seconds later, never to talk to that Capricorn ever again. I'm kind of an idiot, though. I still miss them.

If a Capricorn is in love, sex with them will be about as intense as it comes (sorry/not sorry for that). They will love long, intense foreplay sessions involving oil and candlelight, any sort of fetish anyone can dream up, candied nipples, long johns, and long dildos. They will look their partner deeply in the eye for the duration, which will be exceptionally long, across all measures of time. They will come up with entire scenarios for their partner to play out, usually involving them in some position of power, with their partner cleaning or nursing something, but even in the midst of what some might consider some fucked-up shit, their touch through every part of it will be gentle and loving. Scorpio gets all of the credit for being the sex sign, but the sex act itself was made for Capricorns.

If you want to make sure a Capricorn is ready for an all-night sex marathon, the best way to get things going is for you to concentrate your attention on their knees and legs. Just as Capricorns are a pretty complicated sign, so too are knees incredibly complex parts of the body, allowing a person to walk and exist in the world. Knees are intricate structures, and as anyone with a knee injury knows, when a little part is out of whack, the whole system shuts down. So you must give their knees the same amount of respect that you'd show a Capricorn out of the bedroom. If you want your Capricorn to fall all over you, then massage their knees with some cedar oil and lick and kiss their calves all over. Your Capricorn will be enthralled seeing you down there and will want to reciprocate big-time, trust me.

Don't ever expect Capricorns to keep what you do in the bedroom a secret. Capricorns love to kiss and tell. When discussing their sex lives with their friends, they will reveal how hot their partner is, how "wild" they are in the sack, and how their partnership is building continuously in monumental ways. This is all of course the narrative if the relationship is going strong, as they love to put a positive face on their love goings-on and they like people to know how happy and content they are. If they are not feeling positive about their mate, however, you can be sure that their friends will hear about that, too, in full and over-the-top detail. They will not be giving or, shall we say, generous in these types of situations, and will use a biting tone to describe their lovers. I am sorry to say that in situations where they have judged a love partner to be not up to their standards, on whatever dimension they are measuring them, they can be quite mean.

I am sorry to also say that if you are with a Capricorn in a committed relationship, and you are wondering if they are being faithful, the chances are good that they are probably cheating on you. That is not to say that Capricorns can't be incredibly loyal lovers and extremely honest and true if they truly love someone. But a Capricorn's lustful drive is something that often cannot be contained well, and they also don't think the laws of cheating apply to them. And if you aren't putting in the several hours a day it takes to keep them happy, your Capricorn may be putting it in elsewhere, so to speak.

Capricorn as a friend

Capricorns are exceptionally abiding friends and will be there for the people who mean the most to them, especially in moments of emotional distress. I once had a Capricorn best friend I could call at all hours of the day and night about absolutely anything that was bothering me or even just vaguely on my mind, and they always were ready to listen. I loved the attention and I loved the feeling that my feelings mattered to someone. My Capricorn's quick mind and astute understanding of people was intoxicating. I felt truly safe while this dear Capricorn was in my orbit, and although we had a rather dramatic friend breakup eventually (again, Aries-Capricorn is not the best match always), I am hard-pressed to think of another friend since who is capable of giving me such solace and comfort.

Capricorn friends are pretty exciting. Because of their fondness for status and riches, they always seem to know about good parties. And despite their reputation for being in bed by 5:30 p.m., Capricorns actually like to stay up late, having an amazing time wherever they are. They love food, especially good food, and there is very little they like better than sitting in a cozy party setting, under a luxurious fuzzy blanket (do they call it a throw nowadays?), drinking someone else's fancy cocktails. Or make that whiskey, a deep amber color, a really expensive variety, that they can drink straight out of an old-fashioned glass while they tell hilarious stories that are at least 45 percent pure lies. Capricorns love to spin a yarn and excel at concocting fantastical fictions that have very little basis in truth, especially because they love the reaction these stories get from people. They also love a good dance party, and although you might not find them actually dancing, they will still be part of the action somehow, working some contacts while you shake it in the middle of the floor, making you feel in that second that maybe all of your struggles are worth it. After all, who is this fabulous friend that you have somehow attached yourself to?

The one thing Capricorns are not known for is swallowing any sort of slight or tension/conflict that you might have in your friendship. You won't get too far with a Capricorn by pretending everything is cool if they think that it isn't. I once had a sort of Capricorn acquaintance and I got busy for a while, all Aries-style, and forgot to call her to check in. Well, after a few weeks in which I was happily dating some silly Gemini, she was desperately seething on her own, wondering what dramatic event had happened between us to make me act this way. Of course, when she approached me to "talk about it," I had no idea what the heck she was referring to, as I liked her as much as I always had. We shared some awkward exchanges and I am sad to say that I never really spoke to her again.

I have spent a long time painting this picture of a Capricorn as an independent, strong star who will do anything to both survive and win. They are this, but they are very sensitive, too. Like all earth signs, they are secretly deeply emotional and will need a lot of hand-holding at times, and will demand this of their friends. They definitely love long conversations that go on a lifetime about every thought each of you has ever had, and if you are close to them, they will want this about every minute of every day. Despite their buttoned-up independence, Capricorns really just want to be placidly happy, and they look to time with their friends to achieve this sort of contentedness.

Capricorn friends can be a lot of work, but they are worth it.

Capricorn style

Like their earth sign sisters, Capricorns can get a bad reputation for being happy about a boring dress code. I've known quite a few

Capricorns to go gaga over some rich eggplant tones, and you can often spot a Capricorn dressed in head-to-toe soupy browns and olive Frog and Toad greens. Yes, it's true that Capricorns do like clothes that resemble the earth, and there are extra points if the clothes have a sort of hippie vibe to them and are embroidered with strange circles and patterns that usually mean nothing. Capricorns also really love hats, and if you gift them one, they will keep it forever, thoughtfully wearing it whenever they see you, and remarking on what a considerate gift it was twenty-five years ago.

Capricorns like to be very comfortable and will choose a style of dress that allows them lots of breathing room. They will wear flowy concoctions whenever possible, ones that also somehow make them look sexy. If they have some assets, they will show those off proudly and aren't shy about exuding some good old-fashioned sex appeal. While aiming for extreme comfort, they will have their clothes be a little tight in all the right places and will be kind of whatever when things start just hanging out as the night gets a little long or their work shift is excessive. They love bodies and they love their bodies. Everything alive is blissful to a Capricorn.

Two common clichés about Capricorns are that they are stingy and that they are somewhat corporate in both dress and behavior. In many ways this can be true, as most Capricorns detest wasting money. So if they can get good-quality clothes cheaply, they'd be silly not to. But even though the corporate image is not altogether off the mark, it's also just not the full picture. In many ways, a sign like Aquarius, with all of their weirdness, can exude a corporate vibe, as they will tend to pick clothes that make them feel like they "fit in," because they don't want to get too much attention, lest everyone find out how weird they truly are. But I've known plenty of Capricorns who are fantastically into glitter everywhere, or obsessively wear enormous rhinestone pins. If it's fake and loud, Capricorns tend to love it. Just think of Dolly. It's hard to find a Capricorn who doesn't like a few (or a lot of) items in leopard print. So something that looks like a big cat was just sacrificed at an altar is another safe gift bet for them. It had better be actually fake, though. Many Capricorns are deeply passionate about animal rights.

Texting with a Capricorn

Capricorns, although sometimes sluggish and slow to adopt new things, will always be all over methods of communication that relate to personal connections and commerce. Since in our time texting is a means of quick communication and building up of close contacts, Capricorns love texting. They will text you like nobody's business, because most of the time it is actually in their business's best interest to be in contact with you.

If you are trying to text them to set up a date, their response if they are interested will be quick and to the point. They are of course not nervous at all about making the first texting move, and if you meet and suggest that you should meet up again, whether for something romantic or otherwise, you'd better be serious in your intention, because a Capricorn will text you right there to make sure you have their correct phone number. They will also follow up and make sure that this date or business meeting happens within a reasonable time frame. All of this will be very easy for them. Just remember, they are Capricorns. This is what they do.

If you are a love interest, they will text you compulsively and send you all sorts of nude pics. You'd better have their texts on hidden unless you want everyone you work with to see their entire anatomy, because if they are trying to entice you to remember them (even though you just saw them two hours ago), the full-on display will be on full display. They will check in with you to see how you are feeling every fifteen seconds, and if you want to go someplace later with them they will inquire quite a few times to gauge your minute-by-minute feelings on the matter. Again, if they like you, and especially if they like you a lot, they are the exact opposite of retiring.

Once you get into a regular texting routine with them, they will keep up an emotional rapport with you by text and will provide soothing words and a general cheerleader attitude to you throughout your time away from them. This goes for friend texting, lover texting, and, hell, even business texting. They truly are loyal and caring people (don't listen to all of the other stuff I said earlier), and they will shower you with love by text whenever they can. They will be exceptionally sweet when you are down and need a little love. If you are important to them, they love to show you how important you are, and they will always get right back to you if you are asking for their attention. They know how to be there for you when your spirit needs them, and in this modern age, despite how awful this is to admit, we tend to need each other to be there through texting. A Capricorn understands this reality intrinsically and profoundly.

Like anything else with them, if a Capricorn is very mad at you or perceives you as being unimportant to their life or, worse yet, their career, then all of these principles might not apply. Because if you aren't worth their time in any of these areas, they definitely won't take the time to give you a simple yes or no as to whether they plan to show up at your party tomorrow. If they do show up, it will be very late, and they will probably just be coming for the free food. Still, count yourself lucky, because even as they hide a few dinner rolls in their satchel, they will be bringing the glamour there for you. Take a picture of them at your soirée and of course post it somewhere. Always take a page out of their reference book: it's good for business.

Capricorn: Thanks a lot.
Aries: For what???
Capricorn: You know.
Aries: No I don't?????

Capricorn: You are so elegant
Taurus: You are so elegant
Capricorn: I have oil
Taurus: I thought you'd never ask

Capricorn: I found a book you might like.
Gemini: I've probably already read it.
Capricorn: I doubt it. This is a very obscure text.
Gemini: I've read every book ever written.

Capricorn: I really liked meeting you today
Cancer: Haven't we met before
Capricorn: I don't think so?
Cancer: You don't remember

Capricorn: Do you like the stars?
Leo: Do you mean astrology?
Capricorn: No
Leo: Like Hollywood?

Capricorn: I think you like me
Virgo: I do
Capricorn: Want to come over
Virgo: No

Capricorn: I can talk but only for an hour
Libra: Never mind then! You don't care
Capricorn: No, I do care
Libra: Why would you limit my time then?

Capricorn: If I get my pilot's license, will you fly with me?
Scorpio: Don't get it
Capricorn: Why?
Scorpio: Why would you?

Capricorn: Are you free tomorrow?
Sagittarius: [no response]
Capricorn: Are you free tomorrow?
Sagittarius: Maybe

Capricorn #1: How many bank accounts do you have?
Capricorn #2: 3
Capricorn #1: I have 5
Capricorn #2: Stop flirting

Capricorn: Do you believe in fate?
Aquarius: No
Capricorn: Why?
Aquarius: Stop writing me

Capricorn: You are simply the concept of eternity
Pisces: I am in the present
Capricorn: An eternal ice cube
Pisces: I'm married

The Capricorn imagination

If a Capricorn were a city, it would be Chicago, with its high winds
and cold winters and bustling scene and general sense of bursting
life. Chicago with its big steel skyline, with towers that can with-
stand it all. If Capricorn were a season it would be winter itself, as
nothing grows as beautifully as when it has been through the hard-
ship of cold and formed itself out of earth and rain. If Capricorn
were a type of utterance it would be the kind you make when you
are dumbstruck in love and still trying to keep it together. Perhaps
you really can't, but you will try and try. If Capricorn were a type
of handshake it would be the kind that involves looking the other
person dead in the eye (emphasis on dead) and also kind of turns
into a hug. If Capricorn were an insect, it would be a spider, with
its eight legs that make it stable on any surface and its delectable
ability to convince anyone to come into its place of worship. If
Capricorn were a time of day it might be 11:00 p.m., right at the
moment when you think you don't have enough time, but then you

are cleansed in the notion of midnight and the new day, but it isn't the new day yet, it's still only a possibility. If Capricorn were a number, it would be 20, 10 doubled, with a table set exactly for two. If Capricorn were a type of bread it would be a dinner roll and it would be so buttery you could set your heart on fire with the opposite of buttery hate. If Capricorn were a sign-off it would be "Warmly," except unlike everyone else who uses the word, the Capricorn really would mean it when they wrote it.

The key to understanding Capricorn is to think about the idea of a king. This is not to gender Capricorn in any way—we can use "king" and "queen" interchangeably—but to suggest that Capricorns always engage with an air of royalty, and with a sense of loyalty to one's own cause. Kings hold their own no matter where they are and will attract a group of people around them to listen to their every word. Even the least famous Capricorns will act like they own the place and will expect everyone to realize that they do. Also kings (generally) love attention and will demand it when they aren't getting it. The head of the whole thing is almost always a Capricorn.

The best way to think of a Capricorn is to think of the earth from whose riches they rule. Just as the earth is endlessly rich with possibility, so too is the Capricorn endlessly rich with the possible things it can create. Its soil is the greatest gold and past any idea of what one could commodify from it. Every Capricorn has a sense of the wealth of the lands and waters of the planet and the immense goodness they hold. In a time when we need to revise our respect for our earth in order to combat the ravages of human-induced climate change (among other things), we need Capricorns.

A Capricorn is like a magical forest where every creature that has ever lived or died goes to be itself. In the magical forest of Capricorn, the ponds and tadpoles are lined with gold glitter and the rocks shine with a bright blue biological lacquer. The land of Capricorn is a land of trees, marsh, and soot, and it is a kind land, womblike and bursting with dark red possibilities that lie fallow.

The Famous Capricorn

Fame was made for Capricorns. The trappings, the riches and the luxuries, everyone knowing your name, never having to explain who you are and what you do—all Capricorns love that. Because, as they might say, if you work hard, why shouldn't you be famous? Fame is the drug Capricorn longs for. They can drink cupfuls of it and still not get drunk off of it. No one is happier than a Capricorn about being famous.

I have long been obsessed with Dr. Martin Luther King Jr. He is truly my idol, and when our world seems like it is spinning out of control with hate, I reread his writings and feel better. I thank the universe for him every day. I think I first got obsessed with him when I taught his work in Introductory Writing classes to college students; it is often on the syllabus. In graduate school I had a friend and mentor, an amazing arts educator named Dr. Marit Dewhurst (also a Capricorn), who is also absolutely obsessed with Dr. King. In fact, to this day, on his birthday, she mails out postcards with some of his best quotations to her friends and colleagues, just to remind us all what real hope feels like. I hope one day she will take the practice mainstream and make a mass mailing of all of these cards. Our world today certainly could use it.

Dr. King was a fantastic rhetorician, obviously, one of our American best, and his ability to manipulate an audience is a very Famous Capricorn skill. It is said that all Capricorns have silver tongues, and this just is the truth. One of my favorite pieces by Dr. King is "Letter from a Birmingham Jail." I love its relentless quality and its ability to suggest a world where hate is impossible, because all humans are seen through a lens of equality and love. One of my favorite parts of the letter is almost an aside, stated at the beginning. Dr. King writes:

> While confined here in the Birmingham city jail, I came across your recent statement calling my present activities "unwise and untimely." Seldom do I pause to answer criticism of my work and ideas. If I sought to answer all the criticisms that cross my desk, my secretaries would have little time for anything other than such correspondence in the course of the day, and I would have no time for constructive work. But since I feel that you are men of genuine good will and that your criticisms are sincerely set forth, I want to try to answer your statements in what I hope will be patient and reasonable terms.

The best part of this opening statement is of course its generosity to its readers, who are presumably Dr. King's critics. They are fellow clergymen who have asserted that his nonviolent protests are not a good thing, and Dr. King is there to set them straight. He later states: "I cannot sit idly by in Atlanta and not be concerned about what happens in Birmingham. Injustice anywhere is a threat to justice everywhere. We are caught in an inescapable network of mutuality, tied in a single garment of destiny. Whatever affects one directly, affects all indirectly." This is just such a Capricorn sense of the world, this interconnectedness, that every breath of one person is intrinsically connected to the breathing of all of humanity. But of course what makes this letter a masterpiece of a Famous Capricorn is Dr. King's acknowledgment that he "seldom" "pause[s] to answer criticism."

This is such a Capricorn power move. His admission that he gets a lot of criticism feels self-deprecating, but there is so much strength in admitting that. Just as a famous social media account might get a lot of shit-talking in the comments section, Dr. King gets so many critiques because he's so famous and doing something truly important. He's also a person with not just one but "many secretaries." He has a network of power and he's acknowledging the criticisms of his fellow clergymen only because he feels a moral responsibility to do so. It's a classic Famous Capricorn power maneuver, and Dr. King does it effortlessly.

Famous Capricorn poets like to get earthy and use language to best explain what it means to be a living, breathing thing in the universe. Dara Wier is a Famous Capricorn Poetry Goddess who at this point has authored close to twenty books. One of my favorite poems is her "The Pressure of the Moment," which starts off: "The pressure of the moment can cause someone to kill someone or something." It goes on:

> But if my house is on fire and you notice, I wish you would kill
> That fire. But if my hair is on fire, while I'm sure you'll be enjoying
> The spectacle of it, act quickly or don't act at all.

We can see the essence of Famous Capricorn energy here: What Capricorn doesn't understand a murderous instinct? Everywhere is this desire to "do something," as the poem later states. The persona's hair is on fire, and while the onlooker is probably "enjoying / The spectacle of it," they should really "act quickly" or not bother acting "at all." The poem says never let go, never give up, be a Capricorn and do what the situation requires, and do it well.

Another Famous Capricorn is David Lynch. We can see him exemplifying a Capricorn in his films. He is undoubtedly and undeniably a genius, capturing an American sublime with little fanfare and much obsessive devotion to his art. Most famous for his television series *Twin Peaks*, Lynch was able to get at the heart of what makes living in small-town America so terrifying: the utter banality of it all engulfs one's soul in a profound sense of evil.

Even though Killer Bob (or the devil) in *Twin Peaks* is played by an extremely attractive Scorpio actor, Frank Silva (wish you could call me, baby, from the afterlife), when you see Bob in action you know for sure that he represents the Capricorn essence. He is dogged in his determination to make you feel a sense of doom—not chaotic doom (it's not like getting into a series of pointless arguments/conversations with a Gemini) but something colder and more calculated. When you are in the corner of the pink-lit living room and you see Bob coming at you, he is everything any real poem wants to or should be. He's after you. (Just google "Bob moment and *Twin Peaks*" to see what I mean.) When Bob comes at you with those sexy, murderous eyes, he's a Capricorn through and through.

Something else that David Lynch's work shares with all of the work of Famous Capricorns is that despite how weird and unsettling it seems, there is still an air of conservatism at play. However mystical the scene, it is all about power, the power of language and the surreal being subordinate to the real. Bob behind your bed is horrible, but it is truly scary because the world he suddenly appears in at first seems quotidian. A Famous Capricorn, particularly an artistic one, will maintain a foothold in the real world for as long as possible. The strange ecstasy of the horrific will not be about what is in their imagination but rather about actual possibility, the rich possibilities that every real moment on earth contains. It's the gift that all Famous Capricorns give us freely.

Other Famous Capricorns

1. Muhammad Ali
2. Sade
3. Elvis Presley
4. Michelle Obama
5. Jenny Zhang
6. Richard Nixon
7. Zora Neale Hurston
8. J. D. Salinger
9. Stephen Hawking
10. Sheila Heti

Capricorn playlist

- David Bowie, "Space Oddity"
- Janis Joplin, "Piece of My Heart"

- Sade, "The Sweetest Taboo"
- Francis Poulenc, "The Human Voice"
- Dolly Parton, "Love Is Like a Butterfly"
- Ricky Martin, "Livin' La Vida Loca"
- Aaliyah, "Rock the Boat"
- Annie Lennox, "Money Can't Buy It"
- Marilyn Manson, "The Beautiful People"
- Joan Baez, "Love Is Just a Four-Letter Word"

The Capricorn (a poem)

In the deep deep woods. There is a tiny plant. It doesn't need your water. It doesn't need your shade. It has everything that it needs. It has prayers. I don't remember its name. We were friends once. Oh, but I can't remember its. We used to. Ah yes. The blue. Blue in its entirety. Blue papers in which we wrote the blue words. Moon juices, dripping endlessly from blue vines. But I am frightened of what I will become. The plants will grow. With humor and a sense of hope. They will grow and grow taller than you. And that one plant who you used to know. It will give you shade and bring forth the dark orange fruits. One day it will bend over to hug you and will crush you. No I am frightened of what I have already been. The moon will crush you. You were wrong all along. It's not a tree. It's a rock.

AQUARIUS

January 20–February 18

Truth is always strange,
stranger than fiction.

Lord Byron, born January 22, 1788

The Aquarius

When the official poster for Woodstock surfaced in 1969, the festival billed itself as "An Aquarian Exposition." Go and you would be changed. Stay home and people who went would change things regardless. Although, more than change, the sign of Aquarius has to do with the zeitgeist. The spirit of the times. It also has to do with the future. To be an Aquarius is to be plugged in. Not necessarily in terms of what's happening but what needs to happen. What's lacking in the culture and in the often mythologized "soul" of the collective (what is humanity/why are we here). Think the Summer of Love in 1967, or the mood of the late '60s and early '70s in America—a time when there was an opening in public consciousness and in what people thought was possible. A time for new thought and abrupt departure from ritual. Sparks of this energy have gone off since then—1994, Gen X, Nirvana, the Occupy movement, and all the ways social media has fueled and complicated activism. To be an Aquarius is to question reality. To arrive at change through doubt and disturbance.

It's been said that those born in late January through most of February feel the shape of things to come before others. Not in a psychic manner, but in a "let the bridges I burn light the way" manner. Aquarians have the inclination to be revolutionaries and are naturally intuitive. They are self-starters. That kind of power is difficult to harbor because it doesn't come with a guide. And even if it did, almost every Aquarius is a rebel. Give them a guide and they won't follow it. Tell them there's a dress code and they'll show up wearing nothing at all.

If you've had a conversation with an Aquarius, you know they're bossy and confusing at the same time. They feel like aliens who are fluent in human language. It's difficult to get a read on them (though many Pisces have tried), and it's impossible not to gravitate toward their authoritative nature. Aquarians are ruled by Uranus (the mysterious blue planet associated with discovery, enlightenment, and technology), and they're also ruled by Saturn (the planet closest to the gods and associated with immortality and lasting power).

An Aquarius is typically aloof but secretly sensitive, obsessed with their own eccentricity, and obviously, the stranger in town no matter how long they've lived there. You'll be surprised a person like them can survive in the real world because they're constantly testing it. Aquarius has also been described as the sign of genius and invention, the sign of willpower and one that serves as a reminder to imagine a life closer to the elemental. Or to put it another way, they're basically the hot nerd who went through a punk phase, grunge phase, spiritual phase, goth phase—then came out on the other side rolling their own cigarettes and encouraging everyone to join the community garden. Who wouldn't fuck an Aquarius at least once? Personally, I'm always relieved to find one at the bar, where they always people-watch (even when they're with friends) and wait for someone to be impressed by the fact that they know all the words to Meredith Brooks's "Bitch" (also their karaoke song).

Things you might want to know about Aquarius

Aquarius is a fixed air sign and the eleventh sign of the zodiac. It comes after Capricorn and has inherited their purposeful anger and strong opinions. What they do with that anger is nothing you want to find out about. They can hold a grudge longer than anyone and are the most vicious in a bar fight (or any fight really). Have you ever encountered a drunk Aquarius? They will find a reason to get mad at anyone. Resistance (sometimes just for the sake of resistance) is in their blood. They've also learned an important lesson from Capricorn's rigidity: knowing that pragmatism doesn't always work. In fact, it can leave you stuck and miserable in your own life (shout-out to Capricorns) if you're pragmatic about big things like love and following your true passions. That's why it's safe to say Aquarians fall somewhere closer to dreamer than rationalist.

In the sky, Aquarius is the water bearer, pouring water from an urn. Since they come so late in the zodiac, they've established a belief system that's centered around realism and invention. The two can sometimes work against each other, but this is also what makes Aquarians so resourceful. They don't panic when their environment doesn't give them what they need to thrive. They don't suffer through it either. They're the people who use spit instead of lube, and a cigarette to light a fire. They're basically Shakira in the "Whenever, Wherever" video—rising from the ocean, twerking with horses in the desert, crawling through mud and somehow ending up on a mountaintop wearing nothing more than a crop top in winter. All while being very coy and demanding (I feel like this is a permanent Aquarius mood).

If you watch that video, you'll notice there's no one else in the world but Shakira. It's like she's the only one who survived the apocalypse. Shakira and horses. The horses are every ex an Aquarius has ever had and they're running toward her while also running away from her. If you've ever dated an Aquarius, you know it feels something like that. But their contrarian nature is sexy. It definitely turns me on to argue with one. And they make other people you've slept with seem boring and unambitious. There's something indescribable about the way an Aquarius looks at you. Like they're judging you while also actually seeing you for the first time.

If you earn the trust of an Aquarius, it's truly more impressive than surviving an FBI investigation. Their temperament is cool and discerning. They're a lot like academics—consulting with a variety of sources (a.k.a. people they talk shit with) and doing plenty of research (a.k.a. mildly stalking you) before revealing anything about themselves or making their mind up about you. This can be alarming. At times they can feel clinical and severe. It doesn't help that they're blunt (a lot like a Sagittarius) whenever they do choose to speak. In this illogical world of ours, I'd say these qualities actually make them real friends. An Aquarius has no time for bullshit. And unlike a fire sign, they won't demonstrate that by making a scene or some polemical statement that makes people uncomfortable. They'll simply bounce, cut people out, and treat you to their greatest weapon: Aquarian silence. It wins for them. It saves them a lot of time.

Aquarius as a lover

It's easy to become infatuated with an Aquarius because they tell you little about themselves willingly. The entire time you're with them feels like studying with the hot calculus nerd in your class who doesn't know they're hot but vaguely knows you have a crush on them and still tries to talk to you about calculus anyway. It's maddening. And really sexy. Not exactly intentional on their part, but it does go with their brand of being odd. Talk to their therapist and they'll be as perplexed as you are. They'll tell you how they know their office plant better than the Aquarian in question. But the good news is that their therapist isn't the one fucking them. You are. A little bit of mystery goes a long way. So many water signs have ruined lives by over-communicating. Just as many fire signs have ruined relationships by "telling it like it is." Be grateful for how detached Aquarians are outside the bedroom. It makes them intimate and carnal in bed. A place where, thankfully, you don't need to use words.

Not everyone will find Aquarian mystery to be a turn-on. Capricorns and Virgos won't. They need clarity. They're too boring for an Aquarius, and come with too many rules. Pisces and Cancer will overwhelm an Aquarius emotionally. And a Scorpio is a good creative and friendship match, meaning there'll be lots of deep conversation, but mostly, they'll disagree on important things. This kind of friction works for some couples and not others. Sagittarius, Gemini, Libra, and Aries are all going to keep an Aquarian's interest. These are signs that know what to do with a difficult and withholding person. They're also fairly extroverted (depends on the Libra) and can break through that. Leos, I'm sorry, but your pageantry reads as desperate to an Aquarius. It won't last.

The erogenous zones for Aquarians are their calves and ankles. Use restraints there and also aim for them when you 69. Aquarians can be spacey during sex, making it hard to tell what they like and what they don't. This can lead you to believe they aren't kinky, but that's a lie. They're kinky in a quiet way. You'll have to be the one who takes charge and gets into some ankle play. My one Aquarius boyfriend really liked hate sex (which normal people would call makeup sex). For whatever reason, he got so turned on by being mad at me. And that turned me on too, because as a Sagittarius, it gave me more permission to be a bitch. It didn't last, because we got into a huge fight one night in California around a fire he was trying to build and I almost pushed him in it. Unfortunately, I don't have great aim, so he lived.

Aquarians have awkward body language. Sometimes I think they're playing charades with themselves. They're not Libras. Grace won't be how they capture your heart. Though their idiosyncratic jokes will charm you. The obscure facts they've memorized about the world will make you feel glad you're alive. If they were anyone in a romantic comedy, it'd be the slightly spacey but empathetic friend who's so obviously an old soul, you realize you've been in love with them from the beginning. And Aquarians are capable of a deep, electric love. You'll rarely hear them talk about it, but secretly they're looking. It's almost like the way we never see the wind, although we know it's there. It moves the sea. It goes right through the trees. That's what it feels like in the first months with an Aquarius. The strangeness of it can be perplexing. You'll ask friends to read the messages they send you, to look at photos where their mysticism glimmers and then disappears. Are they into you? Do they want to see you again? They won't be direct about it. They'll rarely answer personal questions with the carelessness and freedom of other air signs (Geminis, for example).

Love and obsession are things an Aquarius processes through the intellect. Remember that at their core they are cerebral creatures. And being cerebral isn't exactly exciting when it comes to love. It can be read as playing hard to get or being disinterested. If you're in love with an Aquarius (or trying to make one fall in love with you), this initial stage of coolness must be survived. They aren't performing. They don't mean to seem apathetic. Just know that every little pathway in their mind is exploding, short-circuiting, rewiring, and their instinct is to analyze as opposed to feel. Their instinct is also to step back and see what you do first.

The ideal romance for an Aquarius is difficult to live up to. It's like their view of the world: hard to reconcile with reality. They want to be in charge and have everyone live as freely as possible at the same time. It's no wonder there've been five Aquarius presidents.

Aquarians in love are bossy when you get past the cool and abstract phase. When you finally know they're into you, they will start telling you what to do. They like to ask a lot of questions, which is also how they disguise their judgment and how they give commands. No Virgo schedules or Scorpio spying here. It's more big picture than that. They'll ask you why you have the job you do, if you're happy, if this is how you imagined your life would turn out, if next Saturday you'd like to go to the moon with them. Lofty questions that are a bit terrifying. Questions that lead to more questions.

Knowledge is a real turn-on for Aquarians. Both the personal kind (acquired through everyday intimacy) and the kind that deeply engages the intellect. If you want to impress them on a date, take them to some eccentric dance performance or experimental theater. They may not even like it, but that's not important. They love to know about everything, especially things outside their element. Aquarians are curious partners. What excites them is seeing their curiosity matched. If you're someone who can surprise them, you have a future together. And the future is where they truly come alive. They're fiercely independent. Clinging to them will only drive them away, but giving them too much space may depress them. They won't ever ask for your attention out of pride. The Aquarian psyche is a real balancing act, like trying to keep an orchid alive.

Not putting all their cards on the table is an Aquarius move. Or rather, they'll set them out but you'll still need to interpret them. They aren't the most transparent lovers. Once I dated an Aquarius who went on a three-day camping trip without telling anyone. By the end of it, I thought he was dead. I had called his phone sixty-seven times. "You called me 67 times" was the first text he sent me after. No explanation, no real alarm, just that statement. Then he proceeded to defend himself and point to an earlier message I should have understood as him asking for space. It was clear he didn't do it out of spite. But he also found it unbelievable that not everyone understood his coded way of communicating. I really wasn't in the mood for a relationship that felt like the *Times* crossword puzzle every week. But it definitely kept me on my toes, so if a temporary disappearing act does turn you on, try an Aquarius.

Aquarius as a friend

If they had to fill a bar, they'd fill it twice. Aquarians seem to know everyone and they're the type of person who needs a lot of friends. Being around people is more restorative for them than being alone. Think of them as anthropologists: constantly observing, fascinated and open, more interested in truth than judgment. They thrive when in a group. They don't need to be lauded either. Given that they believe so staunchly in individualism, the collective holds an important place in their lives. It's what motivates them to pursue their ambitions. Without their friends, they'd go off the rails by being too radical.

The downside to an Aquarian's very social inclinations is that it makes them difficult to get close to. Many people in their world are acquaintances. There's a real magnetic pull toward an Aquarius. We're all drawn to someone who respects, almost fetishizes, individuality. And allowing the individual to be an individual—living freely and without limits—is a core Aquarius principle. It's what they most respect in their friends: their ability to remain themselves even when it's unpopular. That's also why Aquarians are very selective with compliments and praise. They're astute people. They won't say what they don't mean. If I had to count the number of times an Aquarius has complimented me, I wouldn't get past three or four. But they were the type of compliments worth hearing because they were true.

The same way a Taurus takes their time with romance, an Aquarius takes their time with trust. At times being their friend can feel like having a second therapist. They'll listen. They'll ask questions. They'll aspire to know everything about your life, but you'll get a sense that they're withholding what they really think. Aquarians aren't the sign to freely seek advice. If they come to you with a problem, you can be sure they've turned it over in their heads for many months. Their reservoir of personal strength is vast. And while they're dependable, they don't like to talk about their problems because they truly believe they can solve them alone, which they do. We all know every Aquarius is more magician than mortal, more witch than anything else.

The danger to an Aquarius and their four hundred and one friends is that they also have the urge to isolate themselves. It's always like this with anyone who thrives on people. Like how it is with comedians, too. In order to perform the joke you have to have survived the joke. And when the audience leaves, when everyone goes home, you're no longer a comedian. You're someone trying to live alone in a room, just like everyone else. This is what Aquarians are scared of.

The reasons why an Aquarius oscillates between social immersion and isolation is because they're universalists. They either want to be with all people or they want to be with everything that isn't people—the sky, the sea, that one glow-in-the-dark star they've kept on their ceiling. Hope and possibility are things they deeply value. And they find both of these in extremes. Coming after Sagittarius on the karmic wheel, an Aquarius has already learned to privilege freedom. That freedom is mixed with a stern practicality, the lessons Aquarius has learned from Capricorn. To have an Aquarius friend, then, is to know they will resolutely pull you toward the new, toward a yet-to-be-imagined place. Just make sure to pull them out of their rooms when they get a little too heady and pensive.

Aquarius style

Aquarians are loud dressers. They're the person in your friend group who you'll say "Only you can pull that off" to. That's because they don't have many inhibitions when it comes to style. They'll mismatch, wear suede in the rain, leather on the hottest day, and almost nothing in the dead of winter. They follow their own compass and typically stay away from darker colors. Of course, if you point that out to them, they'll show up looking like they're ready to go to a death metal show. I once knew an Aquarius who wore two different sneakers to class. His shoelaces were metallic blue and he drew constellations on his Converse.

Comfort means a lot to an Aquarius. The more comfortable they feel, the closer they are to being free. I don't want to imply that a lot of Aquarians dress like stoners, but a lot of Aquarians dress like stoners. And skaters. And failed actors auditioning for B-level films. Ripped white tees, light-wash denim, vaguely gay-looking running shoes. Aquarians also love capes, crop tops, and shirts they got when they were volunteering for some cause they're really into. Like the environment or fund-raising for some bad band's punk EP.

An important thing to mention is that Aquarians aren't materialists. Their closets aren't sacred to them. They're also not really a place they spend time thinking about. If they get to be overwhelming, they'll give a lot of what they have away. They don't have a problem doing that. It goes with their sensibility of being in the moment. If they're really into wearing acid-wash cutoffs one summer, don't assume they will be the next. They like to change things up, but not in a premeditated way (like a Leo, for example, who thrives on shock value).

There's definitely a glamorous side to Aquarians (stoner aesthetics aside), though it tends to be a little on the weird side, like everything else about them. Don't be freaked out if they show up to your wedding looking like they've come from a rave, or are somehow wearing a shower curtain as an actual garment. For them glamour translates to being experimental. The more esoteric it is, the more value it has. Don't forget that when shopping for an Aquarius. Always go for something that's a little mystical and visually perplexing, like a shawl that's actually a dress that's actually a field of flowers.

Texting with an Aquarius

I'm never really sure what Aquarians are saying. They use words, I guess, but those words require their own translation. Getting a text from an Aquarius is like talking to someone drunk at a wedding. It's either really short and emotionally shocking, or longer than you anticipated and saying something about something else that has nothing to do with the something you were talking about to begin with. What I find even more curious is that you can respond entirely off topic also, and they will go along with it. As if their phones were tapped and all texting were in code, except no one agreed on what the code is. Given all this, Aquarians are actually quite good at making plans and following through. You just might have to text in Middle English or French, and maybe bark, too. Here are some classics.

Aquarius sext

Aquarius: hey wanna come to this bar called my bedroom
You: oh um . . .
Aquarius: the stars remind me of the way you do your hair in winter surrounded by dead trees

Aquarius check-in

You: hey what's up, how's everything?
Aquarius: Just thinking about how King Lear is basically modern life. Also how Crystal Pepsi was a thing in the 90s. [taco emoji]

Aquarius making plans

Aquarius: Can't wait to see you at 7:47 tomorrow night by that sculpture we both like!
You: Oh! Yeah . . .

Aquarius nostalgia

Aquarius: I just miss how everything was in the beginning.

You: What beginning?

Aquarius: You know, like the beginning of time . . .

Aquarius anger

You: Are you mad about something or . . . ?

Aquarius:

You: Okay, we don't have to talk about it.

Aquarius: If we wanted to talk about it and if I was mad, we should pick the right place where we could, you know, talk about it. Should we go see a movie?

Aquarius sadness

Aquarius: Do you ever think about all the places where it's raining right now?

You: But it's not raining right now.

Aquarius: I know but somewhere it is.

Aquarius happiness

You: So I'll see you later?

Aquarius: Yeah. Bring whoever you want! I've invited some people I know from college, high school, kindergarten and the hospital where I was born!

The Aquarius imagination

If an Aquarius were a city they'd be Tokyo—because of all the neon in daylight. If they were part of a book they'd be a footnote. Specific. Nerdy. Needing context. Type of weather: hail. Karaoke song: a disco version of Sheryl Crow's "All I Wanna Do." Cooking utensil: grater. Time of day: just before dawn. Item of clothing: a pair of hologram tights. And of course if they were a vegetable they'd be a blue potato, and a pomegranate if they were a fruit.

I feel lucky to know Aquarius people. They're the right ones to cut your bangs, rearrange your furniture, give you crystals to sleep with under your pillow. If you smoke weed with an Aquarius, you're one step closer to enlightenment. If you skydive with them, you'll see how serious they are about the sky. They think about the sky the way other people think about money. They know the afterlife is somewhere to the left, not up.

"Style" is a word we use often. Walt Whitman wrote, "The greatest poet has less a marked style and is more . . . the free channel of himself." Style is being free of style. Style is accumulation also. Actually, it's what we do with accumulation, with all the things we choose and all the things we don't and whose absence we must also live with. No one knows this better than an Aquarius. They are that free channel of themselves. For them, style is a sea. The sea is cold. Sometimes the sea is greener than blue, and often it's black, like the night. But *sea* always equates to *style*, because the sea knows how to change in order to stay the same. What couldn't we imagine if we let the sea be a sea, allowing it to move us along without trying to build an outpost of safety along its banks? This is what an Aquarius is always trying to find out.

Once I went shopping for underwear with an Aquarius. It was actually his idea. I was sort of in a rut and really going through it. So this Aquarius suggested buying all-new underwear. If I changed that, he said, everything else would follow. So I listened to him (there was something convincing about this) and let him pick out my underwear, which, by the way, I wouldn't even do with the person I'm sleeping with. I came home with crazy shades of Calvin Klein boxer briefs. One of them was neon pink and another electric blue. Since my bed is all white, the colors somehow stained my sheets. There was a big electric blue mark in the middle of my bed. I was livid. I texted the Aquarius and told him it was a terrible idea. "Wait," he said. "It's exactly what should happen. Throw out the sheets, too, don't sleep in white anymore. Sleep in gold." I was upset. Where would I find gold sheets? I ordered them online, I slept in them, a week later nothing was different. The mark was now neon pink on gold. I, a Sagittarius who always wears black and sleeps in white, felt entirely out of sorts. Then one Friday, drinking coffee in my new gold sheets, I got a phone call that my second book of poems had been taken by a publisher. The first person I texted was the Aquarius. He said, "Yes, of course. Electric blue is new style. Neon pink is vigor. And gold—gold is what you get when you change something, when you stop living life the same way you used to live. All you have to do is change," he said. Even the smallest things can cause a major shift.

I tell this story not because it's unforgettable for me (which it is, in some ways), but also because Aquarians, as principled as they are, leave a door open for magic—maybe even all the windows.

They won't refer to it as magic. Ritual. Superstition. Aura. Vibe. Whatever they choose to call it. Being more than capable of living in the real world, they won't talk about all the little spells that make their life work. But they're there. And if they see you need them, they'll make sure to tell you, too. They'll make them available to you in the early mornings when you're struggling. In the Aquarian imagination everyone is their sibling. Everyone is tied to them somehow.

The Famous Aquarius

Before the Summer of Love and before the sexual revolution, there was James Dean in *Rebel Without a Cause*. Blue jeans, white shirt, red jacket. Smoking a cigarette out back with the car already running, not exactly sure where he would go. Dean was a classic Aquarius, and he more or less played one in that movie. The Aquarian spirit is often associated with the '60s and the hippie generation. It strives for a utopia that requires dropping out of everyday life and overturning the machines of capital. There's also a danger in (and an allure to) being an Aquarius. Dean himself died in his race car (a Porsche he'd nicknamed Little Bastard) at the age of twenty-four, crashing into another car at an intersection in California. He had a passion for racing. He hated talking to the press. And in his short-lived stardom, he already had a reputation for being aloof, mystical, and somewhat impersonal. Someone who was an outsider, yet most at home surrounded by regular people, not Hollywood types.

The revolutionary Aquarian spirit is also alive in civil rights heroes like Rosa Parks. Abraham Lincoln, too. Bob Marley and his idea of universalism. Yoko Ono and her call for peace. Thomas Edison's vision and the rebel streak of Galileo. And of course the empire and philanthropy of Oprah—all examples of how instinct and fearlessness work out for an Aquarius when they decide to pursue career paths driven by passion rather than precedent. Things are more likely to go right for an Aquarius if they take a big risk than if they're tempered.

If you're looking to spend a day reading about one single day in a woman's life, a very Aquarian experience awaits you in Virginia Woolf's *Mrs. Dalloway.* It's not surprising Woolf was an Aquarius. Her style was groundbreaking and her characters complex, moody, and unmistakably human. Reading *Mrs. Dalloway*—with its abrupt transitions into the past and future, and its revelation that the present moment is stunning in having arrived at all—it feels exactly like swimming through Aquarian thought. The secret bliss Aquarians find in the everyday is what keeps them going. At their core, they aren't an easily discouraged sign. Though they may scrutinize their life and decisions more harshly than others, it's only because of how aware they are of time and how consciousness resides within it, often outside of our control, no matter how we protest.

Other Famous Aquarians

1. Frederick Douglass
2. Wolfgang Amadeus Mozart
3. Shakira
4. Ellen DeGeneres

5. Jackie Robinson

6. Lana Turner

7. FDR

8. Harry Styles

9. Michael Jordan

10. James Joyce

Aquarius playlist

- The 5th Dimension, "Aquarius/Let the Sunshine In"
- Bob Marley, "Could You Be Loved"
- Harry Styles, "Kiwi"
- Guns N' Roses, "Paradise City"
- Garth Brooks, "Friends in Low Places"
- Dr. Dre, "Let Me Ride"
- Roberta Flack, "Killing Me Softly"
- The Weeknd, "Starboy"
- Regina Spektor, "Fidelity"
- Gucci Mane, "Wake Up in the Sky"

The Aquarius (a poem)

People speak of the future
as if they know it's there

and if they spoke to you
they'd know the future is

they'd know the future's blue.
Ships in the vast dark.

Dark in the blue wheel.

Before the sun has risen
only memory then

and memory now
of stars, of hands

in someone's hair
this close to yours.

You've touched the world
so many times

it does remember you.
It does begin to see.

PISCES

February 19–March 20

We cannot live, except thus mutually
We alternate, aware or unaware,
The reflex act of life: and what we bear
Our virtue onward most impulsively.

Elizabeth Barrett Browning, born March 6, 1806

The Pisces

When in a sea of people at Coachella in 2012, Rihanna rolled a blunt propped up on her bodyguard's shoulders, literally doing so on his head while wearing a PEACE crop top and aquamarine-studded cutoffs—that was Pisces culture. When at a Nirvana show in 1992, Kurt Cobain gave a monologue about how much he loved Courtney Love, asking the crowd to yell "Courtney, we love you" because she was feeling like "everybody hates her"— that was Pisces culture. And in 1905, when Albert Einstein invented the theory of relativity, and seventy-one years later, Steve Jobs introduced us to Apple, forever changing our lives and the way we communicate—that was Pisces culture. Peace, love, and communication. It's the Pisces mantra.

All of us have feelings that run through us and orbit our brain like Jupiter and its seventy-nine moons. A Pisces is a very special person. Not only do they have the capacity to experience more than seventy-nine feelings in a minute, they also live in those feelings at all times (even when they're sleeping). This happens at their expense and mostly for our benefit. The emotional generosity of a Pisces is boundless. You know that banal artsy scene in *American Beauty*, the one where Ricky Fitts is trying to impress Jane Burnham by showing her a video of a floating plastic bag he recorded on a windy day? He's sitting on his bed talking about how much beauty there is in the world. So much that he can "barely take it." And by the end of this he's tearing up, staring at his own "art" in awe, as if he's just witnessed the end of war or world hunger. Jane Burnham is enthralled, of course. When the weird-sensitive-edgy boy has a hard-on for you it's hard to say no. And obviously that boy is a Pisces. Ricky Fitts is a Pisces. He might even be a double Pisces at that. I'm willing to bet there's also Cancer and Scorpio in his chart because all he does in the movie is hang out with Jane in his bedroom and record dead things he finds on the street. He also secretly spies on her, making him the ultimate water sign. And he's full of existential angst and likes to get "deep" while smoking pot. A far-fetched, completely delusional plan he has is running away to New York with Jane and staying with his drug dealer. Absolutely-insane-anything-for-love behavior. Definitely hot and terrifying at the same time. That floating plastic bag is also Pisces culture.

It's poetry. That moment in *American Beauty* is the Pisces heart. Blown open, ready to be taken anywhere and feel anything.

Things you might want to know about Pisces

Pisces is a mutable water sign and the last of the zodiac. Since they come after everyone, they've learned many karmic lessons— devotion, receptivity, commitment, and above all, an unshakable belief in love as a guiding force. They'll make any sacrifice for it, go anywhere to find it, do anything because of it, and some Pisces have even been known to conjure love like witches or lovesick poets. In short, they're an old soul. The oldest. They're also two fish swimming in opposite directions, representing duality. It isn't the duality of a Gemini, which has more to do with artifice, performing for an audience, and being obsessed with the surface of things (this is why Geminis are natural celebrities). In fact, Pisces aren't too interested in the surface of anything. They want to go deep. Their duality has to do with being the emotional antennas of the world. They pick up on both the conscious and unconscious realms of existence. The saying "go with your intuition"—it's how they live constantly, except their way of doing it is more informed than others' because they've gathered more emotional data (a direct result of being last on the karmic wheel). They see through people and situations easily.

Whether they like it or not, Pisces are processors with many receptors. They can discern your mood by looking at you. They can tell what you're thinking by studying your body language or silence.

There is great empathy in how a Pisces approaches people, even their enemies. So much empathy that they temporarily inherit the energy of whoever they're talking to. Even the person selling them a cup of coffee. A Pisces can actually become quite invested in strangers. And strangers will find themselves wanting to reveal the most personal things, often acting against their nature, not realizing they're actually being brought closer to it because most Pisces feel like home. They're mellow, welcoming, and dreamy. Pisces are prone to being whimsical and often get lost in what's possible, as opposed to what's real. This is what makes them charming. They feel like artists even if they're not.

Being around a Pisces is like a return to childhood. One reason for this is because they are enamored with childhood itself. It's the origin of their nostalgia and they like to surround themselves with relics of it—photographs, ticket stubs, mix CDs, playlists, letters, any reminder of the past. Pisces view their early years on earth as a magical time (even if they weren't idyllic). A time when their feelings were unguarded and they could connect with people without worrying about being taken advantage of or getting hurt. Sure, they romanticize childhood, but they romanticize everything that's already happened. It replays alongside all their days like an old VHS tape. If an Aquarius is the future and an Aries is today, a Pisces is the past—sepia-toned, Belle and Sebastian playing in the background, a car full of friends who've known each other forever on their way to a cabin by a lake.

Pisces as a lover

Pisces are obsessive and clingy lovers. They're that person who scrolls through every photo on your Instagram, trying to read between the lines and wondering if you're in love with your friend Becky, because not only is Becky in most of your photos, but the one from two years ago where you touch her hand possibly gives something away. And since most Pisces are in love with all their friends, they assume the same of others. Fair warning: you will get jealous of the bonds between your Pisces and their most trusted people. It will feel like their friendships are huge relationships of their own, full of romantic and sexual tension, and a history that seems intimidating compared to the one you have (especially if you've just started dating). Get used to this. Pisces fall in love with trees and ants and the sky between seven and eight in the morning. They do this every day. Now imagine how they are with people. It's in their nature to fiercely attach themselves to the world and the human landscape is their favorite.

Rereading texts, emails, letters—any form of communication—is another compulsive Pisces trait. They are masters of investigating tone and studying word choice. They're good detectives, a quality they share with Scorpios, although a Pisces inquiry into your life has more to do with sizing you up on a "soul level." Scorpios are manipulative. What they use their findings for depends on their mood. You won't have to worry about this with a Pisces. They just want to get close to you. Really, really close to you. You probably need one of those safety warnings: "Objects in mirror are closer than they appear"—because that's them. They're the objects.

The incredible thing about dating a Pisces is that hardly anything about your past or emotional life will scare them enough to give up on you. Are they terrified of their own interiority? Sure. But they consistently give their lovers the benefit of the doubt and are willing to take on emotional baggage. This can backfire (naturally), though their partners are lucky nonetheless. You can do a lot of finding yourself with a Pisces. It can feel as if you're in therapy 24/7, except your therapist is ready to make out and fantasize about road trips you can take together. As much as Pisces love returning to places where they have a history, they're quite spontaneous. And kinky. Their erogenous zone is their feet. They'll never turn down a foot massage or . . . maybe even something more. (Google "feet" on Xtube.)

In terms of compatibility, a Pisces needs someone who is a leader. Cancers are opinionated enough to fit the bill (though they're more like pretend leaders since they secretly want to be led also). The same goes for Virgos, although this match will feel like one of opposites. Virgos plan and act; Pisces dream and process. Every Pisces is attracted to fire signs, but it's far from an easy relationship if they follow that attraction. An Aries will excite them but ultimately feel too juvenile—exactly why they'll be after them in the first place (remember their obsession with childhood). Leos will perplex them and seem one-dimensional, especially in their need for validation. And a Sagittarius is the ultimate mindfuck for a Pisces. Both signs love to get lost in the world as it could be and not as it is. They like trips and adventure. They're idealists and need someone who understands their creative spirit. Except ultimately, a Pisces wants a forever love. They believe in commitment. And as we all know, Sagittarians are around long enough to remain mysterious and unforgettable. But not much longer.

Air signs are entertaining and confusing to a Pisces. That's because they have a flimsy emotional center. An Aquarius will be too aloof and a Gemini too chaotic. Libras are as close to a good air match as it gets. They'll bond with a Pisces over aesthetics and give them the impression that their intellectual nature is actually infused with emotional longing (which it is, but Pisces are more emotionally evolved, and they know this, so the relationship will get boring fast). Capricorn and Taurus are both too rigid. They aren't able to understand the limitlessness that every Pisces demands in love. That feeling of expansiveness most people never get to because it's at the brink of desire overtaking them. Yes, Scorpios will understand it. But a Pisces is even more devotional. For them, love is a calling.

Pisces as a friend

A Pisces believes that our primary reason for being here is to connect. They've learned that through their past lives and karmic cycles. And so they take that connection very seriously. Their friendships are the most important things to them, more than their romantic partners even. One thing they may struggle with early in life is the ability to discern where to invest their time and who to put their energy into. This has to do with the fact that they take people at their word and are trusting. Perhaps too trusting. No matter how many times a Pisces has been burned by the world, they will retain a high level of belief in people. It's what makes them great friends (and poets).

For all their emotional intelligence, Pisces have a hard time accepting help. Though unlike a Virgo or Sagittarius (signs who share this inability), they're able to open up about their problems and show vulnerability one-on-one. Usually they'll wait and listen to you first. A Pisces also does a lot of calculating before coming to anyone for help. They assess what's going on in your life, rather than privileging theirs, and decide if it's even worth burdening you. Most times they decide it's not. And this is where all great Pisces art comes from. You should probably stop reading this and listen to Johnny Cash. Or Vivaldi, if you want to hear a Pisces really go off.

Something that's troubling about being friends with these water signs is that they're passive-aggressive. They hold grudges though pretend like nothing's wrong. It's not the obvious grudge that you get with a Taurus or Capricorn. One where you know exactly what you've done and exactly what you need to say in order to remedy it. Pisces won't confront you like a fire sign either. They see a grudge as their way of protecting themselves. As a way of not letting you know how hurt they really are. What they don't know is that it's so obvious when they're doing this. They overperform being "fine." It's a little like a soap opera.

If a Pisces has a problem with you they'll hide behind decorum while fuming on the inside. Every single fight I've had with my Pisces exes (three of them) has had to do with their inability to confront what they're actually upset about. As if it would betray something about their feelings and how invested they are— which it would—but come on. Grow up. Be explosive if you need to. Unfortunately, Pisces don't work that way. They keep a lot of their feelings repressed, thinking it's a holy act of generosity when it's really fear.

Pisces style

Given their compulsive texting, grandiose emotions, and endless nostalgia, you might be surprised to know that Pisces are quite understated when it comes to fashion. They're rarely going to wear something solely for attention. In fact, they wouldn't like it at all if everyone in a room was looking at them and making eyes. They'd become over-analytical and have a panic attack. With a Pisces it's all about the little things. Some piece of jewelry given to them by their grandmother, a not especially valuable pair of sunglasses they bought when they were happy on vacation, or a shirt they've managed to keep in their closet for years and have grown attached to because of it. All Pisces are meaning makers. It's how they're able to make it through the day. And their favorite garments are important to them for some odd reason, usually having to do with personal history.

A Pisces will seldom look tacky or like they're trying too hard. They're not fire signs or Geminis. All their fits are a little loose, a little blousy—airy, really—and intriguingly mysterious. They rely on their aura more than their dress when it comes to seduction (so yeah, they do tend to favor basics). While an Aries might walk into a room wearing an attention-grabbing red dress, a Pisces will feel confident wearing light-wash jeans and a see-through tee, stealing the same kind of attention with ease. For them, everything is in the eyes. They direct people to their eyes no matter what they're wearing. And a Pisces knows how to look at you and make you feel both wanted and captivated.

The story behind the clothes is always more important to a Pisces than the clothes themselves. They love to support friends who are designers, artists, or any type of makers. At the same time, invite them to a casual party and they'll shock you because, of course, they have the perfect silver platforms. Pisces taste is classic. There are many black-and-whites, many casual elements. It's very Calvin Klein 1995 to be honest. They also know how to throw in a curveball. Those silver platforms were probably $1,000, not anything you'd wear on Halloween. They probably were the same pair Rihanna wore, but a Pisces would never tell you that. Part of their sex appeal is putting you at ease and making you feel like you've known them forever. Go overboard complimenting them on their shirt and the next time you see them they'll have it for you as a gift (in exactly your size). Pisces are always paying attention to things like that.

Texting with a Pisces

They will send you all the heart emojis and in every color. Throwback photos without need for an occasion. Links to songs and poems about heartbreak even when they're happy. Quotes: "Imagination is more important than knowledge," Einstein. "Bitch better have my money," Rihanna. They'll share tweets, screenshots of their own emails, bad selfies. Pisces are over-communicators. It's more endearing than overbearing. It comes from a place of wanting to be seen, and it's a way for them to preempt judgment, to feel okay that they're texting you at all (and yes, they're paranoid that you don't want to hear from them).

A Pisces is not the type to disappear on you. It doesn't matter if it's unimportant or major, they'll make sure you know they're there. Telling you what they had for breakfast, the last time they cried, how last night they watched *The Big Chill* before bed. In a sense, these are all invitations for you to reveal your own drama. There's nothing a Pisces likes more than helping someone with their emotional life. Sometimes the back-and-forths with them can be so intoxicating, it's like you're in a TV show. You're the main character and they're every sidekick and best friend. Here are some Pisces moods via text.

Everyday Pisces

So I was thinking about your life in the shower and I really think Doc Martens should be part of your brand. Let me know if you wanna hear more!!

Philosophical Pisces

[link to Natalie Imbruglia's "Torn"]

In-love Pisces

I CAN'T BELIEVE THE SUN RISES EVERY DAY OMG. Life is crazy! Hahahaaa

Passive-aggressive Pisces

Yeah I heard something different from another friend who is super-reliable, but maybe you're right. Who knows! Gotta run to a meeting!!

Hurt Pisces

Yeah I'm just shopping, I forgot I don't own any leather pants! TALK LATER! xoxx

After 10:00 p.m. Pisces

Wow I just remembered that one time when you came over and I played you records and you slept in my sweatshirt and we talked about what kind of ants we would be if we were ants and then in the morning you ate half of my bagel and left and I really miss that . . .

Spiritual Pisces

Sometimes when I walk into a bar and hear Stevie Nicks it's just like, god . . . I know why we're here.

Happy Pisces

I was just thinking about the past and how it's so beautiful we'll always have it, even the bad things. Omg lol I'm being so crazy. I just had kombucha and think I'm drunk at work??

Stressed Pisces

Thanks so much!! Everything is great! How are YOU doing haha

Chill Pisces

[mass text to 234 friends]
The sunset is at 7:14 tonight!
[234 emojis follow]

The Pisces imagination

If a Pisces were a city, they'd be San Francisco. Moody, surrounded by water, fog and sun competing with each other at all times. Spiritually, it's as close to Europe in America as possible. That in itself is a Pisces mood. There's something whimsical about being so close to the end of the West. Like the beyond is right there and also nowhere. Like there's not another edge from which to see that far.

If they were punctuation, they'd be a colon. Inclusive, unassuming, housing a never-ending list of mementos. Room? A childhood bedroom. Time of day? The gloaming. And if they were weather, a Pisces would be warm winter rain. Unexpected and soothing. Making room for a melancholy you never knew you wanted.

The Pisces imagination is hopefulness itself. They have that special gift for seeing how dysfunctional reality is yet refusing to be discouraged. This is because every Pisces believes in magic and the unseen. They see art as the highest intelligence and affect as its own religion. For a Pisces, time is a river. And at any moment the river is a different river. The light, the rocks, the life beneath—they're changing. Moving toward something not necessarily perfect but real, and certainly alive. Because Pisces is ruled by Neptune—planet of dreams, receptivity, and creation—it may take them longer than others to decide on a life path. They think of everything they do as a vocation, not a career. There's mindful intention behind their choices, and also a lot of self-torture, even over what may seem insignificant—like buying the right flowers. (Pisces love white tulips, blue hydrangea, and any rose.) They'll easily admit this about their decision-making. It has been going on since they were born—since they were able to think and feel (which was probably before they were born).

A crippling self-awareness comes with the idealism that Pisces are handed at birth. They know that the world does not reward idealists. They also know that only idealists can change the world. How do they deal with this? Well, for one, most Pisces stare at the ceiling for a very long time before going to bed and for at least an hour after waking up. If they didn't have obligations to get to, they could spend their entire day thinking and staring at that ceiling. They could write letters for hours. Two novels are constantly being written in their heads. In one, they have a relationship with everyone who's ever looked at them. In the other, they find that one person on a crowded platform, someone who already knows their name and has the good sense to take them to a charming place with a view for a glass of wine. A view of the city or anywhere overlooking life in action. A place from which a Pisces can see that people don't regret life. That they keep going, no matter the weather.

Pisces are architects of the past. The past continues for them like it's seamlessly the present. They also know that time is not linear. It's not how they experience it. And it's why, if you've ever dated a Pisces and decide to show up to their door ten years later, they'll welcome you the way they welcomed you the first time. They'll remember all the moments when they felt alive with you. They won't hold on to bad things.

One of my Pisces boyfriends liked to get high and record little songs he made up for me on his phone. He'd send them to me in the middle of the night, maybe around three or four when I was sleeping. He wanted to make sure I woke up and listened to them first thing. They were these dreamy, folky ramblings about love and peace and food. Each time I listened to one of them, I'd think, *I really hope the world doesn't crush this person.* All Pisces are pacifists and will only fight intellectually or over their own ethics. They're not power-hungry or greedy. They love animals. (Most people who work for sanctuaries are Pisces.) You can't really say that they're dog or cat people. They're more like cat, snake, bird, ant, wolf, and dog people. The animal kingdom is something they cherish because of its purity.

Arts-inclined as they are, Pisces would make great scientists. They feel deeply connected to the environment and would live outside for the remainder of their lives if they could. Too much of the indoors makes them highly anxious. They need to be reminded that there is a world out there and that they're not alone. It might sound like a paradox, but the people who know they're most connected to others often forget it when faced with their despair. And despair for a Pisces is a slow existential IV drip. It's constantly going. It never seems to run out.

Dance and theater are two other areas where Pisces excel. Any profession where they can use their bodies, preferably in relation to others, is good for them. They make great actors. They're good in business, too. Personal touch and an ability to relate to their clients emotionally is what gets them many deals.

While they might resist going to a party, they'll also be the last to leave. They love being around people. A Pisces will listen to anyone's story and indulge them. Even if they find it sad, boring, unbelievable—they'll listen. And they'll earnestly try to understand why things turned out the way they did. They'll try to see if they're in love with the person telling the story. Most of the time, they are. But they also know what it's like to leave a room being in love with everyone. They're used to forgiving people for being disappointing and they're used to loving flaws.

An ideal day for a Pisces would be one where they wake up alone and then see everyone they've ever slept with and everyone they've almost slept with too. This takes care of the entire population, but what you need to know is, they'd rather go to bed alone. This is because sex is not the most important thing to them. They don't consider it the greatest intimacy. For a Pisces, the greatest romance is friendship. This is what they live for. They have no trouble being alone because they have their memories. They have the photos and songs and all the things they've kept and written. Scrapbooks are for Pisces. A Pisces is a scrapbook.

The Famous Pisces

Since they're the oldest and most knowledgeable ones, they're here to change the world. Albert Einstein. George Washington. Nina Simone. John Lewis. Without Pisces, things would be a lot less comfortable and a lot less beautiful, too. The true portrait of a Pisces is Justice Ruth Bader Ginsburg. Only the second woman to be appointed to the Supreme Court, very tough and deeply compassionate, she's proof that these qualities can coexist and that people who possess them can be of great service to others. Most of the cases Ginsburg took on early in her career had to do with women's rights. And her style and humor are unrivaled on the bench. She's become a cultural icon outlasting nearly everyone. That's the thing about Pisces people—for all the talk about how sensitive they are, they're often the last ones standing.

Elizabeth Taylor, a Pisces who was famously married eight times, was once quoted as saying, "Some of my best leading men have been dogs and horses." She looked for love everywhere. And it became clear to her how abundant it was. It didn't have to start in marriage or end in divorce. While they'll certainly play along with cultural norms, Pisces long to deviate. If they could, they'd float in and out of people's lives without any disturbance and without any attachment. The no-disturbance part is possible for them; the no-attachment is not.

If you want to see a truly Pisces film, watch Spike Lee's *Do the Right Thing*. There is so much tension and so much at stake, but everything is between people and can be solved by them too. As much as it's a film about chaos and race, it's truly a film about love.

Or the potential for it. Having had so many lives on earth, Pisces understand conflict differently than the rest of us. They know it's inevitable and sometimes necessary. They're willing to endure it but are more comfortable in therapy mode, trying to make things work.

Does it surprise anyone, then, that one of the longest, strangest, and most powerful novels of our time, *Infinite Jest*, was written by a Pisces? In it, David Foster Wallace tries to capture . . . well, everything. The uncontainable. The uncapturable. As a reader, you're often deeply uncomfortable and confused. What Wallace gets down in *Infinite Jest* is the mind at work. Layers of experience that are important and unimportant, but cannot be forgotten. All of them point to the future. At times you don't know if you should cry or laugh, or if you should be furious. All of the emotions. All the time. That's Pisces.

Other Famous Pisces

1. Steve Jobs
2. Liza Minnelli
3. Nat King Cole
4. W. E. B. Du Bois
5. George Harrison
6. Michelangelo
7. Justin Bieber
8. Drew Barrymore
9. Ansel Adams
10. Queen Latifah

Pisces playlist

- Lou Reed, "Perfect Day"
- Nirvana, "Come as You Are"
- Chopin, Nocturne in E-flat, op. 9, no. 2
- Rihanna, "Kiss It Better"
- Lisa Loeb, "Stay (I Missed You)"
- Johnny Cash, "Hurt"
- Erykah Badu, "Bag Lady"
- Nina Simone, "Don't Let Me Be Misunderstood"
- Coldplay, "Yellow"
- Teena Marie, "I Need Your Lovin'"

The Pisces (a poem)

The first feeling of the day
and a feeling of yesterday in it.
A feeling that feels itself
moving through everything
once felt, without end
without us, without reason.
Again and again
like a sea losing its shape
for the last time. This hour
of night now arriving
through windows and doors
right at noon.

ABOUT THE AUTHORS

Alex Dimitrov and **Dorothea Lasky** are the duo behind the beloved Twitter account @poetastrologers, better known as the Astro Poets. Dimitrov is the author of three poetry collections and his work has been published in *The New Yorker*, *The Paris Review*, and *The New York Times*. Lasky is the author of six books of poetry and prose. Her work has been published in *The New Yorker*, and she is an associate professor of poetry at Columbia University School of the Arts.